No Limit Hold 'em Theory and Practice

By

DAVID SKLANSKY

and

ED MILLER

A product of Two Plus Two Publishing LLC

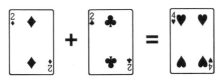

FIRST EDITION

FIRST PRINTING
JUNE 2006

Printing and Binding
Creel Printing, Inc.
Las Vegas, Nevada

Printed in the United States of America

D0187732

No Limit Hold 'em:
Theory and Practice
COPYRIGHT © 2006
Two Plus Two Publishing LLC

All rights reserved. Printed in the United States of America.

No part of this book may be reproduced or transmitted in any form, by any means, electronic or mechanical, including photocopying and recording, or by any information storage or retrieval system without the express permission in writing from the publisher.

For information contact:

Two Plus Two Publishing LLC
32 Commerce Center Drive
Suite H-89
Henderson, NV 89014

ISBN: 1-880685-37-X

Table of Contents

i

ii Table of Contents

iv Table of Contents

About David Sklansky

David Sklansky is generally considered the number one authority on gambling in the world today. Besides his twelve books on the subject, David also has produced two videos and numerous writings for various gaming publications.

More recently David has been doing consulting work for casinos and gaming companies. He has recently invented several casino games including *Hold 'em Challenge* and *All In Hold 'em*.

David attributes his standing in the gambling community to three facts:

1. The fact that he presents his ideas as simply as possible (sometimes with Mason Malmuth and now with Ed Miller) even though these ideas frequently involve concepts that are deep, subtle, and not to be found elsewhere.

2. The fact that what he articulates can be counted on to be accurate.

3. The fact that for many years a large portion of his income was derived from gambling (usually poker, but occasionally blackjack, sports betting, horses, video games, casino promotions, or casino tournaments).

There is little doubt that the majority of the successful poker players today attribute a great deal of their success to reading and studying David's books.

Other Books by David Sklansky

Hold 'em Poker
The Theory of Poker
Getting The Best of It
Sklansky on Poker

Poker, Gaming, and Life
Sklansky Talks Blackjack
Tournament Poker for Advanced Players

Gambling for a Living by David Sklansky and Mason Malmuth
Hold 'em Poker for Advanced Players by David Sklansky and
  Mason Malmuth
Seven-Card Stud for Advanced Players by David Sklansky, Mason
  Malmuth, and Ray Zee
Small Stakes Hold 'em; Winning Big with Expert Play by Ed
  Miller, David Sklansky, and Mason Malmuth

About Ed Miller

Ed Miller grew up in New Orleans, Louisiana. In 2000, he received degrees from MIT in Physics and Electrical Engineering and Computer Science. After college, he moved to Redmond, Washington to work as a software developer for Microsoft.

Looking for a new hobby, he deposited a few hundred dollars online in November 2001 to play small stakes limit hold 'em. After losing his initial stake, he sought to improve his game, and he found the books and website of Two Plus Two Publishing. He participated in discussions on the forums at www.twoplustwo.com, and after a few months he turned his losses into wins at a local cardroom.

By January 2003, he had moved up to $10-$20 and $20-$40 limit hold 'em, and in March he left his job to play poker full-time. After six more successful months playing in the Seattle area, he moved to Las Vegas, where he currently resides with his wife, Elaine.

In July 2004, Ed finished his first book, *Small Stakes Hold 'em: Winning Big with Expert Play*, co-authored with David Sklansky and Mason Malmuth. By 2006, it had sold more than 100,000 copies and had taught countless players to play professional-level limit hold 'em.

In April 2005, Ed finished his second book, *Getting Started in Hold 'em*. Geared for beginners, it provides a perfect introduction to limit and no limit hold 'em cash games and tournaments.

You can find the latest from Ed, including news, photos, and his poker and gambling articles, on his website at www. notedpokerauthority.com.

Introduction

No limit hold 'em is hot. In only a few years, the game has gone from rarely played (except in tournaments) to one of the most popular forms of poker. The last few years have seen millions of new players.

The no limit literature has had trouble keeping up. Relatively little has been written about the game, and most of what has been written is either misleading or is presented in a "recipe book" format. That is, most of the discussion has been of the "If you have top pair, and your opponent bets, raise..." variety. These recipe books give you a taste of how to play the game, but can get you into trouble quickly if you know only the what's and not also the how's and why's.

This is not a recipe book. We don't tell you what to do if you have top pair and your opponent bets. We tell you what factors you should consider when you make your decisions. We teach you how excellent players think about the game. We don't give you a fish so that you can eat today; we teach you how to fish so that you may eat forever (or so the saying goes).

No limit hold 'em is complex, sometimes frustratingly so. If you have $50 in front of you, you should do one thing, but if you have $200, you should do something different. And if you have $1,000, you might do a third thing. If your opponent plays one way, you should do one thing, and if your opponent plays another, you should do something else. To be successful, you have to learn how each of these factors (stack size, opponent play, and many more) affects your decisions, and you must learn how they work together.

While many of the concepts in this book have been known to elite players for years, we expect most of our readers to be taken aback by the depth of discussion. We think a lot of you will say to yourselves, "I didn't know I was supposed to be thinking about all these things while I played. I had no idea there was so much to the game."

This reaction is natural given how the game has been packaged and sold on television. Advice comes in sound bites: "You never want to go broke on a draw," or "Ace-queen is a good hand; ten-seven is a bad hand." Sound bites make for terrible no limit advice. Reading even just the first few chapters of this book should give you a big knowledge edge over your friends and opponents who learned the game by watching television.

This book isn't intended for beginners. We assume that you are familiar with some general poker terms such as "pot odds," "implied odds," and "expectation." We also assume that you have mastered some fundamental ideas like, "Straight draws are worth less in multiway pots when the board is paired," or, more generally, "Some draws are better than others." If these terms and ideas sound foreign to you, we recommend that you read *The Theory of Poker* by David Sklansky or *Getting Started in Hold 'em* by Ed Miller (the whole book, not just the no limit section) before you continue with this book. A quick read of either of those books should bring you up to speed.

Please don't think of this as a cash game book or a tournament book. It's not either. It's a book about how to think about no limit hold 'em, and the concepts we discuss will be useful in both cash games and tournaments. We have a few tournament-specific nuggets for you, but almost everything we talk about should be valuable in either setting.[1]

Periodically throughout the book, we will compare no limit hold 'em to limit hold 'em and highlight some important differences between the games. Many of our readers will be experienced limit hold 'em players who would like to try no limit. (Until very recently, limit was by far the more popular game.) We think comparing the two games will be especially helpful to those players trying to make the transition.

---

[1] For discussion of some tournament-specific scenarios, read *Harrington on Hold 'em, Volume II: The Endgame* by Dan Harrington and Bill Robertie.

But even if you have never played limit hold 'em, please don't glaze over during these sections. Thinking about the differences between the games should give you insight into no limit even if you've never played a hand of limit. Comparing two different games often reveals things that you would miss if you analyzed either by itself.

Also, keep an open mind while you read this book. No limit is an extremely situational game, and sometimes very subtle factors can cause you to change your plays. We don't mean to give you absolutist, "Do this, don't do that," advice. We intend to give you things to think about while you play. The more you think critically about the game and the less rigidly you view it, the better your results will likely be.

The book is divided into two major sections: "Fundamentals" and "Concepts and Weapons." The first section, "Fundamentals," features a series of chapters designed to give you a foundation in expert-level play and thought. "Concepts and Weapons" features shorter, more specific thoughts and insights. Don't ignore or skim the Concepts section simply because it comes second; it contains some of the most important information in the book.

Also, many of the ideas presented in "Fundamentals" are reprised in "Concepts and Weapons." This repetition is intentional; we present particularly important ideas in both formats.

Finally, while we have organized the "Fundamentals" section so that the chapters build upon one another a little bit, most chapters (including those in the Concepts section) will stand alone. You can skip around or read out of order if you like without getting into too much trouble.

We'd like to thank Miriam Miller, Judith Lautner, and Mason Malmuth for their help editing this book. We thank Deva Hazarika, Sunny Mehta, and Matt Flynn for reviewing the manuscript and offering their insights.

We thank Mark Werner from mw2design for designing our cover. Thanks also to Portraits Today by Catherine for the photo of Ed on the back cover. We also thank Creel Printing for design and artwork throughout the book.

Ed would like to thank his family — his wife Elaine Vigneault, his father Raymond, and his mother Mimi — for their understanding and support during the sometimes difficult and sometimes joyous times through which we produced this book.

Finally, we would like to thank Two Plus Two Publishing, LLC.

About This Book
by David Sklansky

I have been reluctant all these years to write a no limit book, even one that dealt mainly with theory, because I know that theoreticians without other talents will still be underdogs to talented non-theoreticians, especially if stacks are large relative to the blinds.

By that I mean that many no limit skills are not theoretical in nature, and they require you to observe and adjust well to your surroundings. I'm talking about skills like:

1. Reading hands and/or assigning probabilities to competing hands

2. Knowing when to "change gears"

3. Using deception

4. Making others play badly (through mannerisms, conversation, or strategy)

5. Playing hands in ways that set up extra profits in the future

A "talented" player who is good at these skills, but who has a shaky theoretical understanding of the game, can often easily beat a less talented player who has mastered the theory. Even if they sometimes make the wrong-sized bets or call with a draw when they shouldn't, talented players will still get the best of it through superior hand reading and other skills.

This fact made me reluctant to write the book because I like my books to be ones that you can "take to the bank." I like you to be able to read my books, play a little bit, and be a favorite in the appropriate games almost immediately. But no limit hold 'em doesn't work that way. No matter what I put in the book, I can't make all my readers immediate winners because these talent skills play such an important role.

I changed my mind about writing the book because of the resurgence of no limit poker. An added reason is that many games and tournament situations involve low stack-to-blind ratios where theoretical considerations are paramount. In any case, whether you are talented or not, your game will be improved by this book. Knowing this material will make talented players world class. If you aren't instinctively talented and can't learn to be, this book will still help you enough so that you can beat games not populated by experts, as well as all games with mainly short stacks.

A theoretical understanding of no limit may not, by itself, allow you to beat every game or opponent. But it's almost guaranteed to make you a better player. Hopefully this book will accomplish that goal.

Some Notes About the Examples

Throughout this book, we'll introduce examples in this format:

"You're playing a $5-$10 game with $1,000 stacks..."

By that, we mean that there are two blinds: a $5 blind to the left of the button and a $10 blind two to the left of the button. Also, every participating player has at least $1,000 in front of them. You might have $1,000, and everyone might have you covered. Or you might have $3,000, and your opponent (or opponents) have around $1,000.

In this scenario, $1,000 would be the *effective stack size*. One player may have more than that, but the relevant players will be all-in after $1,000 in betting.

We have a few examples in the book where there is no effective stack size because multiple participants have significantly different stack sizes. For instance, one player might have $500, one might have $2,000, and you might have $5,000. For these examples, we will state each stack size explicitly.

Most of our examples, however, will use effective stack sizes. This convention simplifies analysis; not all of your hands will work so neatly. We could have devoted literally hundreds of pages to discussing the peculiarities of hands played with multiple different stack sizes including side pots and so forth. We decided that those discussions were beyond the scope of this book.

In our examples we sometimes will count the pot size and neglect a few dollars to make the math easier. For instance, in a $2-$5 blind game, if one player makes it $20, and the big blind calls, we might quote the pot size as $40 instead of $42. We do it to simplify the math, but if you'd like, you can pretend that those missing $2 were raked away.

Also, we'll analyze many hands using expectation equations. We don't expect our readers to solve equations at the table. We, the authors, don't play poker by solving equations ourselves. We provide the equations because they show you how to estimate and combine probabilities. Common sense answers won't always be correct; you should learn the process for getting to an answer the right way.

Having said that, if you don't like working with equations, you can skip them. You can learn how to think about no limit correctly without them. You'll be a lot better off if you read the book without the equations than if you give up entirely.

Part One

Fundamentals

The Skills for Success

You can't learn to be a good no limit hold 'em player until you understand what it *means* to be a good no limit player. What do good players do that mediocre or bad players don't? This chapter will tell you what it means to be a good no limit player, and the rest of the book will show you how to think about the game so that you can acquire those skills.

In many endeavors the answer to the question, "What makes someone good?" is at least somewhat transparent. You have to have quick reflexes to be a good baseball hitter. You have to be a good logical thinker to be a scientist. But what do you need to be a good no limit player? It's not as clear.

New players (and non-players) seem to think the game centers around two things: being a good liar and being keenly aware of tells. Don't let that stone face crack, keep an eagle eye for your opponents' nervous scratches and tics, and you're on your way to riches and glory.

Five buy-ins later, the neophytes realize that there's a little more to the game than that. Then they concentrate on the cards they play. Now it's about playing tight and out-folding the competition. That works a little better, but still it doesn't produce results. So they switch it up and start playing loosely and raising a lot. Reading hands is the key skill now. That strategy produces some big wins — and some big losses. Some who get very good at it become consistent winners.

Most don't. They get hung up in their progression as players. They realize that reading hands is important, but they never get particularly good at it. And their notion of reading hands usually ends at "trying to put their opponents on a hand." When asked what other skills are important to be a good no limit player, they'll come up with a vast array of possibilities, but few that reflect what the good players really do.

The strange truth is that many no limit players, even some experienced ones, don't know what makes one player better than another. You will. Some of the most important no limit skills are:

- Manipulating the pot size
- Adjusting correctly to stack sizes
- Winning the battle of mistakes
- Reading hands
- Manipulating opponents into playing badly

We'll discuss briefly what each of these skills is and why it's important.

Manipulating the Pot Size

All players receive good hands and bad hands. All players win some pots and lose some pots. Not all players make sure that the pots they win (or are likely to win) are bigger than average and the pots they lose (or are likely to lose) are smaller than average. Only the good ones do.

Good players keep the pot small when they are vulnerable, and they build it big when they have the edge. Fundamentally, that's *why* they win. Everyone wins and loses pots. Good players win big pots and lose small ones. The difference is their profit.

That idea sounds simple enough, but putting it into practice requires knowledge and skill. You can't just make big bets with good hands and small bets with bad ones. Your opponents will catch on to that strategy.

First, you have to recognize when you have a good, "big pot" hand, and when you have a vulnerable, "small pot" hand. It's not always obvious. For instance, what if you have

on a

flop? Should you try to build a big pot or should you try to keep it small?

Actually, it's a trick question, because under some circumstances with that hand you should try to make the pot big, and under others it's best to keep it small. The skill is recognizing which situation is which, then planning the entire hand such that your checks, calls, bets, and raises keep the pot the size you want it to be.

Adjusting Correctly to Stack Sizes

No limit strategy changes drastically depending on the sizes of the stacks. Say you're playing in a game with blinds of $5 and $10. If you have $50, then the only decision you make is whether to move all-in or fold before the flop. There's not much else you can do. If you have $2,000, however, then your strategic options are significantly more complex.

Indeed, the sizes of the stacks of all remaining players in the hand should play an important role in every decision you make. You can't even make your preflop play without adjusting for the stack sizes. Later in the book, we'll give you a simple example of a preflop decision that works out three different ways with three different stack sizes. You have the same cards each time, but your different stack sizes necessitate different plays.

Being perpetually aware not only of your stack size, but also of those of your opponents, is a key no limit skill. But that's just the beginning. You also have to know how to adjust your strategy based on those stack sizes. If your opponent has $1,000 behind, you do one thing, but with only $300 behind, you do something else. It's a tricky thing to master, but it's also a fundamental no limit skill.

Winning the Battle of Mistakes

You make money when you win big pots and lose small ones. You also make money when your opponents make big and frequent mistakes (especially in relation to what you hold), and you make small and infrequent ones. If your opponents made no mistakes, there'd be no money for you to win. Your opponents' mistakes are your opportunities for profit.

Everyone makes mistakes. The goal isn't to play mistake-free. Good no limit players try to win the battle of mistakes. Winning the battle of mistakes means making sure that your opponents make more frequent and more costly mistakes than you do.

You do this by creating difficult situations for your opponents. You set traps for them. You recognize how to put the most pressure on them.

All the while, you try to avoid those difficult situations yourself. You look ahead, both to later decisions in the same hand and to future hands, and you foresee the traps and dangers. You avoid them before they cause you trouble — before they cost you money.

At every decision, good players think about the battle of mistakes. "Will this raise help my opponent to play correctly against my hand, or will it trick him into playing incorrectly? Will this call give my opponent the opportunity to make a play that puts me in a tough spot, or will it help me to avoid a sticky situation?"

Reading Hands

Most players know that reading hands is a critical skill. If you can consistently and accurately deduce what your opponents' cards are, you can beat the best players in the world.

Hand reading is deeper than many players seem to think it is. It's not just about knowing what you have and guessing what your opponent has. It's about getting into your opponent's head. "Given how I've played the hand so far, what might my opponent think I have?" Or, "Given what my opponent knows about how I think, what might he think that I think he has?" Or even, "Is he trying to deceive me, and if so, what does he want me to think he has? And, therefore, what sort of hand might he actually have?"

Hand reading is also an exercise in juggling probabilities. Rarely will you be able to deduce with certainty what cards your opponent holds. Usually, the best you'll be able to do is to sort candidate holdings into categories like, "Likely," "Somewhat likely," or "Unlikely." You might observe the way a pot has played out and conclude, "She's probably either got a terrific hand, or she's bluffing. It's unlikely that she's got a fairly good or a so-so hand."

Finally, the hand reading skill requires that you be able to use the insight into your opponents' possible holdings to formulate your strategy. It does you no good to know which hands are likely and which hands aren't if you can't translate that knowledge into the right play. The translation process relies upon logical reasoning, and it too is a valuable skill.

Manipulating Opponents into Playing Badly

This skill is similar to, but separate from, winning the battle of mistakes. Your opponents' states of mind will shape their thought processes. If they've been winning a lot, they might be more prone to play one style. If they've been losing, they might play another. You can make certain noteworthy plays (or just pay attention to the plays you've made "naturally") and take advantage of your opponents' reactions to them.

They also might play one way or another if someone (you) at the table is talking to them, flirting with them, taunting them, or arguing with them. Manipulating your opponents means behaving in a way that gets them to play the way you want them to play. Put them on tilt. Put them at ease. Get them drunk. Make them feel sorry for you. Make them fear you.

From Skills to Success

These are some of the most critical skills for no limit success. There are other important ones as well, but mastering these will give you a big edge in most games. The remainder of the book will offer insights to help you hone these skills.

We take a bottom-up approach to teaching. We don't say, "Here's how to manipulate the pot size in fifty different situations," or "Let's learn about all the different stack sizes." Instead, we offer a series of concepts and examples, each of which is designed to clarify your thinking in one or more of these areas.

We usually aren't going to tell you what to do. We're going to expose you to some ideas and show you some examples. We're not telling you, "This is how you should play in this situation." We're saying, "Here's something to consider as you make your decisions."

If you are reading a section, and you feel like you don't "get it," refer back to this section. Think about the big picture. If you want to be a great no limit player, you want to master these skills. Think about how the concept you're struggling with relates to the skills.

Now that you know what it takes to be a good no limit player, let's get started.

No Limit and the
Fundamental Theorem of Poker

In David's book *The Theory of Poker*, he introduces a concept he calls the "Fundamental Theorem of Poker:"

> Every time you play a hand differently from the way you would have played it if you could see all your opponents' cards, they gain; and every time you play your hand the same way you would have played it if you could see all their cards, they lose. Conversely, every time opponents play their hands differently from the way they would have if they could see all your cards, you gain; and every time they play their hands the same way they would have played if they could see all your cards, you lose.[2]

The basic idea is that, if you could see your opponent's cards, you'd always choose the "ideal" play, the play that serves you best. You'd never pay off with a second-best hand, and you'd never fail to bet when you should. Every time you make a play other than the "ideal" play, you have made a "mistake," and you've cost yourself some money.

Note that we use the term "mistake" in a specific and somewhat peculiar sense. We don't mean that you played badly, or that a more skillful player would have played differently. We just mean that you played differently than you would have if you could have seen your opponent's hand. For instance, say you have $500 left in a tournament with $100-$200 blinds. You're on the button with pocket kings, and you move in. Your opponent in the big blind calls and shows pocket aces. Raising all-in there with kings is clearly correct. But your raise was a "mistake" in our

---

[2] *The Theory of Poker* by David Sklansky, pages 17-18.

terminology because you wouldn't have moved in had the big blind shown you the aces first.

Throughout the book, we will use the term "mistake" in this sense; a mistake is a play other than the play you would make if you knew your opponent's cards, but it's not necessarily a bad play.

The Fundamental Theorem of Poker highlights the value of hand reading and deception. One of your goals when you play no limit hold 'em is to try to deduce your opponent's holding while disguising your own. You try to make few mistakes, while you encourage your opponent to make lots of them. If you do a good job, you will be winning the "battle of mistakes," and over time money will flow from your opponent to you.

Indeed, the format of no limit hold 'em allows the Fundamental Theorem of Poker to blossom fully. In limit poker, many situations arise where you simply cannot entice your opponent to make a mistake no matter what you do. Say you are limited to a $20 bet, and you know that your opponent has a flush draw. If the pot is $200, there's absolutely nothing you can do to encourage your opponent to make a mistake. You can bet $20, and he will call, just as he would do if he saw your cards. The 11-to-1 pot odds make the bet and call automatic plays, and neither player has any real opportunity to make a mistake.

In no limit, however, you can choose whatever bet size you want. That ability allows you to deceive your opponents more fully and to encourage them to make mistakes. You could bet $150 into the $200 pot, and the player with the flush draw might no longer be correct to call. If your opponent likes to draw to flushes, and he isn't so concerned about the exact odds he's getting, he may be willing to call your $150 bet even though it's a mistake.

Say you know your opponent well enough to know that he will call a $100 bet correctly, and he will fold to a $200 bet correctly, but he'll mistakenly call bets in between. You can target your opponent's weakness by betting the exact right amount to encourage his mistakes.

> No limit hold 'em permits you to exploit the weaknesses in your opponents' playing styles by betting just the right amounts to induce them to make mistakes.

Manipulate your opponents and create situations where they are likely to make mistakes. Don't let them off easy. Place them in situations where their natural tendencies lead them astray.

For instance, some players (and we'll talk about these players more later in the book) are particularly suspicious (especially if you've given them even the slightest reason to be suspicious in the past). They seem to always be worried that every bet is a bluff. Consequently, they tend to call bets (particularly some big ones) that they shouldn't call. These players make for very profitable opponents in no limit hold 'em, and the reason is that they are very likely to pay off with second-best hands when they shouldn't. That is, they systematically tend to make one certain type of mistake.

If you were playing limit hold 'em, there would be only so much you could do to exploit this weakness. You could bet for value somewhat more often against these players, but your bet size would be fixed (and small relative to the pot size). And you'd play many hands exactly the same way, whether your opponent was suspicious or not.

In no limit, however, you can exploit this weakness to its fullest. You can vary your bet size on the river to make it the largest you think your suspicious opponent is likely to call. By betting more against suspicious opponents than against unsuspicious ones, you tailor your play to exploit your opponents' weaknesses and set up situations where their natural tendencies will be their downfall.

And betting more on the river isn't the only thing you can do to exploit this weakness. You can also manipulate the betting and pot size on earlier betting rounds to encourage them to make big river calls even more often than they already do. We'll learn more about this idea in later chapters.

In any event, you should set up pots where your opponents will make mistakes without even thinking about it. Likewise, you should avoid making plays that your opponent can't help but respond to correctly. (We'll give you some examples of these plays later in the book as well.) If you give your opponents enough opportunities to make mistakes, they'll make some. Furthermore, you should try to avoid situations where you are likely to make a mistake. Plan ahead for bets later in the hand (and even for future hands), and don't allow yourself to fall into a difficult situation where you're likely to make a mistake. To win the battle of mistakes, you have to maximize the number of mistakes your opponents make and minimize the number you make.

> **Good no limit players magnify their opponents' weaknesses and make plays to which the expected response is a mistake. Good players also actively avoid falling into situations where they are likely to make a mistake.**

> **Bad no limit players make things easy on their opponents by making plays to which the expected response is also the correct response. Bad players also don't plan ahead, and they wander into traps set by their opponents.**

If you read and understand all the concepts in this book, you'll be well on your way to playing like the good players.

Thinking In Terms of Expectation — Playing the Nuts on the River

You are heads-up and last to act on the river with the nuts. Specifically, say you have

and the final board is

After some bets on the previous betting rounds, the pot contains $100. You and your opponent each have $500 left. Your opponent bets $50. How much should you raise?

Some players might instinctively want to raise a small amount, $50 or $75 maybe, to avoid "scaring their opponent off." But your goal shouldn't be to maximize your chance of getting called. Instead, you should *maximize your expectation*.

When you are heads-up and last to act on the river with the nuts, your expectation on a bet or raise is given by (ignoring check-raises or bet-reraises)

$$EV = (P_{call})(S)$$

where:
P_{call} is the chance you will be called by a weaker hand, and S is the size of your bet or raise.

To find the right bet size, you have to estimate the chance of being called by a weaker hand for bets of different sizes. Specifically, let's consider three potential raise sizes for this example: $50 (small), $150 (medium), and $450 (large and all-in). If you make the small $50 raise, you think your opponent will likely call with most of his possible hands. Maybe you expect him to call your minimum-sized raise about 80 percent of the time.

If you make the medium $150 raise, you expect your opponent to fold any hand that doesn't include a seven (making a straight). However, since he bet the river into this scary board, you think he has a relatively good chance of having a seven. Let's say he's got a 40 percent chance to have a seven and call the raise. (Please ignore the chance that he has a ten-seven with you, so your straight will always be bigger than his.)

If you make the large $450 raise, your opponent will again likely fold anything except a seven, and we've already posited that he'll have that hand 40 percent of the time. But say your opponent is a little scared of big bets, and you aren't sure he'll call such a large bet with just a seven (he'll fear you have the hand you have, ten-seven). Say you think there's a 50/50 chance he'll call an all-in raise if he has a seven. Thus, you think he'll call you about 20 percent of the time (half of 40 percent).

To find out which raise size is best, you should calculate the expectation for each size. The expectation for the $50 bet is $40.

$$\$40 = (0.80)(\$50)$$

The expectation for the $150 bet is $60.

$$\$60 = (0.40)(\$150)$$

Finally, the expectation for the $450 bet is $90.

$$\$90 = (0.20)(\$450)$$

The small "don't chase them away" raise works out to be the worst of these three options; moving in makes you the most money on average over the long run.

And while we made up the percentage chances you'd get called for this example to make the mathematical process easy to understand, in practice moving in is likely to be the best play in this scenario.

A one-card straight is possible, but you have that hand beaten because you hold the top card also. Anyone without a straight will be hard-pressed to call a decently-sized raise, and anyone with a straight will be hard-pressed to fold. Your only real decision is whether to make a tiny raise to try to get two pair and trips to call or to forget about those hands and try to get the most out of a trapped straight. Because you have so much money behind, your best play is to move in and hope your opponent has a seven.

Final Thoughts

Expectation is at the heart of every no limit decision. You shouldn't bet a certain amount "because you want to make sure you get called," or because "you're trying to look weak." You should bet that amount because it maximizes your expectation.[3]

---

[3] On rare occasions you might choose a play that gives you a slightly less than maximum expectation because it significantly limits your risk. These occasions usually arise if you are on a limited bankroll or are in the end stages of a tournament. They can also arise when you

Now your bet might maximize expectation *because* it's likely to get called or it looks weak, but those factors are only a means to the end: making the most profit by maximizing expectation. Throughout the book, we'll analyze many decisions by evaluating which option has the highest expectation. Thinking in these terms will make you a clearer thinker and a better player.

---

want to avoid giving a "live one" any chance to win so much that he might be inclined to quit.

The Pot Size Philosophy

This will be a brief section, but don't let that fool you. It's one of the most important in the book. It's a simple (and seemingly obvious) philosophy for playing deep stack no limit, but one that you ignore at your peril. We call it the pot size philosophy.

Big pots and big bets are for big hands.

For a moment, take a 30,000-foot view of no limit. Ignore specific hands, situations, and bluffs. Just think in general terms. On most hands you don't bet much. On a few hands you bet a lot. If you want to win, you have to, on average, bet more on your good hands than you do on your bad ones. If you consistently get it backwards, if you build big pots with bad hands, but keep the pot small with good ones, you'll get crushed over the long haul.

Obvious, right? Except many players frequently get it backwards. They slowplay and milk with their good hands and make too many big, daring bluffs. Sometimes they do it in the name of deception. A little deception is good, but it's only a balance to normal behavior. And normal behavior should be big pots and big bets for big hands.

For instance, some no limit players opine that that they are more likely to call a big bet on the end than a small one if all they have is a bluff-catcher. They figure that, with a good hand, most players would try to "milk" them by making a reasonable-sized, callable bet. So a big bet must be a bluff.

Sometimes these players are right. Against some rare opponents, they might have it close to exactly right. But, *as a general principle*, calling big "bluffs" but folding to small "value bets" is horrendous strategy.

If you don't understand why, think about how easy such a strategy would be to exploit. In principle, the most profitable general betting scheme against players like that is to bet small when bluffing and bet big when betting for value. That way, you risk little when bluffing, but you get the most value for your big hands.

Naturally, a bettor has to mix that pattern up to avoid being too readable against most opponents, but he wouldn't have to mix it up against someone who calls big bets and folds to small ones. It would be a double whammy for the perverse caller: He'd tend to lose both more money and more often to value bets, and he'd snap off bluffs for less money and less often.

Habitually playing big pots with small hands and small pots with big hands will leave you swimming upstream against the Amazon. Even if you're the best swimmer in the world, eventually you'll make a mistake or tire and be carried away.

The pot size philosophy, however, is about far more than which bluffs to call. It should be with you at every decision you make. Look at your hand. Look at your opponent. Look at the size of the stacks. Think about how the action might go down if you bet $30. Then think about what might happen if you bet $60. What about if you checked?

Do you want to play a big pot with your hand in your position against your opponent? If you do, choose the action now that makes a big pot likely by the river. If not, choose the action most likely to produce a small pot.

Keep in mind that the biggest pots aren't necessarily always made by the biggest bets preflop or on the flop. Sometimes a small initial bet is most likely to trigger an avalanche of money. Sometimes a check-raise will be the best tactic.

The decision will depend on the board, on the size of the stacks, and on your opponents' proclivities. You'll need to think about what your opponent might have, what your opponent might think you have, and how your opponent might view a check or a bet of various sizes. You'll need to gauge how big the bets and raises are likely to be throughout the hand, then look at the stack sizes and work backward to see when, if, and how the big pot will be built. Then you pick the option most likely to get all the money in the pot.

If you want a small pot, then you have to go through the same process. The only difference is that you'll select the option least likely to produce a big pot.

Deep stack no limit hold 'em is largely about building big pots when you want them big and small pots when you want them small.

The Pot Size Philosophy — An Example

Say you are playing $2-$5 no limit with $500 stacks. You are in the big blind with

Someone opens from middle position for $20. You call. The flop is

so you flopped a set.

Obviously, you want a big pot. Your goal should be to get the remaining $480 into the pot. It's going to be hard to do that if your opponent raised with T♠7♠ or 2♥2♣. But if he has aces, ace-king, or even a flush draw, you have a decent shot at his stack.

The first thing you should do is assume he has a hand that he might go all-in with. Pretend he's got pocket aces or ace-king, and formulate your plan based on that assumption. Why so optimistic? You're optimistic because the other possibilities, though likely, are largely irrelevant. No matter what you do, you're likely to achieve the same result in many cases. If your opponent has pocket nines or kings, then you're destined to get stacked almost no matter what. If he has flopped two pair, then you're destined to stack him, unless he outdraws you. (Note: These hands are "destined" only because of the size of the starting stacks. If you were playing ten times deeper, with $5,000 stacks, your destiny might be different.)

If he has a weak hand, and he's not a habitual bluffer, there's almost no way you can play it to make out big. If he has ace-high, then you might catch him for a little something if you check the flop and an ace happens to come off on the turn. But against most players, you won't make much extra profit even in that circumstance. You'll have only two streets to get $480 in on a $40 pot. That's going to require excessively large bets on your part, and any decent opponent with only one pair will rightly be suspicious. You'll usually have to be content with only a small win if the flop gets checked.

Against opponents who aren't habitual bluffers, your playing decisions matter most when your opponent has one of only a few holdings: good, but not great, hands like aces, ace-king, or a flush draw. Thus, tailor your strategy to maximize performance against those hands.[4]

The way to get the most money out of the good, but not great, hands is to make sure that it's "too late" by the time your opponent suspects he's beaten. Don't let him suspect when there's only $200 in the pot and $400 left to go. Give him the bad news of a big bet only once there's more like $500 in the pot and $250 left to go. Even though he'll suspect he's beaten, he may feel "pot committed" (in many cases, he'll be right) and pay off.

So, working backward, you want your last bet or raise to be about $250 (or somewhat less). How should you construct the

---

[4] Note that this trick of narrowing down your opponent's holdings to the "important" ones works best against conservative opponents. Against a habitual bluffer who bets the flop and often the turn with weak holdings, allowing him to bluff makes the most money. You become more concerned with making money against his weaker hands, because they are so profitable to you (assuming you allow him to bluff). In that setting, you would check multiple streets.

betting to get the first $230 in without raising too many suspicions?

Generally speaking, the last $250 bet will materialize either as a river bet or a turn raise. You might get it all-in on the flop, but if that happens, it usually won't require much planning on your part. It will just require an opponent who wants to get it all-in as well.

That first $230 to be bet can be broken up in roughly two different ways: a $70 bet and a $160 bet, or a $30 bet, a $70 bet, and a $130 bet. (The numbers are obviously only approximate. This whole planning process is approximate; the plan may need to be changed or abandoned entirely, depending on what actually happens.) That is, bets generally escalate in size during no limit hands, and so you should break your $230 down into two or three "chunks," each one bigger than the last.

Which option you choose, the two- or three- "chunk" option, depends on your opponent. The $70 and $160 option has the upside of offering your opponent few chances to gauge your hand strength.

Say you bet $70 on the flop, and he calls. Then you bet $160 on the turn. Should he call? Move in? Fold? Anyone with aces or ace-king will have an extremely tough decision because there is so little information for him to go on. Sure, you're betting strongly, but you don't know that his hand is as strong as it is. Maybe you are trying to push him off something weaker. It'll be hard for him to tell, so often he'll end up guessing. Whenever your opponents guess in critical situations, you're looking good. Sometimes they'll guess wrong, and you'll be rewarded with their stack.

The downside to the two-chunk option is that it forces you to overbet significantly on the flop. First, you're betting $70 into a $40 pot. Then you're betting $160 into a $180 pot. Those big bet sizes (compared to the size of the pot) will make some opponents skittish. They may see the big pot brewing and lay down quickly if they are particularly timid (or astute) players.

Your flop overbet will seem out of the ordinary to some adept opponents. They may figure out that you are trying to manipulate them into playing a big pot, and this may allow them to abandon ship. That's why it's so important to think about not only what your opponent might have, but also what your opponent might think you have, and how your opponent might interpret your bets. Some opponents will get snookered by the overbet, seeing it as a sign of semi-weakness. Others will see the overbet as a threat.

The three-chunk option, bets of $30, $70, and then $130, doesn't require overbetting at any juncture. If you bet $30 initially, it'll be into a $40 pot. The $70 bet will be into a $100 pot ($40 plus two $30 bets). Then the $130 bet will be into a $240 pot ($100 plus two $70 bets).[5]

The downside is that, since those three bets are intended for at most two betting rounds, your opponent has to make a bet or raise somewhere along the line. That is, if you are to get your $250 final bet in on the river, you somehow need to get $30, $70, and $130 in on the flop and turn. You can't get all three bets in if your opponent just calls twice; you'll just get the $30 and $70 bets in and be left with $380 on the end.

If you can count on your opponent to raise at least once with aces or ace-king, three chunks may be the way to go. Particularly, if you can count on your opponent to raise the flop and then bet the turn if checked to, then three chunks are surely your best option: bet $30 on the flop and get raised (hopefully about $70 more). Then check and call on the turn (hopefully about $130). Finally, bet $250 on the river. (Or you can check-raise all-in on the turn.)

If your opponent is less aggressive, though, then you may have to put in the raise. You could check-raise the flop: check, allow him to bet $30, and raise $70 more. Then bet $130 on the turn and $250 on the river.

Unfortunately, that's a "strong arm" line; check-raising can be very intimidating, particularly if you have a lot of money behind. You may lose your opponent, especially to the $130 turn bet. (Check-raising the flop and checking the turn usually won't

---

[5] Depending on your opponent, you may want to bet slightly more on the $70 and $130 chunks, leaving less than $250 for the final bet.

work either, because most opponents will merely check the turn back.)

You could also check and call on the flop, planning to check-raise the turn. But again, that's a "strong arm" play, and you'll lose many players on the big check-raise.

The right line will differ from opponent to opponent and situation to situation. If your opponent calls big bets too often, but doesn't put in enough raises, then two chunks should be best. If your opponent is hyper-aggressive, but looks to make tough laydowns, then go with three chunks, and let him put in a raise. If you recently got caught on a big check-raise bluff, then any option that involves check-raising becomes more attractive. Your opponents will remember the bogus check-raise and look you up.

The overall philosophy, however, is the same no matter your opponent or situation. You have a big hand, and big hands are looking to win big pots. Break down the future action, and figure out how you can best construct the big pot. Figure out how big you want your last bet to be, and work backward from there. How can you maximize the chance that your opponent is still around when that big bet comes down? How many "chunks" will you need to get there? Do your opponent's tendencies naturally suggest one line or another?

Perhaps this process seems cumbersome or superfluous to you now. So many things can happen; perhaps you figure you should play one street at a time. But this sort of bet planning and pot size manipulation is the key to successful deep stack no limit. Learn to think this way during every hand, and you won't regret it.

The Importance of Implied Odds

Say you have $500 in a $2-$5 blind game. In middle position, you make it $20 to go with

Everyone folds to the big blind, who has you covered. He says, "raise." As he goes to his stack to cut off enough chips for his raise, he accidentally shows you his hand (though he's not aware that he did it):

Should you always fold? Or does that decision depend on how much he raises? Clearly if he raises all-in, $480 more, you should fold. You are roughly a 4.5-to-1 dog, while you would be getting barely more than even money (520-to-480) to call.

But hopefully just as clearly, if he raises the minimum, $15, you should call like lightning. Why is that?

Including his raise, the pot would be $55 (your $20 plus the big blind's $35). So you are risking $15 to win $55. But that's not all, for almost no matter what cards come, you can expect the player with aces to bet the flop. Say he will usually bet the size of the pot: $70. If you don't flop a jack (or if you do, but he flops an ace also), you'll fold. But if you flop a set and he doesn't, you almost always win that $70, plus the $55 that was in the pot, plus even more.

So really you are risking $15 to win at least $55 plus $70, or $125. That's immediate odds of 125-to-15 or about 7.33-to-1. Since the odds of you flopping a jack without him flopping an ace are about 8-to-1 against, calling shows an immediate profit if you can win an average of about $10 more than that over the course of the hand.

In practice, you'll win significantly more than $10 more on average. To fail to hit that mark, your opponent would essentially have to refuse to give any more action at all. That is, with A♠A♣ on a J♣7♥2♦ flop, he would have to give up immediately every time his flop bet is called or raised. If you meet someone who actually plays that weakly, you can steal almost every pot from them.

In any event, while you'll lose eight times out of nine when you don't flop a set, you'll make, on average, significantly more than eight times your $15 investment those times you do, so you have an easy call.

So where did your opponent with the aces go wrong? He made the mistake that we'll call "offering too high implied odds." That is, he raised too little, so even though you called as a big underdog, you could afford to gamble because you'd be adequately compensated if you got lucky.[6]

> **Avoid offering your opponents too high implied odds. Make sure that you bet or raise enough with your good hands so they can't profit by playing for a longshot.**

---

[6] When the stacks are deep, you also must know when to get away from hands on the turn and river to avoid offering too high implied odds. We discuss this idea in the next section.

How big a raise would be "enough?" Since the pocket jacks will flop a set (with no overset) one time in nine, if he raised an amount equal to one-eighth (offering you odds of 8-to-1) of your total possible win, calling would be break-even at best. Your total available win is $520, the $500 in your opponent's stack and the $20 you already raised. (Remember, once you bet, the money is no longer yours.) So if he were to raise $65

$$\$65 = \frac{\$520}{8}$$

you could not possibly make any money with your jacks. To see that for sure, let's play the hand nine times.

Eight of those nine times, you will call the $65 raise, fail to flop a set (or flop a jack while he flops an ace), and fold to your opponent's $170 (pot-sized) bet. That's a loss of $520.

$$\$520 = (8)(\$65)$$

The last time, you'd flop a jack, raise the pot-sized bet all-in, and (hopefully) get called for a total win of $520 (your opponent's $500 plus your $20 raise). Actually, you wouldn't even win the full $520 because sometimes your opponent will catch an ace on the turn or river and win instead.

The bottom line is, if your opponent reraises only a small amount, you can call him, hoping to get lucky and bust him. If he reraises about $65 or more, though, there's nothing you can do. You have to fold.

Imperfect Information and Implied Odds

The previous example was idealized because you knew exactly what your opponent had: pocket aces. You could play perfectly against him, always folding without the required implied odds and making the most when ahead. In that situation, the player with pocket aces had to raise a relatively large amount, $65 in a $40 pot, to protect himself from you.

Real poker is played with hands facedown, though. If you have pocket jacks and all you know from your opponent's reraise is that he has a "good" hand, but not necessarily pocket aces, then your situation is weaker.

For instance, we said before that about one-ninth of the time you'll flop a jack without him flopping an ace. But about one-one-hundredth of the time, you'll both flop a set, and if you don't know he has pocket aces, you'll almost certainly get stacked. Now your EV for a $65 reraise is -$4.80.

$$- \$4.80 = (0.88)(- \$65) + (0.11)(\$520) + (0.01)(- \$480)$$

The remote threat of getting stacked if you both flop a set costs you almost an extra $5 a hand. That means that your opponent with secret pocket aces doesn't have to raise as much to keep your call from being profitable.

Also, if your opponent sometimes will reraise preflop with smaller pairs or unpaired hands like ace-king (as almost everyone will), then your implied odds situation is much weaker still. Sometimes when you hit your set, you won't get your opponent's stack. Meanwhile, when you don't hit your set, the raiser will get you to lay down what turns out to be the best hand. In this situation, the most typical in real play, the raiser needs to raise less still to avoid offering you too high implied odds.[7]

So, putting you in the raiser's shoes for a moment, the more your opponent can narrow down the range of hands you might have, the larger of a percentage of your total stack you must bet

---

[7] Also in this situation, the player with aces need not reraise so much because he has to balance out the threat of giving a pair the right implied odds with the risk of scaring out hands like ace-king, ace-queen, or king-queen.

immediately to avoid rewarding your opponent's ability to take advantage of his knowledge.[8]

> **The more your opponents know about the exact nature of your hand, the more you have to bet immediately to avoid offering them too high implied odds.**

Here's another example. Say you are playing $5-$10 blind no limit with $2,000 stacks. Someone raises to $30 in early position, and you call on the button with 6♦5♦. Both blinds fold ($75 in the pot and $1,970 left to bet). The flop comes J♣7♣3♠, giving you a gutshot. Your opponent bets $100. At that point, he tells you (he's not lying) that he has a set of jacks. Furthermore, he promises to bet all the rest of his money on the turn no matter what comes.

If you call and miss your straight, you lose $100. If you call and make your straight, you still have to dodge a board pair on the river to win. Ten cards out of forty-four pair the board, so 23 percent of the time (10/44) you'll lose $1,970, and 77 percent of the time (34/44) you'll win $1,970 + $75 = $2,045. So your expected win if you catch your straight on the turn is $1,132.50.

$$\$1,132.50 = \left(\frac{34}{44}\right)(\$2,045) - \left(\frac{10}{44}\right)(\$1,970)$$

Thus, your implied odds are $1,132.50-to-$100 or about 11.3-to-1. Your chance to catch your straight is 4/45 or about 10.25-to-1. Since your implied odds are greater than your chance to make the straight, you should call.

Let's say that the preflop action and flop cards are the same, but now your opponent tells you (again, he's not lying) that he

---

[8] Again, when the stacks are deep, knowing when to get away from your hand will allow you to make smaller bets. Keep reading.

either has a set of jacks or A♣K♣ (for a big flush draw). And again, he promises to bet all-in on the turn no matter what happens.

First, there are three ways to have a set of jacks (J♥J♦, J♠J♦, J♠J♥), while only one way to have A♣K♣. So there is a 75 percent chance he has the set and only a 25 percent chance of the flush draw.

Knowing that, you have to fold to the all-in turn bet if you miss, even if you catch a pair, since even though you are now ahead of the flush draw hand, he's three times more likely to have the set and have you still drawing to the gutshot.

So again, you lose $100 if you call and miss your straight. But if you call and catch your straight, the math changes.

If you call and catch the 4♦, 4♥, or 4♠, then you are the favorite over both the set and flush draw. The set has a 23 percent chance to outdraw you (10/44), and the flush draw has a 20 percent chance (9/44), so weighting the jacks at three times the likelihood, he has on average about a 22 percent chance to outdraw you.

$$0.22 \approx \left(\frac{1}{44}\right)\left[\frac{(10)(3) + (9)(1)}{4}\right]$$

If you catch the 4♣, then 75 percent of the time, you are ahead and will be outdrawn 23 percent of the time (10/44). The other 25 percent of the time, you are drawing dead, the equivalent of being outdrawn 100 percent of the time. So he has about a 42 percent chance to outdraw you.

$$0.42 = \left(\frac{1}{44}\right)\left[\frac{(10)(3) + (44)(1)}{4}\right]$$

That is, three times out of four, you'll have a 22 percent chance (9.75/44) of being outdrawn. And one time out of four, you'll have a 42 percent chance (18.5/44). Together, this represents an aggregate 27 percent chance to be outdrawn.

$$0.27 = \left(\frac{1}{44}\right)\left[\frac{(9.75)(3) + (18.5)(1)}{4}\right]$$

Note that your chance to be outdrawn when your opponent always had the jacks was 23 percent. So things are now worse for you. How much worse exactly? Well, now your expected win is approximately $970.

$$\$970 = \left(\frac{32.06}{44}\right)(\$2,065) - \left(\frac{11.94}{44}\right)(\$1,970)$$

Thus, your implied odds are $970-to-$100 or 9.7-to-1. Your chance to catch the straight is still 10.25-to-1, so now you can't call profitably. Adding a little uncertainty about your opponent's hand turned a profitable call into an unprofitable one.

Put another way, your opponent made a mistake by betting only $100 when he told you he had exactly jacks. He offered you too high implied odds. With some uncertainty about his holding, though, his $100 bet is enough to make you fold.

While you will rarely play a poker game where you will know your opponents' hands with such certainty as in this example, the general principle applies: The more accurately your opponents can read your hand, the more you have to bet in proportion to your stack to prevent them from calling profitably. The more accurately you can read your opponents' possible holdings, the larger the bets you can call to try to bust (or bluff) them.

Don't Justify
Their Optimistic Calls

In the last section, we learned to avoid habitually offering your opponents too high implied odds. But there's another related rule: Don't justify your opponents' optimistic calls either.

What is "justifying your opponents' optimistic calls?" Well, say you bet one-fifteenth of your stack with a good hand. Your opponent calls with a gutshot, because she figures that she'll hit it one-eleventh of the time, and that she'll stack you if she does and make fourteen times her investment.

If she's right, and she does stack you when she hits her straight, then, in addition to offering her high implied odds, you have made the error of "justifying her optimistic call." If, on the other hand, you thwart her by folding before she gets your whole stack in, then you have done well.

Many no limit players' eyes are bigger than their heads. They often call decently-sized flop bets with longshot draws because they assume that if they get there, they'll stack you a large percentage of the time. If they are wrong, though, and they get your stack only a small percentage of the time, then they will lose money in the long run on these calls.

You can use this loose-calling tendency against your opponents if you refuse either to offer too high implied odds or to justify optimistic calls. That is, before you bet with good hands, you should mentally decide whether you are willing to pay off a big bet with the hand or not. (Obviously, sometimes you will decide one way, but change your mind later in the hand. Nevertheless, you should always be asking yourself, "Am I willing to lose a lot?")

> **Whenever you bet or raise, always have an answer in your head to the question: "Am I planning to pay off a big bet on this hand, or will I fold if it comes to that?"**

If you are willing to risk losing a lot, then you should usually avoid offering too high implied odds to players with the most likely draws. Bet enough so that if they call, they will lose money over the long term even if they do get you to pay off a big bet when they get there.

If you aren't planning to pay off a big bet (because you don't think this player will often bluff), though, then consider whether your opponent will call too often with weak draws, hoping to bust you. If she will, then use the fact that you aren't justifying her optimistic call to your advantage. Bet an amount that will look small enough to her, but that you know actually is too much for her to call because you know that you won't go broke.

For instance, say you have

on the button with a single opponent and a flop of

There is $100 in the pot, and you have only $800 left in your stack. With such a strong hand and so little left to bet, you likely will be betting your entire stack before the end of the hand. So if your opponent assumes he can call a flop bet, hoping to bust you on a happy turn card, he's right. He can bust you that way.

In that case, you should bet enough on the flop to avoid offering your opponent too high implied odds for the likely draws. In this case, the strongest likely draw is middle or bottom pair, a hand like 9♠8♠. With five outs (ignoring the backdoor draws for simplicity), he will get there about 5/45 times, or he's 8-to-1 against. With $100 in the pot and $800 left in your stack, he's got $900 total he can win.

If he gets there with a nine, which will happen 3/5 of the time he improves, you have eight outs (three aces, two queens, and three treys). If he gets there with an eight, then you have only the two queens. So even if he gets there on the turn, you'll draw out on the river 12.7 percent of the time.

$$0.127 = \left(\frac{3}{5}\right)\left(\frac{8}{44}\right) + \left(\frac{2}{5}\right)\left(\frac{2}{44}\right)$$

So, on average, when he gets there on the turn and all the money goes in, he'll win $900 87.3 percent of the time, and he'll lose $800 12.7 percent. His expected win in that circumstance is $684.10.

$$\$684.10 = (0.873)(\$900) - (0.127)(\$800)$$

He's 8-to-1 to make his hand, and he stands to win $684.10 if he does. You should bet at least $684.10/8 = $85.51 to avoid offering too high implied odds. If you bet any more than $85.51, then you will profit from his call. A pot-sized $100 bet would be fine. Slightly more than the size of the pot, perhaps $120, would be even better if you think your opponent is likely to call such a bet with middle pair.[9]

---

[9] You don't have to figure this precisely while you play. Just realize that you should offer him less than about 10-to-1.

But what if you have $5,000 left rather than only $800? Now a willingness to go to the felt indiscriminately can be costly. To avoid offering too high implied odds to someone with middle pair or a gutshot, you'd have to bet many times the pot. And if you do that, you're likely to get action mainly from flopped two pair and sets.

While A♥Q♥ is likely to be tops on a Q♠8♦3♥ flop, it is no certainty. And when you commit to $5,000 in betting to protect the $100 in the pot, those rare times you are beaten will destroy you. Instead, you should estimate how much you're likely to lose while finding out that your ace-queen is no good. Let's say for simplicity that you'll lose an average of $684.10 (as you did in the previous example) figuring out your ace-queen has been outdrawn. (The better your opponent plays, the higher this number will be, almost by the definition of "good" versus "bad" player.)[10] You should now bet an amount large enough to make sure your opponents won't profit by trying to outdraw you, but small enough so that they might *think* that you have mistakenly offered them too high implied odds.

Since $85.51 was a large enough bet to avoid pricing your opponent in for an average loss of $684.10 before, it still is now. So you should bet more than that. But you shouldn't bet so much that your opponent will never call. Once you have bet enough to offer too low implied odds, you want your opponent to call. So don't blow them out of the water. Bet an amount that they might call.

Keep in mind that your better opponents will look at your remaining stack and try to estimate how much they can get out of

---

[10] In practice, it's very difficult to make such an estimate with any real precision. For the purpose of this text, we will often make "estimates" with the foresight of Nostradamus. We are primarily teaching the mathematical processes for coming to conclusions, not telling you whether to raise or fold in specific situations. Thus, the actual numbers we choose are largely irrelevant. It's the process we use to come to a conclusion from those numbers that is important.

you if they hit their draw. Then they will compare that amount to your bet and try to decide whether they can draw profitably or not. Ideally, you want to bet an amount that you know is too much for the likely draws to call, but that is small enough that it might tempt your opponents.

> **When betting good hands with deep stacks, bet enough to make your opponents' draws unprofitable, but not so much that they won't often call.**

Final Thoughts

These implied odds concepts are at the very heart of deep stack no limit hold 'em. The single most important variable in any no limit decision is the size of the remaining stacks. The next most important variable is how loosely or tightly your opponents bet those chips. Every time you have a decision, you should ask yourself, "How much money, on average, can this hand make me?"

The first piece of information you need to answer that question is how much money is available to win and how likely it is that you will win it. Then you need to decide what action to take to maximize what you will win. These implied odds ideas are at the root of that winning thought process.

Bet-Sizing

One of the trickiest things to learn in no limit is how to size your bets correctly. We've already introduced the idea of maximizing expectation when you have the nuts on the river. But what if there are more cards to come?

The right bet size depends on your goals for the bet, the size of the stacks, psychology, and a number of other factors.

Ironically, though the ability to size your bets is the defining feature of no limit (as opposed to limit), many players spend almost no time thinking about how much to bet. They'll just default to a "standard" amount, or they'll let their emotions decide for them.

In this section, we'll give you some theoretical guidelines for deciding how much to bet. There's no "cookbook" formula for deciding the right bet sizes, but after you read this section you should know what factors to consider when you make your decision.

The Basic Rule

Generally analyses should start with the simple case and add complexities. We'll do that too, and thus we offer the (hopefully obvious) basic rule.

> **If your opponent's hand is worse than yours, and it's fairly obvious what it might be, bet more than he can profitably call.**

For instance, say you have

on a

board. Your opponent has checked to you in a $100 pot. Both you and your opponent have $400 behind. Based on the flop action, you think your opponent almost certainly has a diamond flush draw. (Ignore, for now, how you would know his hand so precisely. We'll soon get to imprecise situations.)

Nine river cards (any diamond except the two on board and the two he has) give him a winner. Therefore, he is a 3.9-to-1 dog (9/44) to beat you. Bet enough so that you offer him implied odds of less than 3.9-to-1.

Because you know his hand exactly, his implied odds are no better than the pot odds because you can fold if a third diamond comes. That is, if he draws out, his total win will be $100 plus whatever you decide to bet. A $40 bet offers 3.5-to-1 pot odds ($140-to-$40), so bet at least that much. (That $40 bet is the theoretical answer. In practice, you can expect him to call much more than $40 since he thinks he can often win a bet on the river if he hits.)

When Your Opponent Could Have One of Several Draws

In the last example, we knew exactly what our opponent's draw was. In practice, you rarely will. You may know that he's likely to be drawing, but you won't know whether he has a straight draw, a flush draw, bottom pair, etc.

Say you again have A♥A♠ on the turn in a $100 pot with $400 behind. But now the board is J♦T♦6♣9♣. You are fairly sure your opponent has a draw, but you don't know whether it's a diamond draw or a straight draw. It could even be a backdoor club draw with a hand like A♣T♣.

Whatever draw he has, he's likely to have about eight or nine outs (though big combination straight, flush, and pair draws are also possible). So he's still likely to be approximately 4-to-1 against to make his hand.

Unfortunately, your opponent won't make it easy on you and tell you which draw he has. If any of the "obvious" draws comes in, that is any diamond, king, queen, eight, or seven, he may bluff even if the card didn't complete his hand.

Now you can't just fold on the river if a diamond comes and your opponent bets. Depending on exactly how much he bets and how often he bluffs, you may still fold, or you may call. But either way, you lose money: if you call, sometimes you'll be paying him off, and if you fold, sometimes you'll be getting bluffed out.

Since your opponent can now sometimes make money from you on the river, his implied odds are significantly better than the pot odds. A bet offering slightly worse than his pot odds doesn't cut it anymore. You have to bet a larger amount to prevent him from calling profitably.

> **If your opponent could hold one of several draws, bet a larger amount than you would if you knew which draw he had.**

Don't Bet Too Much

Once you observe the basic rule and bet more than your opponent can call profitably, you should now root for him to call. That's because calling would be a mistake (if your opponent knew what you had), and you want your opponents to make mistakes even if they sometimes draw out and it costs you the pot.

While moving all-in anytime you know you have the best hand might prevent your opponent from calling profitably, it's still a dumb thing to do. Huge bets will blow your opponents out of the hand and *force them to play correctly*. According to the Fundamental Theorem of Poker, you should avoid plays that force your opponents to play correctly. Put them to a decision; let them make mistakes.

> **Bet more than your opponents can call profitably, but don't bet so much that you blow your opponents off their hands. Bet an amount that entices them to make a bad call.**

How Big Do You Want Their Mistake to Be?

We've limited your bet sizes to a range: Bet more than they can call profitably, but bet less than what would almost certainly blow them off their hand. Now we need to figure out what the right size is within that range.

You want to choose the size that will maximize your expectation. Roughly speaking, your expectation is equal to the approximate value of the mistake times the chance that they'll make the mistake.

By "value of the mistake" we mean how much money, on average, your opponent loses to you by making the mistake. Say your opponent can break even by calling a $100 bet (and profit by calling a bet smaller than $100). If you bet $101, then your opponent is making a mistake by calling, but it's a tiny mistake. The value of that mistake is less than $1 (less than because sometimes your opponent will draw out and win the extra dollar).

On the other hand, if your opponent calls a $1,000 bet, then he's made a huge mistake. Let's do a little math to get a feel for exactly how big these mistakes are.

Say you bet $100 into a $200 pot, and your opponent is a 3-to-1 dog. Ignore future betting for the moment. If your opponent calls, on average it will be break-even for him.

$$\$0 = \left(\frac{1}{4}\right)(\$300) + \left(\frac{3}{4}\right)(-\$100)$$

Now say you bet $150, and your opponent calls. On average, your opponent expects to lose $25 on a call.

$$-\$25 = \left(\frac{1}{4}\right)(\$350) + \left(\frac{3}{4}\right)(-\$150)$$

If you bet $200, and your opponent calls, on average he will lose $50.

$$-\$50 = \left(\frac{1}{4}\right)(\$400) + \left(\frac{3}{4}\right)(-\$200)$$

If you bet $600, and your opponent calls, on average he will lose $250.

$$-\$250 = \left(\frac{1}{4}\right)(\$800) + \left(\frac{3}{4}\right)(-\$600)$$

So when you bet $50 more than break-even, he loses $25. When you bet $100 more, he loses $50. When you bet $500 more, he loses $250.

> In general, the value of your opponent's mistake will be proportional to the excess amount you bet beyond the break-even point.

This is an important concept, so we'll repeat it. Your opponent's expected loss (and, thus, your gain) is proportional to the *excess* amount you bet (and he called), beyond what would have been break-even, not the total size of the bet. If $500 is a break-even amount, then you double your profit by getting $600 called versus $550. (A conclusion worth noting is that $600 will almost always be better than $550 in this scenario, as it offers double the profit potential. Your opponent would have to call $600 less than half as often as $550 to make the smaller bet better, and in practice, that will almost never happen.)

The value of your opponent's mistake is only half of the expectation equation. To get your total expectation, you have to multiply the value of the mistake by the chance your opponent will make the mistake. Again, a big all-in bet may offer your opponent the opportunity to make a huge mistake, but if your opponent will never be dumb enough to call, then you don't gain anything.

Say you are fairly sure your opponent has a flush draw, and a $100 bet will be break-even for her. You are choosing between three bet sizes: $150, $200, and $500.

You think that your opponent will call the $150 bet about 70 percent of the time, the $200 bet about 40 percent of the time, and the $500 bet 5 percent of the time. To find the best bet, you have to multiply the size of the mistake by the chance your opponent will make it:

$$\$35 = (\$150 - \$100)(0.70)$$
$$\$40 = (\$200 - \$100)(0.40)$$
$$\$20 = (\$500 - \$100)(0.05)$$

The best bet is the $200 bet. It doesn't get called the most often, but it has the highest expectation.

> **Bet the amount that maximizes your expectation: the value of your opponent's potential mistake times the chance your opponent will make the mistake.**

Expectation and Multiple Possible Hands

In the previous example, you maximized your expectation against a single, known hand. If your opponent can have one of several draws, you should maximize your expectation against the range as a whole. Sometimes doing this will mean allowing your opponent to draw profitably with the strongest of his possible draws.

Put another way, if your opponent can have a 4 out draw, an 8 out draw, or a 15 out draw, the bet size that maximizes your expectation might allow the 15 out draw to draw profitably if your opponent will call incorrectly those times he has the 4 or 8 out draws.

Say you think your opponent has one of two draws: one that's 4-to-1 to come in and one that's 2-to-1. You think your opponent will have the 4-to-1 draw 75 percent of the time and the 2-to-1 draw 25 percent of the time.

Again, for simplicity, assume that there will be no betting on the river (we'll adjust for river betting at the end). The pot is $1,000.

The break-even point for the 2-to-1 draw is a $1,000 bet ($2,000-to-$1,000). The break-even point for the 4-to-1 draw is a $333 bet ($1,333-to-$333).

You're considering two bet sizes: $1,500 and $500. If you bet $1,500, you're fairly sure your opponent will fold either draw (and be correct to do so). If you bet $500, you're fairly sure your opponent will call with both draws (correctly with the 2-to-1 draw, but incorrectly with the 4-to-1). If you bet $1,500, you will win the pot and no more. We'll call this the "baseline" and assign it a value of $0. You don't win anything from your opponent's mistakes, but you don't lose anything by giving away a profitable call either.

If you bet $500, then you gain because the 4-to-1 draw calls incorrectly, but you lose because the 2-to-1 draw calls correctly. The value of your opponent's mistake of calling with the 4-to-1 draw is $100.

$$- \$100 = (0.20)(\$1{,}500) + (0.80)(-\$500)$$

The value of *your* mistake by allowing your opponent to call with the 2-to-1 draw is $167.

$$\$167 = \left(\frac{1}{3}\right)(\$1{,}500) + \left(\frac{2}{3}\right)(-\$500)$$

So you gain $100 when your opponent calls incorrectly with the 4-to-1 draw, and you lose $167 when he calls correctly with the 2-to-1 draw. But he has the 4-to-1 draw three times more often (75 percent versus 25 percent), so your total gain against the baseline is $33.33.

$$\$33.33 = (0.75)(\$100) + (0.25)(-\$167)$$

Even though you made a mistake by allowing your opponent to draw correctly sometimes, your opponent made a bigger mistake by drawing incorrectly the rest of the time. Overall, in this case, you maximize your expectation with the smaller bet.

> **Choose your bet size to maximize your overall expectation, even if that sometimes means that your opponent can draw correctly against you.**

We ignored possible river betting in our analysis. In reality, the fact that your opponent can have one of several draws will mean that his implied odds are greater than his pot odds. Thus, according to the rule from earlier, you should bet a larger amount than you would if you knew your opponent's hand. So you might want to bet significantly more than $500 to ensure that his calls with the 4-to-1 draw are still significant mistakes.

Don't Take Away Their Rope

In the first example of the section, you had A♥A♠ on a Q♦7♦2♣4♠ board, the pot was $100, you and your opponent each had $400 behind, and your opponent was on a diamond flush draw. Our conclusion was that you should have bet at least $40 because he was 3.9-to-1 to make his draw, so you should have offered him no better than 3.5-to-1 pot odds.

Let's reconsider the same example, except now you hold Q♥Q♠. You have top set instead of an overpair, and the 4♦ and 2♦ make your opponent's flush, but give you a full house. Your opponent now has seven outs instead of nine, so he's 5.3-to-1 to beat you (7/44). By our earlier reasoning, you should offer no better than 5-to-1 pot odds, so you should bet at least $25 (offering $125-to-$25).

But our earlier reasoning doesn't hold anymore! Why not? Because if the 4♦ or 2♦ comes, not only do you not lose, but you stand to win your opponent's remaining $400 on the river. Let's compare two expectations: one where you make a big bet, forcing your opponent to fold, and another where you check, allowing him to draw for free.

If you bet a lot, forcing your opponent to fold, you'll win the $100 pot every time. So your expectation is $100.

If you check, then you win $100 whenever no diamond comes (35/44), win nothing when a non-pairing diamond comes (7/44), and win $500 ($100 plus $400) when the 4♦ or 2♦ comes (2/44). Your expectation if you check is $102.28.

$$\$102.28 = \left(\frac{35}{44}\right)(\$100) + \left(\frac{7}{44}\right)(\$0) + \left(\frac{2}{44}\right)(\$500)$$

Because your opponent will occasionally make a second-best hand and get stacked, you'd prefer that he draw for free than that he fold. The lower bound of your betting range isn't $25 — it's $0.

Obviously, you'd rather bet and have your opponent call than check. But you should bet an amount that you're fairly sure your opponent will call, even if that's less than $25 (although in this case it wouldn't be).

> **If your opponent could catch his draw, but still be second-best, tend to bet an amount you're fairly sure he'll call. Don't miss a chance to stack him by blowing him out too early.**

Your Opponent Thinks He May Have the Best Hand

In the preceding discussion we have been focusing on hands where your opponent thinks he has to improve to win. In those cases your bet is highly related to the number of "outs" you think he has. But that is a minor consideration when you think he has a legitimate made hand that you can beat.

For instance, if on the turn you have bottom two pair and you put your opponent on an overpair, he has eight outs. But that fact is largely irrelevant to your bet-sizing decision. Your bet should be significantly more than the minimum one-third pot-sized bet that having eight outs would suggest because your opponent isn't counting on having to improve to win. Your opponent is likely to call a sizable bet, so make one.

However, even when you're choosing a large bet size because your opponent may think he has the best hand, you still should consider whether he has outs. If he has no outs, and you think that he will call X dollars 100 percent of the time or 2X dollars 50 percent of the time, the two options have equal expectation. But if he has outs, the bigger bet is better because you now gain something when he folds.

You Might Not Have the Best Hand

Our analyses thus far have assumed that you always have had the best hand, and your opponent always has been drawing (or second-best). In practice, unless you hold the nuts, you will never be certain that you hold the best hand.

> **The more likely your opponent is to have you beaten, the less likely you should be to bet at all.**

If you are sure you have the best hand, then the trick to bet-sizing is to find the amount that causes your opponents to make the biggest aggregate mistakes (given your hand and their possible ranges).

But if you aren't sure, then betting at all could be a mistake for you. The larger the chance that you're beaten, the bigger that mistake becomes. As the chance you're beaten rises, you may be better off just letting your opponent draw.

Checking is usually best if you aren't the favorite,[11] and you act last. If you are out of position, however, sometimes you should

---

[11] You aren't the favorite as calculated by combining the chances that you are beaten already with the chances you will be outdrawn.

make a small bet even if you aren't the favorite. You do this if you frequently expect your opponent to make a large bet if you check. This sort of "small bet to stop a large one" is called a "blocking bet," and we analyze it in more detail in the "Blocking Bets" chapter starting on page 135.

Final Thoughts

You now have a solid theoretical understanding of how to size your bets. As a quick summary, here are the rules we learned:

1. Bet enough so that your opponents can't call profitably.

2. If your opponents could have one of several draws, and that fact means that you'll sometimes lose money on the river, bet more to cut down their implied odds.

3. Don't bet so much with the best hand that you blow your opponents out of the pot. You'd prefer they sometimes make a bad call than that they fold every time.

4. Size your bet to maximize your expectation, which is the size of your opponent's possible mistake times the chance he will make the mistake.

5. If your opponents might have one of several draws, size your bet to maximize your expectation against the total range of hands. Sometimes that will mean letting them draw correctly with strong draws if they'll also draw incorrectly with weak ones.

6. If your opponent might make a second-best hand that would cause him to lose a lot on the river, keep him in the hand. It's usually better to make a small bet that gets called than to blow him out of the hand with a big bet.

7. Ignore the number of outs your opponent might have if you think he has a hand that he believes may be better than yours without improvement. In that case, your bet should be much more than what his outs might indicate.

8. Don't forget that you may not have the best hand. The more likely you are to be behind, the less likely you should bet at all. If you aren't the favorite, checking is usually best if you act last, but if you are out of position, sometimes you should make a blocking bet instead.

The Hammer of Future Bets

I (Ed) was watching a poker tournament on TV once, and I heard the commentator say:

"He's moved all-in. The all-in bet is the strongest play you can make in no limit."

It sounds right, but actually it's not. Bets show more power the more money you leave behind. Betting $500 all-in on the turn isn't nearly as strong a move as betting $500 with $2,000 more behind.

Hopefully that fact is obvious: for the same size bet, having extra money left over for future betting is more threatening. But actually this concept of the "hammer of future betting" runs deeper than that. A small bet with money behind can be more powerful than a larger all-in bet.

This idea is correct due to the concept of "reverse implied odds." Drawing hands often benefit from implied odds. You risk a relatively small amount to take a chance at winning a large amount. You call a $50 bet with a gutshot for the chance to win your opponent's $1,000 stack. Your potential loss is limited, and your potential win can be great.

Reverse implied odds work the opposite way. You risk a relatively large amount to try to win a small amount. This situation arises most often when you have a decent made hand that has little chance to improve. And if you are also out of position the effect is stronger.

An example might be

on a

board. The pot is $500, and you and your opponent both have $3,000 behind. You check, and your opponent bets $500.

You could easily have the best hand. Your opponent might be betting any of a number of possible draws. Or she could be betting a made hand that beats yours. You aren't sure.

Unfortunately, you can't just call the $500 and find out whether you win or not. You may have to face another bet. Or you may not. It's up to your opponent whether to bet again on the river.

If your opponent is tough, she'll bet the river when she has the advantage and check it when she doesn't. Having the advantage doesn't mean necessarily having the best hand, however. It means usually having the best hand, but bluffing sometimes as well, and mixing the two up in such a way so that you lose no matter what you do. If you fold, sometimes you'll have been bluffed out, and if you call, usually you'll be paying off a better hand. Neither play wins for you.

If you call the $500 and check the river, you do so praying that your tough opponent checks behind you. Say she does check behind, and you win. Great, except you won only $1,000 for your trouble — the $500 originally in the pot and the $500 turn bet. You had to risk your whole stack, $3,000, for the chance to win that $1,000. Reverse implied odds forced you to put $3,000 at risk for the chance to win $1,000.

That's why the hammer of future betting is so powerful. If your opponent had been all-in on the turn, you'd have been in a much stronger position, even if the all-in bet had been $1,000 instead of $500. If she had bet $1,000 all-in, you would be getting straight $1,500-to-$1,000 or 3-to-2 odds to call. With money behind, however, you are in a sense laying odds, risking a lot to win a little.

Final Thoughts

When you possess the hammer, you take advantage of it by betting weak hands *before* the last round when you think your opponent's hand is mediocre. On the other hand, you avoid using the hammer if you think it will hurt you. In practice, this means that with a deep stack and a good hand you should often check the turn against a player you think has a weak hand. A player with a weak hand is likely to fold to a turn bet, fearing "the hammer" of a river bet. However, if you check the turn, he might well pay off a river bet.

Bluff-Sizing

We discussed sizing bets when you think you likely have the best hand. Now we'll talk about sizing bluffs. The principles involved are simpler.

The Basic Rule

As with bet-sizing, we'll start from the basic principle.

> **Bet enough to "get the job done," but not much more.**

A bluff involves two components: having a hand (or range of hands) in mind that your opponent might have, and betting enough to get your opponent to fold those hands.

You don't bluff to get your opponent to fold. You bluff to get your opponent to fold *if she has a specific hand (or a specific range of hands)*. You'll almost never know for certain what hand your opponent has. Given the way the hand was played, you may think your opponent probably has one pair. But every once in a while, she'll surprise you and show you the nuts (or some other much better hand).

Obviously, no amount of money will get your opponent to fold the nuts. That's not your goal. If you think your opponent probably has one pair, and you want her to fold when she has one pair, bet enough to get her to fold one pair and not much more.

So when sizing a bluff, first decide what hands you are targeting. Then size the bluff to get the job done.

Here's an example of bluff-sizing done horribly wrong according to the basic rule. At the 1979 World Series of Poker Main Event, Hal Fowler (an amateur) was heads-up against Bobby

Hoff (a no limit expert) for the title. For this hand, the effective chip stacks were about $200,000 each.[12]

There was a raise and call before the flop. The pot was about $20,000 at this point. The flop came

The action went check-check. The turn was the T♣. Again, it went check-check. The river was the 7♠.

Fowler now moved in — $190,000 into the $20,000 pot. Hoff folded, and Fowler proudly showed a bluff.

While the play succeeded (and Fowler went on to win), Fowler's bet-sizing was atrocious. Any jack made the nuts, so if Hoff "had it," he wasn't folding no matter how big the bet. And if Hoff didn't have a jack, then he would have folded to any reasonably-sized bet.

Fowler risked $190,000 when he could have risked $15,000 or $20,000 and won just as often. Fowler got away with it, as Hoff happened not to have a jack, and the details of this hand faded into obscurity.

On the other hand, if Hoff had turned up with a jack, this hand would be recounted today as one of the biggest blunders in WSOP history. Don't repeat this error.

---

[12] David witnessed this hand personally, but after twenty-six years, the details are a little fuzzy. The suits and order of the cards and the stack sizes might be slightly wrong, but it doesn't really matter for the story.

A Little More
About Getting the Job Done

Perhaps this is obvious, but it's worth saying anyway. The amount needed to get the job done is not always easy to figure out. Furthermore, it's not necessarily linear either. That is, you can't think of it like:

"Well, $20 will get him to fold a pair of deuces. $25 will fold treys. $50 will fold sixes, and $100 will fold kings. $200 will fold two pair, and $500 will fold a straight."

Things don't work that way at all. Finding the right amount is a psychological problem more than anything else. "If I bet $X, what will he put me on, what will he view his pot and implied odds as, and will he see his pair of queens as profitable?" You have to get into your opponents' heads and see your bets from their perspectives.

Indeed, sometimes a smaller bet will be more likely to get the job done than a bigger one. Obviously, when that's the case (or even if you suspect that's the case) then a small bluff is almost certainly a better play than a big one — less risk and higher chance of success.

> **There's no formula to tell how much it will take to get the job done. You have to analyze each case separately.**

An Exception to the Basic Rule

You may want to bet more than it takes to get the job done if you plan a follow-up bluff on the next betting round. That is, if you plan to bluff the turn, and, if called, also bluff the river, you don't necessarily want to make your turn bet as small as possible.

A planned follow-up bluff provides an extra incentive to make a larger bet: you may win a bigger pot on the second round bluff.

For instance, say you bluff $500 into a $1,000 pot. Your opponent calls. The pot is now $2,000. You bluff again, and this time your opponent folds. You've won $1,500 — the $1,000 that was in the pot originally plus your opponent's $500 call.

If you had bet $800 instead of $500 on the first round, then your second round bluff would have won $1,800 instead of $1,500. Sometimes this extra incentive to bet more will affect your bluff-sizing. See the next chapter "Bluffing on the Turn and River" for a more detailed analysis of this situation.

When Bigger Bluff Sizes Will Fold More Hands

You usually won't be able to read your opponent's hand accurately enough to know exactly what two cards you're up against. You'll have a general idea: "I think she's probably got a pair of queens, but she also might be slowplaying a set or have a straight draw."

Different strength hands will require different bluff sizes to "get the job done." If your opponent has a busted draw, then maybe almost any bet (say a quarter pot-sized bet) will likely be enough to get a fold. If your opponent has a pair, then maybe he'll call a quarter pot-sized bet, but fold for a two-thirds pot-sized bet. And maybe he won't fold a set no matter how much you bet.

Finding the right bluff size is again a matter of maximizing your expectation. For instance, say you are choosing between two bet sizes: quarter pot-sized and two-thirds pot-sized. (Let's say the pot is $300, and the candidate bet sizes are $75 and $200.)

You think your opponent has one of three hands: a busted draw, a pair, or a set. You think she has a busted draw 30 percent of the time, a pair 60 percent, and a set the other 10 percent.

A $75 bet will get the busted draw to fold 80 percent of the time (you'll get bluff-raised occasionally) and the pair 20 percent.

A $200 bet will get the busted draw to fold 90 percent of the time and the pair 70 percent. The set will never fold. The expectation of the $75 bet is then $60.

$$\$60 = (0.30)\big[(0.80)(\$300) + (0.20)(-\$75)\big] +$$
$$(0.60)\big[(0.20)(\$300) + (0.80)(-\$75)\big] +$$
$$(0.10)(-\$75)$$

The expectation of the $200 bet is $145.

$$\$145 = (0.30)\big[(0.90)(\$300) + (0.10)(-\$200)\big] +$$
$$(0.60)\big[(0.70)(\$300) + (0.30)(-\$200)\big] +$$
$$(0.10)(-\$200)$$

Thus, in this example, $200 is the better bluff size. You're better off trying to get both the busted draws and the pairs to fold rather than just the busted draws.

At the table, obviously you can't solve equations like this. (And you wouldn't know the percentages precisely anyway, so even if you could solve equations, it wouldn't necessarily help you much.) Just think about what hands you think your opponents might have, and what hands they might fold for what bet sizes. Choose the size that seems to give you the most benefit for the least risk.

Bluffing on
the Turn and River

WARNING: The following discussion assumes that you are in a game where your opponents are capable of laying down fairly big hands when they think they should. If you aren't in such a game, please ignore the advice in this chapter.

In many ways, deep stack no limit strategy revolves around a single threat: a big, multi-street bluff for all the chips. On most hands the threat never materializes, for if it did, soon the bluffers wouldn't have much money left with which to bluff. But the specter of the daring play hangs over any player with a strong, but not nut, hand.

The possibility of being blown away on the turn or river sometimes keeps players with top pair from building big pots on the flop. A holder of top pair who tries to press his perceived advantage with a $100 flop bet may eventually be faced with an extremely hard to call $1,000 possible-but-not-probable bluff on the river.

Hence, deep stack no limit proficiency necessarily means proficiency with the big turn and river bluff. This section covers some important concepts for that situation.

An Example of the Play

You are playing a $10-$20 game with $2,500 stacks. A strong player in middle position opens for $80. You call on the button with and the blinds fold, so the pot is $190. The flop comes

giving you a double-gutshot straight draw. Your opponent bets $150, and you call ($490 in pot).

The turn is the A♣. Your opponent checks. At this point, it's reasonably likely that he plans to fold if you bet a "standard" amount. So you bet $500. Your opponent thinks for a while, and then, to your surprise, calls. ($1,490 in the pot.)

The river is the J♥, pairing the top card and completing the front-door flush. You move all-in for $1,770, offering your opponent slightly worse than 2-to-1 to call. Hopefully your opponent will think for a while and then fold.

Your turn bluff is a somewhat "automatic" play; your opponent raised preflop and continued on the flop. If it turns out that he doesn't have much (in this case, less than a pair of aces), usually he'll check and fold the turn. To show an immediate profit, your opponent must fold about 50 percent of the time. Given the action, it's likely he will. (Of course, it's even better than that because he will sometimes call and lose to your straight.)

Of course, showing an immediate profit isn't enough to justify the bet, by itself, as you might make more by checking. Nevertheless, in many situations and against many opponents, the turn bluff is a no-brainer.

A river bluff is somewhat more daring. By calling the big turn bet, your opponent establishes that he has a fairly good hand. A reasonable read would be an ace (ace-king probably) or one of the two available flush draws (hearts or clubs), perhaps with an extra draw like a straight draw or flopped pair. He could have other hands — a set, two pair, or a straight draw perhaps — but checking and calling after betting the flop is most consistent with a good, but not great, hand.

With a great hand, your opponent might have bet again on the turn, hoping for a raise. Or he might have check-raised the turn. Or he might have checked and called the turn, but bet big on the river. Check-call on the turn and check on the river is likely not a monster.

The J♥ on the river is unlikely to please your opponent. If he has a club draw, he missed. If he has an ace, he can't like that the flush came in or the possibility of three jacks. And if he has hearts, he'll be worried, given your big bets, that you flopped a set and now have a full house. With a flush he should probably call getting almost 2-to-1 on the river, but a few opponents won't, letting their fear get the best of them. And with anything less than a flush, you'll usually get most opponents to lay down.

Two Principles
for Turn and River Bluffs

This section won't be about deciding when to try the turn and river bluffs. Finding those situations correctly requires accurate hand reading more than anything else. This section is about how much to bet on the turn and river. Or, more specifically, it's about how to divide your remaining money between the turn and river. There are two important principles for dividing your remaining money:

1.   Save enough on the turn for a credible bluff on the river.

2. Bet as much as you can on the turn while still retaining a credible river bluff.[13]

Save Enough on the Turn for a Credible River Bluff

Say the pot is $1,000, and you have $2,000 remaining. If you were to bet the pot on the turn, $1,000, you would have only $1,000 remaining to bet on the river if called. In that case, the pot would be $3,000 plus your $1,000 bet, so your river bet would offer odds of 4-to-1 to your opponent. If your opponent called your pot-sized turn bet with a made hand (likely), he'll probably call again getting 4-to-1. So $1,000 is not a credible river bluff.

Failing to leave enough for a river bluff hurts you two ways. Obviously, it limits your bluffing options. Instead of the turn and river bluffs, you are limited essentially only to a single street bluff. You can't take advantage of a scary river card if you don't have enough left to make it scary.

But it also takes the teeth out of your single street bluff. A $1,000 turn bluff will be much scarier if you have $3,000 or more behind than if you have $1,000 or less. With little behind, your opponent just has to decide how often you are bluffing and compare that percentage to his pot odds.

With a lot left, though, he has to worry about winning a little when he's right, but losing a lot when he's wrong. Many times you won't follow through on the river, and he'll be left with a "paltry" $1,000 win. But sometimes you will follow through, and he'll have a far tougher decision for far more money. (It's tougher for him because you'll bluff $1,000 on the turn and give up on the river more often than you'll bluff $1,000 and follow through for

---

[13] Note that we are talking about bluffing sequences where you will eventually move all-in. If you are extremely deep, you may make big bluffs on the turn and river, yet still not be all-in. Those situations are more complex to analyze than what we will talk about here.

$3,000 on the river. So, from his perspective, you're far more likely to have him beaten when he sees the $3,000 bet than when he sees the $1,000 one.)

Overall, the turn and river bluff play is much stronger when you have a credible threat left after your initial turn volley. How much is credible?

It should be significantly more than the size of the turn bet, and it should offer your opponent relatively short odds on a river call. As the odds get longer than about 2.5-to-1 or so (a bet two-thirds the size of the pot), your opponent will call more and more often. For instance, in a given situation your opponent might fold 75 percent of the time against a pot-sized bet (offering 2-to-1), but 20 percent or less against a one-third pot-sized bet (offering 4-to-1).

On the turn, you may simply not have enough money to try a turn and river bluff. And, since the turn portion loses teeth without the river portion to back it up, you may not be able to bluff profitably at all. From the start of the hand make sure your river bluff will be credible before you launch the play.

Bet as Much as You Can on the Turn While Still Retaining a Credible River Bluff

The flipside to the first principle is that you should bet as much as you can on the turn while still maintaining a "credible" river bluff. Generally speaking, your opponent's chance of folding on the river will look like a logistic curve (also known as an s-curve).

LOGISTIC CURVE

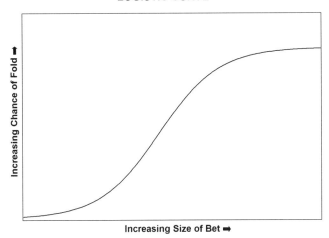

For all bet sizes that are only a small fraction of the size of the pot, your opponents will fold roughly the same number of hands: perhaps only busted draws and the very weakest made hands. For all bet sizes much larger than the size of the pot, your opponents will also fold roughly the same number of hands: almost everything except the nuts and perhaps a couple of other extremely strong hands.

In the middle, usually around the half-pot to one-and-a-half pot range, will be a sharp change in the fold percentage, where your opponents fold stronger and stronger hands to bigger and bigger bets. The optimal size for the river bet is the smallest amount that keeps your opponent folding most of the time.

That is, to find the right theoretical size for your river bet, start at the right-most edge of the graph and follow it left until it begins to drop significantly. Stop there and look at the corresponding bet size. That's about how big your river bet should be.

LOGISTIC CURVE

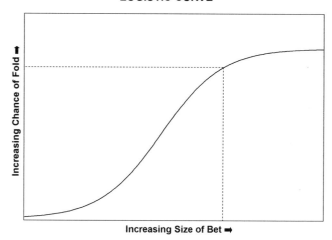

Why is that the right size? Well, if you bet more than that, then you risk significantly more for only a small increase in your chance of success. In a $1,000 pot, it makes no sense to bet $2,000 for an 80 percent chance of folding when you can get a 75 percent chance for $1,000. You'd lose an extra $1,000 20 percent of the time, while making an extra $2,000 (swinging a -$1,000 failure to a +$1,000 success) only 5 percent of the time.

But there's a more subtle reason that's just as important. The less you bet on the river, the more you can bet on your turn bluff. Betting more on your turn bluff serves two purposes:

1. Increases your chance of success, at least somewhat

2. Improves your potential reward on the river bluff if you get called on the turn

Say you have $4,000 to distribute between bluffs on the turn and river. The pot on the turn is $1,000. You are trying to choose between $1,000 and $3,000 bets or $500 and $3,500 bets.

You think a $500 bluff will succeed on the turn about 30 percent of the time, and a $1,000 bluff about 50 percent. If you've bluffed $1,000 on the turn, then you think a $3,000 river bluff into the now $3,000 pot will work about 70 percent of the time. If you bluffed $500 on the turn, then you think a $3,500 river bluff into the now $2,000 pot will work about 80 percent of the time.

Which series is better? When you bluff $500 and $3,500, you can have one of three outcomes: you can win the initial $1,000 if your turn bluff succeeds, you can win $1,500 if your turn bluff fails, but your river bluff succeeds, or you can lose $4,000 if you get called down.

You'll win $1,000 30 percent of the time. You'll win $1,500 80 percent of 70 percent of the time, or $(0.8)(0.7) = 56$ percent of the time. You'll lose $4,000 the other 14 percent. Thus, the EV of this sequence (assuming you have no chance to win by making the best hand) is $580.

$$\$580 = (0.3)(\$1,000) + (0.56)(\$1,500) + (0.14)(-\$4,000)$$

When you bluff $1,000 and $3,000, you can also have one of three outcomes: you can win the initial $1,000, you can win $2,000, or you can lose $4,000.

You'll win $1,000 50 percent of the time. You'll win $2,000 70 percent of 50 percent of the time, or $(0.7)(0.5) = 35$ percent of the time, and you'll lose $4,000 the other 15 percent of the time. (Note that we've set the numbers so that both sequences ultimately succeed roughly 85 percent of the time.) The EV of this sequence is, thus $600.

$$\$600 = (0.50)(\$1,000) + (0.35)(\$2,000) + (0.15)(-\$4,000)$$

Betting somewhat more on the turn and somewhat less on the river increases your overall EV by $20 even though, the way we set the numbers, your total chance of success drops slightly from 86 to 85 percent. It's because your turn bluff succeeds more often and because you win a bigger pot, $2,000 versus $1,500, when your river bluff succeeds.

You have to find the sweet spot. Dividing the bets $2,000 and $2,000 wouldn't work at all: It would violate the first principle by not leaving a credible bluff for the river.

> **When bluffing on the turn and river, maximize the size of your turn bluff while still leaving enough for a credible river bluff.**

Final Thoughts

While the concepts in this section are intended for a very specific play, the turn and river bluff, the ideas represent the same general deep stack philosophies we present throughout the book:

- The threat of a big bet is more powerful than the big bet itself. Bluffs are most effective when the threat of an even bigger and harder-to-call bet looms on the horizon.

- Effective deep stack play relies on planning and stack management. Make no bet or raise without planning out the bet, pot, and stack sizes for the remaining streets.

Bet-Sizing for Information

Betting or raising "for information" is a popular tactic among many poker players, particularly unschooled ones. They see betting primarily as a way to find out "where they're at," and they don't really think about the value of the information compared to what they pay for it. Information has value only if it

- Is specific and accurate.

- Allows you to make more profitable decisions now or in the future.

Obviously, there are shades of gray. Perfectly specific and accurate information is the best, but in poker that's usually only a pipe dream. Information that is highly reliable, though, is generally worth a lot more than merely suggestive information. That is, knowing that your opponent has either pocket aces, pocket kings, or ace-king is likely far more valuable than simply knowing that he has a "good hand, probably." The former information may be worth paying something (or taking on extra risk) to get. The latter probably isn't.

The information also has to allow you to make more profitable decisions now or in the future. If you have pocket aces in the big blind, and your opponent moves all-in, how much would you pay to see your opponent's hand before calling? Hopefully nothing, since you're calling no matter what you see. The information is perfectly specific and accurate, but it won't allow you to make a more profitable decision, so it's worthless.

Quantifying the Value of Information

Sometimes you can put a specific price tag on what information is worth. For instance, say, instead of pocket aces in the big blind, you have pocket kings. Now it's worth something if your opponent shows before you call, as you can fold if you see aces. Say your opponent has raised $100 all-in, and you think (correctly) that she would do this with pocket aces through nines, ace-king, and ace-queen. With kings, you're calling against every hand except aces. When she has aces, you're roughly a 4.5-to-1 dog, so calling costs you $64 (assuming, for simplicity, that the $1 and $2 blinds get raked away).

$$- \$64 = (0.82)(-\$100) + (0.18)(\$100)$$

So avoiding aces is worth $64. But usually you won't see aces; usually you'll see something else. She can have aces six ways, kings one way, queens through nines six ways each, ace-king eight ways, and ace-queen sixteen ways. The chance you'll see aces is approximately 11 percent.[14]

$$0.11 \approx \frac{6}{(6 + 1 + 6 + 6 + 6 + 6 + 8 + 16)}$$

Thus, getting to see if your opponent has aces is worth $(0.11)(\$64) = \$7.04$. If you had queens instead of kings, the

---

[14] For more insight into how this calculation is performed, see "An Essential Hold 'em Concept" beginning on p.118 of *Poker, Gaming, and Life* by David Sklansky.

information would be worth twice that, or $14.08, as you would be exactly twice as likely to see a hand you would fold to.[15]

Now what if the information weren't perfectly specific and accurate? Say you have pocket kings again, but instead of showing her cards, your opponent answers the question "Do you have aces?" Half the time that she has aces, she says "yes," and the other half, she says "no." She always says "no" when she doesn't have aces.

She'll still have aces 11 percent of the time, but she'll tell you she has aces only 5.5 percent of the time. So this information is worth $(0.055)(\$64) = \$3.52$. Even though it's not perfect, it's still worth something. The information would be worthless, however, if she tainted her "yes" answers with enough hands you can beat that you would have to make the call regardless of what she says.

Paying for Information

Most information at a no limit table won't be as easily quantifiable, at least not on the spot. But the criteria for value — accuracy and specificity, and allowing for better decisions — are always important. If you are thinking about taking an extra risk to get information, ask yourself how accurate it will be and how you will change your play based on it.

In limit hold 'em, though a popular tactic, paying for information is usually dubious. Throwing in an extra raise you otherwise wouldn't, or calling a bet you otherwise shouldn't, often doesn't work out.

We've written often that aggressive players in limit usually respond too unpredictably to allow you to alter your play profitably. Limit pots are usually so large compared to the bet size that the information has to be quite specific and accurate to allow you to fold. And the cost of making a bad calldown is relatively

---

[15] Jacks wouldn't be worth three times, though, as ace-king and ace-queen could now be made 16 ways each instead of 8 and 16.

small anyway, so even when you can profit, you don't profit much.

In no limit, though, the right information at the right time could save your whole stack. So the potential upside is much greater than it can be in limit. Also, the information tends to be somewhat more reliable. In aggressive limit games, a flop bet can be almost a dare to raise. If you follow through and actually raise, you'll often be met with a three-bet, sometimes made seemingly on principle alone.

In no limit, only the most reckless players would raise and reraise so blithely since the penalty for putting in a "light" raise (with a weaker-than-average hand) can be so much harsher. Instead of being charged an extra small bet in a pot ten times its size, light raisers can be met with enormous reraises that they can't call.

Also, a mere call transmits much more information in no limit. In limit, a flop call can frequently mean almost any range of hands: any pair, overcards, any draw worth discussing, and other holdings so bad we don't have the stomach to mention them. Such a call is, by no means, a sign of a strong hand.

In no limit, though, good players call with far more consideration. Typically a call will signify a good made hand, a strong draw, or occasionally something weaker. But even the weaker calls often portend an ominous turn of events.

In any event, betting top pair on the flop and getting called in limit is usually a good thing. In no limit, it's often a sign of trouble ahead. If the pot's $150, you bet $120 with top pair, and two good players with $1,000 stacks call, you very likely should give up on the turn.

(One exception to this rule is when the bet and call are small, compared to the stack sizes. If the pot's $20, you bet $15, and one or two players with $1,000 stacks call, you aren't necessarily in trouble. They could be "fishing," relying on the implied odds of the deep stacks to reward their speculation on weak holdings.)

Big bets and calls are telling. Small bets and calls aren't nearly so. Thus, you sometimes have the opportunity to "pay" for information by making a somewhat larger bet than you otherwise might. If your opponents will call $15 with lots of hands, but $30 with only good ones, it often behooves you to bet $30. You don't do it because the $30 bet makes you more profit; you do it because it helps you to save a large chunk of your stack when beaten.

It's often cheaper to bet $30 with a mediocre hand and give up if called than to bet $15, get called in two places, and have to follow up for $60 or more, out of position and clouded in uncertainty. So look for opportunities to bet a little bit extra if it will give you reliable and useful information about your opponents' hands. These information bets are particularly useful when you are out of position, as they chip away at your opponents' advantage.

An Example

You're playing $5-$10 with $1,500 stacks. One player limps, and a tight and straightforward player makes it $40 to go from two off the button. You are next to act with A♥K♠.

You might sometimes call, but you can do something clearly better against this specific opponent. That's because she's straightforward in the following way: if you reraise her, she'll put in the third raise always and only with pocket aces or kings. With any other hand, she'll either call or fold (depending on the hand and how large your raise is). This is true regardless of the size of your reraise; a third raise always means pocket aces or kings, and she will always reraise with aces or kings. (You could change "always" to "nearly always" and the following logic would still probably hold. But as soon as your opponent mixes her play up to any degree, this play doesn't necessarily work as described.)

In this situation, it makes sense to make a small reraise, perhaps making it $80 or $100 to go. You are reraising to see if she puts in the third raise. Your reraise is small because you don't want her to fold ace-queen, ace-jack, or king-queen if she happens to have one of those hands. You also keep it small to avoid risking more than necessary to find out if you are up against aces or kings.

Indeed, this reraise doesn't give you information only about the initial raiser's hand. It gives you information about all of your other opponents' hands as well (the button, the blinds, and the limper). Just calling might encourage an enterprising player to call with some unreadable hands or to take a shot at both you and the initial raiser by putting in a big semi-bluff raise. By reraising, you all but eliminate that possibility, since you very well could be holding pocket aces. So not only does your reraise tell you about the initial raiser's hand, it also keeps the remaining players' actions more "pure," allowing you to make better decisions.

Another Opportunity to Gather Information

If you have a pocket pair, and you aren't sure if you have the best hand, you'll often be in a position to try to gather information through a flop bet. Say the preflop betting has led you to the conclusion that your opponent likely has a pocket pair with you, but you aren't sure whose pair is higher. If an unthreatening flop like

comes, you can use an information bet against some opponents to clarify the situation. If you make a substantial bet, some straightforward players will tend to raise with a big pair (say pocket aces or kings), but just call with a smaller pair. Since you have only two outs when you are beaten, you can use their response to help you play when you aren't sure about your pair.

Final Thoughts

As with any play, betting slightly more for information is not without its perils. Against perceptive, skilled hand-readers, an information raise might invite a big bluff. Or, more generally, they might pick off bets slightly larger than average as information-gathering attempts and feed you intentional misinformation.

Many players make a very obvious information-gathering attempt. If they find themselves under the gun with a good, but potentially vulnerable, hand such as pocket jacks, they often make a big raise. In a $2-$5 game, they might make it $40 to go under the gun. This uncharacteristically large raise is designed to scare out the riff-raff, while limiting reraises only to hands bigger than jacks. The play works poorly in the best of circumstances. It puts too much money at risk, out of position, with a hand that isn't strong enough, and it encourages everyone to play more correctly.

Against a player who can read it for what it is, this play is truly horrendous. The big jacks raiser is out of position and has told everyone else almost exactly what hand he has (usually jacks, possibly tens or maybe ace-king). That's a terrible situation to be in when you're playing deep stack no limit.

So use the information-gathering play wisely. Try it most against straightforward and unaware players (players who will almost never just call your information bet or raise with a great hand or raise it with a merely good one). You can use it against better players also, but use it sparingly, and mix up your play. Make sure those bigger-than-average bets are often big hands as well. But, used correctly, the information you glean can be worth far more than what you have to pay for it.

If you'd like to know more about the concept discussed in this chapter, read "Paying for Information" starting on p. 31 of *Poker, Gaming, and Life* by David Sklansky.

Playing the Nuts on
the River — More Examples

Early in the book we introduced the concept of expectation in terms of a simple example where you made the nut straight on the river and had to decide how much to raise. While we didn't want to delve too deeply so early on into the details of playing the nuts on the river, we do have more things to say on the topic. We'll say them here.

Making a big all-in bet with the nuts is very likely to be the best play in some circumstances. Here's an example of those circumstances. The blinds are $5-$10, and you have $500. Everyone has you covered.

Two players limp to you on the button with

You call $10. The small blind calls, and the big blind checks. The flop is

Everyone checks to you, and you check. The turn is the 7♠. Everyone checks to you, and you check again. (Obviously you would check the flop and turn only under certain circumstances.)

82

The river is the 3♠, and the small blind bets $50. Everyone folds to you.

The small blind likely has a weak hand, a bluff or a marginal value bet. If that's the case, even a minimum $50 raise probably won't be called. But there's some chance the small blind was slowplaying along with you. Though unlikely, TT, J7, 77, or 33 are possibilities. In that case, expect even a $440 all-in raise to be called.

Since there are few possible hands that would call a $50 raise, but not $440, only a big raise makes sense.

> **If your opponent is likely to be weak, but possibly could be sandbagging a big hand, with the nuts you should often assume strength and make a big bet.**

This isn't to argue that you should *always* make a big bet when you have the nuts on the river. Far from it. Often the natural play of "selling your hand" for a modest bet is optimal. We provided two examples (here and in the earlier chapter) where making a big raise was the best play because, at least for some players, this seems to be the more counterintuitive play.

Another Example

Oftentimes you might want to make a small or medium bet with the nuts as well. A great time to make a modest bet is when you think your opponent in all likelihood doesn't have a very good hand, and if he does have a good hand, he's probably planning to check-raise.

For instance, say you have $1,000 in a $5-$10 game, and you're on the button with A♥4♥. After a few players fold, someone makes it $30 to go. You call, and the blinds fold. The flop comes K♥T♠7♥, giving you the nut flush draw. Your opponent bets $50, and you call. The turn is the 3♣. Your opponent checks, and you check. (The pot is $175.)

The river is the 5♥, giving you the nuts by completing the obvious flush draw. Your opponent checks again. This is a good time for a modest river bet, maybe $60 or $80. Given the action, your opponent probably doesn't have much. If he has one pair, he might be willing to make a curious call since your action looks like it might be a bluff.

Furthermore, if he happens to have a big hand (e.g., a flush), he might check-raise, reopening the betting. An aggressive player might even see weakness in your modest bet size and try a check-raise bluff. A small bet loses only when your opponent has a hand that's good enough to call a bigger bet, but not good enough to check-raise with. (King-ten might be such a hand.) Given the action, that possibility is somewhat remote.

Two Other "Big Bet" Situations

Now that we've gotten the mundane small bet out of the way, there are two more important situations when you should often bet big. The first is when your opponent has shown strength throughout the hand, and you have made the nuts on the river in a surprising or unlikely way.

For instance, you're playing $10-$20 with $4,000 stacks. An early position player makes it $80 to go, one player calls, and you call one off the button with

The blinds fold.
The flop comes

giving you a small flush draw. The preflop raiser bets $200, the middle player folds, and you call. (The pot is $670.)

The turn is the 8♥, giving you a gutshot to go with your flush draw. Your opponent bets $400, and you call again. (The pot is $1,470.)

The river is the 7♣, giving you the nuts with a runner-runner straight (but not completing your obvious flush draw). Your opponent bets $600. A big raise is probably the best option; you should strongly consider moving in (making it $2,720 more).

Your opponent has raised preflop and bet every street, so it's likely she has a good hand. She might have something like top two or a set. By calling on the flop and turn, you appear perhaps to have been drawing, but the draw you'd "obviously" be on, the flush, didn't get there. She might interpret your huge raise to be a likely bluff made with a busted flush draw.

> **When your opponent has shown strength, and you've made a surprising or unlikely nut hand, consider making an extra-large bet or raise.**

In the previous example, making a large raise was correct principally because your opponent wouldn't suspect that you have the hand you do, and so she would be more likely than usual to interpret your big bet as a bluff.

Some players (we'll call them "suspicious" players) tend to interpret many extra-large river bets as likely bluff candidates. They figure, "Why would he bet so much unless he was trying to get me to fold?" Against these players, you should obviously make extra big bets when you happen to make the nuts.

Indeed, your opponent doesn't have to be completely "suspicious" (defined specifically as more likely to call a big bet than a small one) to get you to increase your bet size with the nuts. He can also be less likely to call a big bet than a small one, but not less likely *in proportion* to the size of the bet. (We'll call such a player "semi-suspicious.") That is, if you think he'll call a $600 bet 40 percent of the time and a $300 about 70 percent of the time, you should still choose the larger bet because it maximizes your expectation.[16]

---

[16] Interestingly, players who rely solely upon game theory to determine their calling frequency would behave semi-suspiciously under our definition. For more on game theory and calling frequencies, see pages 188-9 of *The Theory of Poker* by David Sklansky.

Value Betting on the River

We have already discussed how you size your river bets when you have the nuts or when you don't have much at all. What about when you are merely fairly sure that you have the best hand? Do you make a value bet and, if so, how much?

This is a trickier problem than the one when you have the nuts because when you add into the equation the fact that you might be beaten (or get raise-bluffed out) it forces you to back off from bigger bets even if they have a decent chance of being called by worse hands than yours.

Suppose, for instance, that you reckon that your opponent has a 20 percent chance of having you beaten, a 60 percent chance of having a worse hand than you that he might call with, and a 20 percent chance of having nothing. You are thinking about betting with the intention of folding to a big raise.

Say the pot is $1,000, and he has checked to you. You know that he will always at least call any size bet with his top 20 percent of hands, fold all his bad hands, and call with the others with a frequency that depends on your bet size.

You estimate that a $200 bet will always get called (except by the 20 percent of "nothing" hands). A $500 bet will get called by the mediocre hands half the time. And a $1,000 bet will get called by the mediocre hands 30 percent of the time.

If there were no chance that you are beaten the answer is clear — bet $1,000. Thirty percent of $1,000 is better than fifty percent of $500 or one hundred percent of $200. But what about when there's a twenty percent chance you are beaten? To find out the new answer, you must do the math.

Assuming your opponent will never check-raise bluff, the expectation of a $200 bet is simply $80. (It's $880 if you include the 80 percent chance of winning the original $1,000 pot.)

$$\$80 = (0.60)(\$200) + (0.20)(-\$200)$$

The expectation of a $1,000 bet is -$20. (It's $780 if you include the original pot.)

$$- \$20 = (0.60)(0.30)(\$1,000) + (0.20)(- \$1,000)$$

That's a negative expectation, though it shouldn't be surprising because, if he will call only 30 percent of the 60 percent of the time he has the mediocre hand, he will actually be more likely to have a big hand when he calls (or raises). (It's 20 percent versus 18 percent.)

So is $500 the best option? Let's see. The expectation is $50 (or $850 total).

$$\$50 = (0.60)(0.50)(\$500) + (0.20)(- \$500)$$

It's still not as good as the piddling $200 bet. Thus, throwing in a small chance you are beaten dramatically reduces your correct bet size to one that is likely to be called by lesser hands. And it might even reduce it to zero. Here's why.

Let's look at what happens when your opponent will sometimes check-raise bluff. Suppose if you bet $200 your opponent will raise $2,000 with his good hands and some of his worst hands (perhaps half of them). That means he will call your $200 bet 60 percent of the time, fold to it 10 percent, and raise you out the other 30 percent (sometimes with a bluff). You can't call the raise because you are getting odds of only $3,400-to-$2,000, and he will have you beaten two out of three times.

You will win $1,000 ten percent of the time, $1,200 sixty percent, and lose $200 thirty percent. That's an expectation of $760. But if you simply checked behind you would win the $1,000 pot eighty percent of the time for an expectation of $800. The possibility of a check-raise bluff has now made a small bet no good either.

And this is, in fact, an important consideration in real life games. Against players who have the guts to try check-raise bluffs occasionally, you are forced to check down decent hands that could show a profit with a small bet against more timid souls.

The above analysis assumed that you were in last position and were checked to. If you are first to act, you can't close out the action by checking, so it gets more complicated.

Continuing with the same example, except this time you are first, if he will never raise bluff or bluff if you check, it reduces to the same question as if he checked and you were last to act. Among the three alternatives, betting $200 is best, and it gives you an expectation of $880 total.

But what about the scenario where he will raise big with his top 20 percent plus half of his non-calling hands? We showed that betting $200 now gives you a total expectation of $760 and, thus, it is better to check behind for an expectation of $800.

Does that conclusion change if you are first? Yes, it does. Say, if you check, he will make a big bet with those same 30 percent of hands he will raise with (one-third of which are bluffs). Again you must fold. That means that a check will win the $1,000 pot only 70 percent of the time for an expectation of $700. The $200 bet is now once again the better play (because it has an expectation of $760). But it still might not be the best play.

Suppose a $500 bet will scare your opponent away from raise-bluffing. Remember, we postulated he will call a bet that size with half his mediocre hands. Making a $500 bet means you win $1,000 fifty percent of the time, win $1,500 thirty percent, and lose $500 twenty percent. As we calculated before (in a different way), that's an expectation of $850. So in this case a $500 bet would be better than a check ($700 EV) or a $200 bet ($760 EV) or a $1,000 bet ($780 EV).

Final Thoughts

As you may have noticed, deciding when and how much to value bet on the river can be complicated. In our example, if you had the nuts, you bet one amount. If you might have been beaten, you bet another amount. And if you might have gotten bluff-raised, you didn't bet at all — that is, if you were last to act. If you were first to act and might have gotten bluff-raised, you bet, and it was a different amount than either of the other two bets. Here are the main ideas to take from this section:

- If you are last to act and might be beaten, your bets should tend to be smaller than they would be if you were fairly sure you had the best hand.

- If you are last to act and are worried about being check-raised as a bluff, you should check some decent hands you might otherwise bet for value against a more straightforward player.

- If you are first to act, you should tend to bet an amount large enough to discourage your opponent from bluff-raising you, but not so large that you lose too much when you are beaten.

Absolute
and Relative Position

Position is undeniably an important factor in every hand. "Having position" often represents an enormous edge. But many people think that having the button always gives you the ultimate positional advantage. Unfortunately, the position story isn't quite that simple.

Sure, there's no better place to start a hand than on the button. And on most hands, the button will be an important asset throughout the hand. We'll call having the button having "absolute" position. That is, you are last to speak no matter what.

But sometimes being last to speak isn't all it's cracked up to be. Specifically, say you are on the button in a four-handed pot. One player limps, and the next raises. You call, as does the big blind and the limper. What's likely to happen on the flop?

When someone raises preflop, for better or for worse, the early players will often check automatically to the raiser. These checks don't mean quite what they normally might —weak hands. They merely mean, "Ok, you raised preflop. We'll let you take first crack at the pot."

So while you are technically last to speak, you aren't the last to speak *meaningfully*. If, as the early players expect, the raiser bets, you are, in a very real way, second of four to speak. The first two players checked bad and good hands alike, and you must commit your chips now without any more clues.

Of course, having the button is still valuable. If you call, and the two checking players fold, then you go back to having all the positional advantage. Or, for that matter, if you end up heads-up on the turn with any of the other three players, you will be positional king. But as long as the pot is multiway, the player everyone expects to bet is on your right, and that player does, indeed, bet, you are in a poor "relative" position.

Absolute position is position relative to the button. The closer you are to the button, the better your absolute position. Relative position is position relative to the likely bettor. The closer you are to the right of the likely better (acting directly before the bettor), the better your relative position.

You can have both absolute and relative position at the same time. If a couple of players limp, you limp on the button, and the small blind raises, you'll likely enjoy both kinds of position on the flop.

Similarly, you can get socked with a double position whammy. If several players limp, the small blind raises, and you're in the big blind, then you are out of position relative to the button and will act directly after the raiser.

One of the major mistakes that bad players tend to make is that they play too many big pots out of position. Limping in and calling button raises is one way they get themselves into these situations. Another is that they call raises from players directly on their right. This is especially dangerous in early position.

For instance, in an eight-handed $10-$20 blind game with $2,000 stacks, someone opens under the gun for $100. If you are next to act, calling can be fraught with positional peril (not to mention the danger of a reraise behind you). This call is doubly dangerous if a couple of loose and tricky players are behind you. They'll call $100 with lots of hands just to take advantage of the fact that you'll be sandwiched between them and the raiser.

This danger is triply menacing if you pick the wrong sort of hand to call with. Moderately big offsuit cards like K♥J♦ or A♣T♠ would typically be terrible hands in this situation. Why? Because being at a positional disadvantage hurts moderately-strong hands (such as top pair with a shaky kicker) more than any other type.

Moderate hands pick up a lot of pots when no one else makes anything better. But finding out whether anyone made anything better can be expensive. When you have position, though, you'll often get to see the raising war happen before you have to commit any money.

But out of position, your money goes in first, and only afterward do you begin to find out where you stand. Thus, these hands can be solid winners in position, but solid dogs out of position. That's a big swing.

The hands least affected by being out of position are those that provide instant feedback: the small pocket pairs. On the flop, you know instantly whether you are a big favorite or a big dog; you don't need to see anyone's betting first. Small pocket pairs will show a healthy profit against loose and aggressive players (those willing to make and call big bets after the flop against your set) even in the worst of positions.

However, don't underrate relative position even with a small pair, as you'll consistently win less on your big hands when out of relative position. For the reasoning behind that contention, read on.

Position and Hand Reading

As a good player, you'll bet, call, and raise more often when you have position. This statement is true both for absolute and for relative position. Playing hands out of position is riskier, and so fewer hands will be profitable.

Unfortunately, your observant opponents know that just as well as you do. They know that many hands can be losers out of position, and they know that you know that. So — and here's the problem — when you do play a hand out of position, they will know that you have a stronger hand than average. In certain circumstances, they may be able to put you on a very narrow range of hands merely because you called out of position.

For instance, say you are playing in a loose ten-handed game with observant, but not excellent, players. The blinds are $5-$10, and the stacks are $2,000. One player limps, and you limp in middle position with

Two players limp behind you, the small blind calls, and the big blind checks. The pot is six-handed for $60 total.

You flop the nuts,

Everyone checks to the player on your right, who bets $60. What should you do?

Unfortunately, neither raising nor calling is terrific. You have the nuts, but the pot is only $120, and you have over $1,900 more that you'd love to get in the pot. Making that happen, however, will generally be quite difficult.

One of your main problems is that you are out of position, both absolute and relative. Two players are between you and the button, and you act directly after the bettor. You know you have the best hand, so that's not the problem. The problem is that, no matter what you do, your opponents will *know* you aren't worried about your hand.

The player on your right probably has a decent hand. After all, he was willing to bet the pot into five opponents on a somewhat scary board. He might have something like A♣J♣, but he's unlikely to be messing around with anything much worse than that. (He might have had only the A♠ for his bet, but since you have that card, that theory is out.)

So no matter what you do, whether you call or raise, thinking opponents will interpret your action as if you had announced:

"I know the board is scary, and any one of my five opponents could show up with a flush. And the player on my right just made a strong play by betting into a big field on this scary board. And I'm way out of position, both absolute and relative, so if someone does have a flush, I stand to lose at least my entire bet here and possibly more. But I'm not worried."

"Why aren't you worried?" they'll wonder. "Probably because you have a monster hand," they'll conclude. So even if you only call, if they have a hand as strong as ace-jack, they'll fold. (Again, we're assuming your opponents are aware, observant, and play decently.)

Being out of position, you can't hope to conceal the strength of your hand. Your only hopes for future action are either that someone misunderstood the situation or that someone else happened to flop a monster also (e.g., a king-high flush) and thinks that their monster is bigger than yours.

Being out of position, whether absolute or relative, hurts you in two major ways: it often forces you to commit to marginal hands without much information (or fold the best hand), and it sometimes prevents you from concealing the strength of your big hands.

The Corollary

Being out of position can force you to tip the strength of your hand earlier than you'd otherwise like to. It does the same for your opponents: When they are out of position with big hands, often they'll be forced to make a "strong" play whether they like it or not. You need to pay attention, identify those situations, and make big laydowns when necessary!

Don't assume that calls are always weaker than raises. Remember, an out of position call can mean a lot of strength, particularly when you know your opponent can't have merely a strong draw.

For instance, you are playing a $10-$20 blind game with fairly good players. You are on the button with a $2,000 stack. An early player raises to $60, a knowledgeable player in middle position calls, and you call on the button with A♥Q♥. The big blind calls. (Pot is $250.)

The flop comes Q♣7♦2♥. The big blind checks, and the preflop raiser bets $200. The middle position player calls, you call, and the big blind folds. (Pot is $850.) The turn is the J♠. The preflop raiser checks, and the middle position player bets $700. Unless the bettor is a very wild player, you have a clear fold.

Your middle position opponent has shown consistent strength out of position on a drawless board. He's likely to have a big hand, probably either queen-jack or a set.

He called an early position raise preflop with several to act behind him. Depending on how loose he is, that fact alone is not necessarily a conclusive indicator of strength. Loose players might well call with a hand as weak as T♥8♥ in such a situation.

But then he called an almost pot-sized bet on a drawless flop in terrible relative position. Again, that fact doesn't, by itself, mean he has a monster: He might have called with a hand as weak as pocket eights, hoping that you and the big blind would fold, leaving him heads-up with a pair and position against the preflop raiser.

Unfortunately for him (if his hand is somewhat weak), you called. Your call is "strong" also. While you might ordinarily splash around a little on the button, you probably wouldn't do it on a Q♣7♦2♥ flop when faced with a sizable bet and a strong out of position call. So your thinking opponents have to worry that you might be the one who flopped a monster.

So the turn bet is the clincher. It's a major show of strength in the situation. Your middle position opponent knows he might be out of position against a strong hand, and he doesn't care. He makes a pot-committing bet. (Starting with $2,000 stacks, by the turn he's bet $960 total, so he has only $1,040 remaining. If you raised all-in, he'd be getting about 3-to-1. Unless he's been bluffing outright, he'll probably call.)

As long as he's rational, the worst hand you should expect to see from him is ace-queen. Queen-jack or a set are more likely. (A set of jacks is possible as well as any of the flopped sets.) You have $1,740 left, and there's only $1,550 presently in the pot. To continue profitably, you have to win a significant percentage of the time, and it's unlikely that you will.

Playing out of position forced your opponent to show strength early in the hand and allowed you to get away from a seemingly good hand, preserving most of your stack.

Final Thoughts

Absolute position, playing from or near the button, is valuable. But so is relative position. Indeed, getting to watch all your opponents respond to a bet before you have to is often more valuable than having the button.

Before you enter a pot, think about who the likely flop bettor will be. Think about your hand and what flops can come. Will the position of the likely bettor put you in a tough situation, or will it allow you to exploit your opponents? A little forethought about relative position will allow you to avoid potentially sticky situations while putting the squeeze on your unwitting opponents.

Raising Before the Flop

In limit hold 'em, one raises before the flop usually for one of three broad reasons: for value, for isolation, or to steal the blinds. With a premium hand like

or

raising is generally for value. Since these hands tend to be better than those your opponents will call with, you theoretically make money for every extra bet that goes into the pot.

With a marginal hand like A♥9♦ or Q♠J♣, raising is generally for isolation. You hope that raising will force out others with similar strength (or even dominating) hands like K♥T♥ or A♣T♦, leaving you in a heads-up pot with the blind money as overlay.

Sometimes in late position, raising is done in an attempt to steal the blinds. If everyone folds to you on the button, raising instead of calling with a hand like T♠8♠ gives you the opportunity to win a tidy profit without even seeing a flop.

While a proper limit preflop strategy includes a little "light" raising for deception, the size of the preflop bet, for the most part, forces you to stay in line. Since the bet size only doubles on later rounds, often twenty percent or more of the final pot size at showdown will originate from the preflop betting round. That is to say, your implied odds on your preflop investment will often be modest — perhaps 8-to-1 or less.

For instance, if you are playing $20-$40 limit hold 'em with $10 and $20 blinds, preflop raising will typically bring the bet to $40 or $60. But in such a game, the final pots are often no more than $400 or so. So if two players call a $40 preflop raise, at least $120 of that final $400, thirty percent, is due to the preflop betting. Raising "light" habitually will leave you taking the worst of it far too often for too large a percentage of the total betting, and no matter how well you play after that, you may never dig yourself out of the hole.

No limit, particularly when played with deep stacks, is an entirely different story. In a $10-$20 blind no limit game, you will often see $100 preflop raises made with $5,000 or more behind. If $10,000 pots occur even occasionally, $200 or $300 total in preflop betting can be just a drop in the bucket.

While that's not a license to make pointless calls and raises because "it's only $100," it does give you more flexibility to play and even raise with marginal hands if you can "make it up" after the flop.

Reasons to Raise

There are at least six main reasons to raise before the flop in no limit hold 'em. Depending on the stack sizes and your opponents' tendencies, some reasons may become more important than others at different times. The six reasons to raise before the flop are:

1. For value
2. For isolation
3. To steal the blinds
4. As a semi-bluff

5. For deception
6. To manipulate the pot size

Raising for Value

Raising for value is the most straightforward reason to raise. You have a strong hand likely to win a showdown, and you'd like to force your opponents either to fold or to risk more money (presumably with you having the best of it). The shallower the money, the more importance raising for value gains relative to other preflop considerations.

For example, you are playing $10-$20 blind with $4,000 (deep) stacks. You are in the small blind with

Two players call $20. You raise to $100 (for value), the big blind folds, and both limpers call. You likely have the best hand of the three, so you have gotten much the best of it on your $100 bet. But there is $3,900 left to bet, and your raise has changed the course of the hand. Having raised preflop might allow your opponents to read your hand better or make sharper postflop betting decisions for the remaining money. If that's the case, your $100 "value" raise may not be worth quite what you think it should be.

Now contrast that example with a similar one. You are playing $10-$20 blind, but with only a $100 (extremely shallow) stack. (Please ignore for now how you arrived in a situation with such a tiny stack.) You are in the small blind with A♦Q♠. Two players call $20. Raising to $100 is now a no-brainer. With no wagering left, you should get your money in with the best of it and hope your hand holds up.

The shallower your stack, the more compelling raising for value becomes. Put another way, the larger the percentage of your stack (or your opponents' if theirs are shallower) a preflop raise constitutes, generally, the stronger your hand "hot and cold" must be to make the raise.[17]

If a raise is only two percent of your stack, you need not raise with all your strong hands, and you need not necessarily have a strong hand to raise. If a raise is twenty percent of your stack or more, you should typically raise with all your strong hands and rarely otherwise.

Raising for Isolation

A common play in limit hold 'em, raising for isolation is not as useful in no limit. First, here's an example of raising for isolation taken from limit hold 'em so the concept is clear.

You are playing $20-$40 limit hold 'em with $10-$20 blinds. You are on the button with A♥T♥. Everyone folds to an aggressive player two to your right who open-raises. The next player folds. You have an automatic reraise for isolation.

You have a good hand that should compare favorably with the range of hands an aggressive player might open with two off the button. (For comparison, he might open with any pocket pair, any suited ace, any offsuit ace down to ace-eight, any offsuit king down to king-ten, and queen-jack.) But with so little money in the pot, your overlay will come from the blind money as much as any value you might get from your lone opponent.

While your hand is good, it is not so good that you should encourage calls from the blinds. So you reraise for isolation, hoping to knock out the blinds and play heads-up with position, dead blind money in the pot, and, on average, a somewhat better hand.

---

[17] "Hot and cold" strength means having the ability to win often when all-in.

In no limit, however, raising for isolation doesn't work nearly as well. There are two reasons:

1. The blind money often represents a much smaller percentage of your expectation for the hand.

2. The punishment for accidentally isolating someone who has a better hand is far greater.

While a somewhat crude view to take, the isolation raise may be seen as an attempt to chop up the blind money with one other player. With $10-$20 blinds, a typical isolation raise might be worth $15 to $30 if successful. In limit that can be quite a tidy haul, even if your opponents play badly. But in no limit played with deep stacks, $15 isn't much to win if the alternative is to play a hand *in position* against a bad player or two, each with several thousand dollars behind.

Furthermore, if you get reraised, it usually costs you a lot more in no limit than in limit. In limit, if someone reraises you (presumably with a better hand than yours), you call, and it costs you a fraction of a bet (only a fraction because sometimes you'll win the hand).

In no limit, if you get reraised, usually you'll have to fold, forfeiting your entire equity in the pot. Thus, getting reraised costs you a fraction of a bet in limit, but lots more in no limit.

Raising for isolation, a common play in limit, is both riskier and less lucrative in no limit.

There is one major exception. If a particularly bad player with a deep stack enters the pot in front of you, you should frequently try to isolate him. Your goal here isn't to chop up the blind money; your goal is to get an exclusive shot at the bad player's stack. You'll win a lot more on average playing raised pots, heads-up, with position against one terrible player than playing unraised pots, four-handed, against one terrible player and a couple of tough ones.

Raising to Steal the Blinds

Just as raising for isolation has less value in no limit than limit, so does raising to steal the blinds.[18] There are two reasons:

1. The immediate odds aren't as compelling in no limit as they are in limit, so the blinds would have to fold significantly more often to show the same profit. For instance, in a limit game with $10 and $20 blinds, there is $30 in blind money, and a raise is $40, so you are laying 4-to-3. In no limit, typically you'd have to raise to $60 or $80 to have a similar chance to win the blinds, so you'd be laying 6-to-3 or 8-to-3 instead.

2. If you are a better player than those in the blinds, you may make more by allowing them to see the flop and make expensive postflop mistakes than by shutting them out immediately.

As a consequence of these differences, limping first in even on the button, almost never right in limit, can be a good no limit play. For instance, say everyone folds to you on the button with J♥9♥. In limit you should typically raise, hoping to win the blinds. In no limit, raising will frequently still be right, but against some opponents limping might be even better.

Assuming you play better than the blind players, you certainly want to play a jack-nine. But this relatively weak hand doesn't rate to be a big favorite against two random hands. So you aren't forgoing much value by failing to raise. You are missing your chance to win the blinds outright, but the reward for that is

---

[18] Again, we are referring to no limit games where the stack sizes are hundreds of times the size of the big blind. No limit tournaments with stack sizes of only a few times the blinds and antes are a different story.

small, and you might make more allowing your weaker opponents to see a flop.

Raising as a Semi-Bluff

While blind stealing is technically a type of semi-bluff, here we are talking about semi-bluff raises after at least one other player has entered the pot. Such semi-bluff raises are virtually non-existent in limit hold 'em, because almost everyone will call your raise once they have already limped or raised themselves.

In no limit, though, you can raise a larger amount and get people to fold. Thus, the semi-bluff raise has its place.

The math behind the preflop semi-bluff is rather simple. You risk the amount of your raise. You hope to win the money that is presently in the pot. Your hand also has some value when your opponents call (rather than reraise) and allow you a chance to catch a great flop. Thus, a preflop semi-bluff is profitable when the following EV expression is true:

$$(\text{chance everyone will fold})(\text{pot size} + \text{raise size}) +$$
$$(\text{chance one or more will call with no raises})$$
$$(\text{value of hand on the flop}) > (\text{raise })$$

where "value of hand on the flop" is the amount of money the hand is worth (also known as EV) if you see a flop with it (a value obviously dependant on the present pot size).

So which hands should you semi-bluff raise with? In general, you should semi-bluff with the *best hands that you would not ordinarily have played*. This maximizes the "value of hand on the flop" term in the EV expression above.

For instance, say an aggressive player with a large stack is clearly often raising light. You would like to take a pot away from him with a semi-bluff reraise. You think that in response to your reraise he will fold his weak hands, move all-in with his strongest hands, and call with the rest.

Now let's say that you think *calling* his raise with queen-jack suited would be profitable, but calling with queen-eight suited would be unprofitable, and calling with seven-deuce offsuit would be clearly unprofitable.

In such a situation, queen-eight suited is the sort of hand you should semi-bluff reraise with. It has no (or rather negative) value to call with, but it is among the strongest of those hands with no calling value. You should prefer semi-bluffing with queen-eight suited over seven-deuce offsuit, because those times your semi-bluff gets called, your hand has more value.

Moreover, you should prefer semi-bluffing with queen-eight suited over queen-jack suited because queen-jack suited is a profitable calling hand. To justify semi-bluffing with queen-jack suited, you must show not only that the bluff will be profitable, but also that it will be more profitable than merely calling, a tougher standard.

This last idea, that you should often choose to bluff with a somewhat weaker hand over a stronger one, leads to a rather curious inversion in the blinds (particularly the big blind). Typically, as we have just deduced, you should bluff with the best hands you would not ordinarily have played. But say you are in the big blind and five players call. Ordinarily you would check with all but your best hands. That is, you would play every hand.

In this situation, consider making your big semi-bluffs with your very worst of hands: 9♥3♣, J♦2♠, and the like. Keep in mind, though, that we are talking about big raises that will rarely be called: usually everyone will fold, and when they don't they will reraise you (perhaps limp-reraising with a big hand).

Choose your very worst hands because seeing a flop with those hands has less value than seeing one with a decent, but not good, hand like queen-eight suited. Since you can see the flop with certainty if you check, bluff-raising costs you that money you would make if you happened to flop great (because one way or the other you won't see a flop).

To summarize, compare two situations. In both situations, you are playing a $2-$5 game with deep stacks.

First, you are in middle position at a tight table. Uncharacteristically, three players have limped in front of you. Normally you would fold both Q♥8♥ and 7♣2♦. But every once in a while you should semi-bluff raise to perhaps $40 or so, and you should do so with Q♥8♥ and not 7♣2♦. You lose nothing by choosing your better hands, and you gain those few times someone calls you (but doesn't reraise). Remember though that with somewhat better hands than that you usually don't raise (because calling is profitable), and with better hands still, you do (because you can reraise for value).

Second, you are in the big blind at a tight table. Again, three players have limped in front of you, not including the small blind. Normally you would check both Q♥8♥ and 7♣2♦. But every once in a while you should semi-bluff raise to perhaps $40 or so, and you should do so with 7♣2♦ and not Q♥8♥. Queen-eight has more value if you see a free flop than seven-deuce does, so you give up less when you make the play with seven-deuce.[19]

Raising for Deception

In limit hold 'em, you should occasionally raise with a weak hand you would normally just call with (or even fold) to avoid being too predictable. But your deception will likely net you just a few extra bets on this hand (and that's only if you hit your hand) and maybe a few more on future hands. Meanwhile, you've put extra money in with a weak hand, immediately taking the worst of it in the process. As a result, raising for deception must be used sparingly in limit hold 'em.

In no limit, however, particularly when played with deep stacks, a deceptive preflop raise can set you up to win someone's whole stack by tricking them into discounting or excluding certain

---

[19] Note that this can invert again if players are relatively likely to call, but not reraise. Then you may again be better off with a stronger hand in the event that you have to see a flop.

weak hands from your range of possible holdings. For instance, a timely $20 preflop raise with

could net you $1,000 after the flop if you manage to find an opponent with

on an

board. The preflop raise may convince your opponent that you are likely overplaying ace-king or aces up rather than sitting on a straight.

Obviously, this is not to say that you should adopt the perverse strategy of raising every eight-six and calling every ace-king. But it is to say that well-timed preflop deception can have significantly more value in no limit than in limit.

For instance, say you are two hours into a session in a $2-$5 blind game, and you have played far tighter than you normally would simply due to a dearth of profitable opportunities. You've limped a few times, folded after the flop, and generally made few waves. Three players limp to you in late position, and you pick up 6♠5♠. You make a modest raise to $20. Since your opponents have seen you play few hands and raise almost never, they are likely (more so than usual) to assume that you have a premium hand.

If you get a couple of callers and the flop comes something like J♦6♥5♣, your small preflop investment is likely to net you far more action than usual from aggressive players. Where they would normally be on guard for someone with small cards, they won't expect it from you. Instead, they might try to take the pot away from you.

Raising to Manipulate the Pot Size

In no limit, the size of the game is determined primarily by the size of the blinds. A $10-$20 blind game with $1,000 stacks plays "bigger" than a $1-$2 blind game with $1,200 stacks. Bigger blinds mean bigger preflop pots, which, in turn, mean bigger bets on later betting rounds.

If you are the best player at the table, you will probably have a long-term positive expectation, no matter the size of the blinds. But there is often a "sweet spot," that is, there is a blind size, given the stack sizes at the table, that will maximize your earn. If the blinds are smaller than the optimal size, the game will play too small, and a lot of the money in people's stacks will remain unbet.

If the blinds are larger than the optimal size, the game will play too big, and people will run out of money too early in the hand. That is, you will often be all-in on the preflop or flop betting rounds, nullifying your skill advantage on the tricky turn and river betting rounds.

Let's assume you are playing a full no limit game where everyone has a $5,000 stack. You are the best player at the table. Clearly $1-$2 blinds will not maximize your earn: Preflop pots will be in the $10-$20 range, and by the river the big ones might max out at $300-$500 or so. Rarely will two players get all-in.

You might as well be playing with $500 stacks instead of $5,000, and that hurts your expected take.

If you doubled the blinds to $2-$4, that would roughly double your expected earn. Every bet would be approximately twice the size it would be at $1-$2, and you still would rarely get all-in against someone.

If you increased the blinds twenty-fold to $20-$40, however, that would not increase your expected earn twenty-fold over the $1-$2 blind game. With blinds that big, you'll now end up all-in for the big pots. The average bet size will be something less than twenty times the average $1-$2 bet because you will now sometimes run out of money. $20-$40 blinds would certainly increase your earn significantly over the $1-$2 blinds, perhaps as much as ten or fifteen times. But it would not be a full twenty times.

Starting at the other end, $500-$1,000 blinds would hurt your long-term earn considerably with $5,000 stacks. With forced bets so large, virtually every hand will play all-in preflop. Racing against another hand might be fun, but it leaves many of your skills unused, and that slashes your advantage over your opponents.

Cutting the blinds to $100-$200 makes the game "smaller," but it gives you more room to maneuver, and therefore should increase your earn.

With $5,000 stacks, the "sweet spot" should be somewhere between $10-$20 blinds and $100-$200 blinds. But, other than switching to a different game, what good does knowing the "sweet spot" do for you? After all, you have no control over the structure of the game.[20]

If the game is too big, there isn't much you can do. But if it's too small, you can start raising a wider range of hands preflop. For instance, say you are playing in a game where everyone has a

---

[20] Well, if you are in a cardroom, you could ask the floor personnel to increase the blinds, and if everyone at the table agrees, they should accommodate you.

$5,000 stack. Three players limp to you on the button, and you have A♣5♣. If the blinds are $25-$50, you should probably limp for $50. But if the blinds are $5-$10, you might want to make a small "sweetener" raise to $20 or $30. The goal is to make the pot bigger, thus making the game "play bigger." The bigger preflop pot will cause the postflop betting to be bigger, and your expectation will increase with the size of the bets.

Of course, raising a so-so hand like ace-five has some drawbacks. Since you usually won't flop the best hand, you may actually give up a little immediate value by raising. That is, if you win less than your share of pots, you take slightly the worst of it immediately. Also, you reopen the betting, and someone who limped in with a big hand could force you to fold by making a big reraise. Finally, a knowledgeable opponent might interpret your raise as a sweetener and use that knowledge against you.

Even so, often the value of making the game play two or three times bigger will offset all the drawbacks and make these sweetener raises right. In fact, if you are an excellent player stuck in a game with small blinds, you might well be right to raise almost every pot you play.

Final Thoughts

We hope that you now understand these six reasons to raise. Most good preflop raises can be justified using one or more of these reasons. The most important thing to take away from this section, however, is that preflop raising in deep stack no limit isn't necessarily as simple as "I have a good hand, so I raise." There are numerous reasons to raise, and some of them have relatively little to do with your preflop hand strength. Whenever it's your turn to play preflop, think about these reasons, and consider whether raising might be the best play.

Sizing Your Preflop Raises

Lots of no limit teachers give a rather peculiar piece of advice. They recommend that you always make the same size raises, no matter what hand you hold. Whether you have

or

raise the same amount every time.

They may tell you to alter your raise size based on your position. Or to alter it based on the number of limpers. But never to alter it based on what's in your hand.

Their rationale is that you can betray information about the quality of your holding by raising different amounts. So, to keep your opponents guessing, always raise the same amount.

This advice strikes us like cutting off your leg to cure your athlete's foot. Sure, you don't want to give away extra information through your raise sizes. And sure, some players do manage to do just that. But, as we saw in the last chapter, you can raise preflop for a variety of reasons, and some of those reasons prefer differently-sized raises. If you artificially limit your options to avoid giving away information, you soften up your entire preflop strategy.

111

> **Different hands in different situations
> call for differently-sized raises.**

Embrace it. Different hands in different situations call for differently-sized raises. If you are worried about giving away information, you need only to *mix up your play occasionally*.

For instance, say you want to raise 6x the blind. Every so often, raise only 3x instead. And vice versa — raise 6x occasionally when you would normally raise 3x. Mathematically, you can calculate an optimal percentage of the time to swap your plays. But, in practice, that isn't necessary. Just do it often enough so that your opponents know you might be mixing things up, and they have significant doubt about whether you hold a 3x hand or a 6x hand. (Or, rather, so that they *should have* significant doubt. Some players seem to think they are clairvoyant and are happy to "put you on a hand," no matter how suspect their evidence might be. Your job is just to make sure their evidence is sufficiently suspect.)

We'll divide this section into two parts: one for deep stack play, and one for short stack play. In deep stack games, the reasons for raising are often quite different than they are in short stack play, and thus, raise sizing works differently also. Obviously, sometimes a deep stack concept will apply to a short stack situation, or vice versa. So don't get hung up on the distinction; it's mostly just an organizational tool.

Deep Stack Raise Sizing

Here's the fundamental idea for deep stack raise sizing:

> **Big raises make big pots. Small raises
> (and no raises) make small pots.**

Do you want to play a big pot or a small pot? The answer to that question will usually tell you how much to raise.

Now it's hard to know exactly what you want before you've seen the flop. After all, you don't know if you've flopped a big hand yet or not. But certain hands and situations lend themselves to making lots of money in big pots, while others tend to end up on the short end in big ones, but do just fine in small ones.

For instance, flopping a small set is the classic "big pot" situation. Take 4♥4♠ against someone with A♠K♥ on a K♣9♥4♦ flop, and often that's "all she wrote" for your opponent. But, especially against good players, if the preflop pot is small compared to the stacks, your opponent will figure out what's going on before you get their stack.

Say you are playing $5-$10 with $1,500 stacks. You raise to $30 on the button with pocket fours, and your opponent calls in the big blind with ace-king. The flop comes king-nine-four, and your opponent bets $60. There's still over $1,400 left in his stack, and your challenge is to figure out how to get it.

If your opponent is a tight player, that may be a tough task. If you make a move early in the hand, either by raising the flop or turn, a good player instantly will know that he's in trouble. He's out of position, deep stacked, against a (hopefully) good player, with only one pair and no chance for improvement if beaten.[21]

If you just call a flop bet, you'll likely see a follow-up bet on the turn. If you call that, expect your good opponent to become extremely wary. He'll likely check the river or make a blocking bet, and don't expect him to call a big bet or raise.

So instead of making $1,400 more off the hand, expect to make more like a few hundred instead. What can you do about that? Make the pot bigger preflop by raising more.

Raising to $60 instead of $30 changes the complexion of the hand entirely. Now the pot is $120 preflop, and after a $120 bet

---

[21] Of course, this depends on your and your opponents' general playing style. Some people play a "wild" style with lots of aggression with strong and weak hands alike. Against those players, you'll likely get all your money in anytime you have two relatively big hands against one another.

and call on the flop, your opponent will have only $1,160 left in what is a $360 pot. If he follows up with a roughly pot-sized bet on the turn, you can raise all-in, and he'll be hard-pressed not to call. After all, it will be only $800 more to him, and he'll be getting $1,880-to-$800 or 2.35-to-1 to call. That would be a tough laydown (and often not a good one either). By doubling the size of the preflop raise, you got over $1,400 after the flop instead of a few hundred.

Unfortunately, there's an obvious downside to making big raises with "speculative" hands like pocket fours. The bigger your raise, the more getting reraised costs you. When you raised to $30, if the ace-king player had reraised to $100 or so, you could call. It would be $70 more to you, you'd have position, and there'd be $1,400 left in the stacks (or 20-to-1 stack odds). That's definitely a profitable situation, especially since stacking your opponent on a king-nine-four flop in such a big pot will be almost automatic.

On the other hand, when you raised to $60, if the ace-king player had reraised to $200, your situation would be grim. Now it would be $140 more to you, and there'd be only $1,300 left, so your stack odds would be less than 10-to-1. Even with position, you can't salvage this hand. Sure, you'll certainly get it all if the flop comes K♣9♥4♦, but if it comes Q♦J♦4♠, you won't. And if it comes Q♦J♦6♠ or K♣8♥5♦ or even 9♠2♦2♥, you'll be out $200.

So you can profitably call a reraise after the $30 raise, but you're forced to fold after the $60 raise. That's the downside. But as long as you mix up your play well, you shouldn't get people playing back at your big raises too often.

Having said that, don't raise *more* than you need to get the job done. If a $60 raise will build a big pot, don't raise $100. That's exposing yourself to unnecessary risk.

> **When raising with a speculative "big pot" hand like a small pocket pair, raise enough to brew a big pot, but no more.**

Suppose now instead it is you with A♠K♥ on the button. In this case a raise to $60 makes no sense. You rarely can win a big pot with this hand, but you might win a moderate amount if you run into ace-nine or king-ten. So why would you try to get those hands to fold?

Make Bigger Value Raises Against Straightforward Players

When you raise for value (because you think your hand is the strongest), make bigger raises against straightforward players. Straightforward players tip you to their big hands earlier and more reliably. As a result, you can get away from bad situations more quickly and cheaply. Suppose you are in the big blind against one limper. While a $60 raise out of position with ace-king might be bad against a tough player, it could be perfect against a straightforward player. Notice that this is different from the previous example where you were in position against random hands in the blinds.

Say the straightforward player will play as follows: He will fold the flop if he misses, call the flop if he flops a good pair or draw, and raise the flop if he flops two pair or better. Now it's fine to make a big raise with your ace-king, even though you are out of position. Since you will know roughly where you stand after seeing the flop and your opponent's reaction to your bet, you won't hang yourself in a big pot. A big preflop raise nets you extra value from the small pots, while you're still safe from playing a big pot.

Make Bigger Raises Against Players Who Fold Too Much Postflop

Some players, particularly many who play medium-sized games, are too timid. They fold too much. Or, more specifically, they call preflop raises liberally with marginal hands, but then fold to the big bets on later streets far too often. They know that big pots and big bets usually mean big hands, and, when they look down, they never seem to see a hand that's big enough.

These are some of the easiest no limit opponents to beat. Raise preflop when you have position. Your hand isn't so important because they'll so often be folding. Then, you essentially make big bets until they fold. Obviously, you shouldn't just bluff off your stack to them every time they make a hand; you need to do some hand reading. Bluff when they are likely to be weak, and check it down when they seem stronger. But with position, aggression, and their folding tendencies on your side, you'll end up with most of the pots.

Since you'll end up with most of the pots, they might as well be big pots. When such a player has entered the hand, make a bigger raise than normal. The bigger the pot, the more expensive a mistake your opponent's bad fold will be. Just make sure you don't raise so much that you don't have enough left to bluff with on later streets. And don't do it so often that your opponent catches on and starts trying to trap you. You don't need to raise every time you get the button; just raise more often than you normally would. You can read more about strategies against timid players in the section "Adjusting to Weak-Tight Games" starting on page 191.

Make Smaller Raises Against Players Who Call Too Much Postflop

The opposite of the above tip also works out. If your opponent calls too much, his mistaken calls are worse the smaller the pot is. Keep the pot small preflop and let your opponent hang himself on your good hands and big bets postflop.

Here's another way to think about it. Why raise $60 with fours to get your opponent to go broke with ace-king when you can raise $30 and achieve the same goal? Less risk, same payoff.

Short Stack Raise Sizing

When sizing raises with deep stacks, it is crucial to think about how big you want the eventual pot to be. That's not so important when you have a short stack. With a short stack, you generally raise preflop with one of two outcomes in mind:

1. Stealing the blinds and antes

2. Finding someone willing to gamble with you for all your chips

In other words, there's little subtlety to short stack raising. By putting any raise in, essentially you're saying, "Anyone want to play with me for everything?" You might be bluffing, and you might abandon ship with a decent hand if someone comes over the top, but you aren't looking to "see the flop and go from there."

So raise sizing is generally simpler too. There are only a few important concepts.

If You Want Action

If you have an excellent hand like a big pocket pair or ace-king, you will usually want action. (There are some exceptions in atypical tournament situations.) If you want action, raise as much as you can get away with and still get called. That amount will vary from game to game (and with your image), but with a big hand, the bigger the raise and call, the better.

In cash games you will want action on most of your raises with a short stack. The best strategy with a short stack in cash games is a tight one. You can't get away with playing for implied odds without money behind, so you have to avoid the small cards and play high percentage hands.

Most of the time, you'll raise preflop and push all-in on the flop. The bigger the preflop raise, and the less you leave for the flop, by and large, the better you'll perform. Just make sure you don't raise so much that you never get called.

If You Don't Want Action

When everyone folds to you on the button or in the small blind, often moving all-in is better than folding, especially with very small stacks like ten times the big blind or smaller. This fact can have you moving in with some weak-looking hands such as

Usually with those hands, you'd prefer not to get called.[22]

In tournaments, this is especially true. You'll often raise to steal the blinds and antes. Since the stacks are generally short, and the antes bloat the initial pot, blind-stealing becomes very lucrative. And it's even more true because most players happen to fold too often in the big blind. In the section "Calling Preflop All-in Raises," we provide charts to guide your calling decisions in the big blind, but most typical players tend to play significantly tighter than they should.

The most important raise-sizing rule when you don't want action is this:

---

[22] Though you aren't relying on not being called to profit. Many times, these all-in raises are correct even if your opponent plays perfectly against you. That is, you would show a profit even if you turned your cards face up after raising. We will expound on this concept later in the book.

> **Don't raise an amount that will leave you unsure of how to respond to a reraise.**

On TV tournaments you see this all the time. Someone raises preflop, another player comes over the top, and the first player goes into the tank. Should I call? Should I fold? They may start asking questions, "Do you have a pair? You have ace-king, don't you? I can beat ace-king."

Some of this behavior is theatrics, and some of it is just pausing a moment to take in everything before acting. But many times, the players who are raised really aren't sure how to respond. Whenever that's the case, they've frequently made a mistake sizing their initial raise. Why?

Let's assume that being unsure what to do means that it's a close decision. Now, that's not always a fair assumption, but that's really what we're talking about here anyway.

In concrete terms, say the blinds are $100-$200, and with A♥J♠ and a $2,400 stack, you make it $700 to go. An opponent reraises, putting you all-in, and it's folded back to you. There's $3,400 in the pot, and it's $1,700 more to you, so you are getting exactly 2-to-1. You have to win one-third of the time to make calling profitable.

If you think your opponent is a loose reraiser and that you will win significantly more than one-third, then you have an easy call. If you think he's a tight reraiser and you will win significantly less, then you have an easy fold.

But if you think you will win about one-third of the time (and that will often be just about right when reraised holding ace-jack), then it doesn't much matter what you do now. But that means your initial $700 raise was probably wrongly sized.

Almost all the hands that your opponent might reraise will be a favorite over ace-jack. Some, like pocket aces, are a huge favorite. Others, like pocket sevens, are only a tiny favorite. Take a weighted average, and the range comes out to about a 67 percent favorite.

You are indifferent to calling and folding, so calling is fine. But moving all-in in the first place would certainly have been better. This is a little tricky, so think about it carefully. The result of moving all-in is that your opponent will likely fold the weakest of the hands he might reraise you with.

Say he'll reraise a $700 raise with pocket sevens, but fold those sevens to an initial $2,400 all-in raise. This is typical and maybe even correct behavior. He'll reraise with the pocket sevens, hoping that you'll fold. He's a favorite over ace-jack (and most other unpaired hands), but he's not a 2-to-1 favorite, so he'd rather you fold. And of course he'd be delighted if he got you to fold pocket eights or nines.

But when you raise all $2,400, he must now compare his pocket sevens to the hands that you might raise all-in with. Since he's getting only $2,700-to-$2,400 (or 9-to-8) on his call, he must win at least 8/17 (47 percent) of the time to call profitably. With pocket sevens, he'll fear that you have a bigger pair too often to allow him to win almost half the time. So he'll fold.

Obviously, he'll call like lightening with pocket aces. So, and here's the tricky part, if you raise all-in, you'll be a much bigger underdog *when called*. While sometimes you got to play against pocket sevens before, now almost every time you get called you'll see something like pocket kings or ace-king. Thus, it might seem that raising all-in is bad.

But it's not. Since, after your $700 raise and all-in reraise, you were indifferent to calling and folding, you might as well call. He'll have pocket kings and ace-king just as often, so you are playing against those hands with exactly the same frequency. What's different is that, while you played against pocket sevens at a slight disadvantage before, you now pick up the blinds instead. By raising all-in, you've turned a small loss into a small profit every time your opponent has a marginal reraising hand.

The above analysis, however, does not mean that it is always better to move all-in with fairly good hands than to raise smaller. That is true only if the smaller raise can't be easily gotten away from. And the size of the smaller raise is up to you.

Suppose the blinds are $100-$200, and the stacks are $3,000. If you raise to only $500 you can easily fold ace-jack to a move in reraise. You're getting only $3,800-to-$2,500 odds, and that's not enough. (Even if he raised a bit less, you would still have to fold as you would have to put in the rest on the flop.)

Final Thoughts

Preflop raise sizing is important. Don't listen to pundits that tell you to keep your raises a constant size. Don't get lazy and just raise the "table standard." Controlling your raise sizes intelligently will help you control your opponents, the pot sizes, and many other factors.

Make smaller raises in early position, with "small pot" hands, and against players who call too much postflop. Make larger raises in late position, with "big pot" hands, and against players who fold too much postflop. Plenty of other factors are worth considering as well — how your opponents will read your raise size, whether you want your opponents to call or fold (though be careful with this one), and more.

And always mix up your play enough to stay unreadable. Seemingly random raise sizes are just as unreadable as constant ones, but they allow you more freedom, control, and profit.

A Preflop Strategy

This section will detail a preflop strategy for playing in a full (nine- or ten-handed) $5-$10 blind no limit game where most players (including you) have stacks of at least $1,000. We assume that you are one of the best players at the table, but that no one particular player is a "live one." Your opponents make plenty of mistakes, but they aren't overly weak-tight or loose.

You should know, however, that we were reluctant to write this section at all because hand values are extremely fluid in deep stack no limit. Whether a hand is playable or not, and how you should play it if it is, depends strongly on numerous factors. Among these factors are the following:

- The precise relationships between the size of your stack, the size of your opponents' stacks, the size of the blinds, and the size of the ante

- The starting standards of the players who have entered the pot, as well as those who haven't yet acted

- The postflop tendencies of your opponents, particularly their willingness to make bad folds in large pots or bad calls (or raises) in small ones

- The predictability of your opponents' play, both preflop and after the flop

- Your image

- The psychological impact previous hands may have had on you or any of the other players

122

Many more factors also enter into preflop decisions, making them quite complex. Thus, trying to develop "one preflop strategy to rule them all" is folly.

So before we begin, we want to make one thing unmistakably clear:

> This strategy is but one of a great many possible strategies that a good player could use with success. Our inclusion of it in this section does not, in any way, imply that another strategy is inferior or losing. Nor does it imply that deep stack no limit hands can or should be categorized and ranked or that this, or any other, strategy should be followed rigidly. *We absolutely do not hold that this strategy is, in any way, the one "correct" strategy.*

We will say, however, that this strategy should be easily good enough for most games you will encounter. That is, if we took a very good player aside and said, "We'll give you a choice. Either you don't play poker tonight, or you promise to adhere exactly to this preflop strategy," the good player should be more than willing to play and adhere to the strategy. He might win more if we cut him loose and allowed him to play however he pleased, but he should still be a solid winner when forced to play this strategy. So while this is certainly not a "perfect" strategy, playing it shouldn't get you into trouble either.

Finally (we'll get past the disclaimers soon), we provide this section as a service to those players who would feel completely lost without some basic preflop guidance. If that's you, then keep reading. If it's not, then you can feel free to skim.

No Limit Hand Values

In deep stack no limit, preflop hands have value based mostly on how well they extract money after the flop from your opponents. They don't have value based on how likely they are to win a showdown. That is, T♠9♠ is a far better no limit hand than

K♣5♠, even though K♣5♠ wins a showdown more often when the hands are all-in and pitted against one another.

If you like to think in terms of A♥7♣ "beating" J♠T♠ because ace-high beats jack-high, or even of Q♣Q♠ "beating" 4♥4♦ because a pair of queens beats a pair of fours, stop now. These notions are worthless in deep stack no limit. Indeed, they are worse than worthless, because they lead you to the wrong (sometimes to absurd) conclusions about how to play.

> **In deep stack no limit, preflop hands derive most of their value from how well they extract money after the flop from your opponents. Comparing hands based on how often they win a showdown or on their poker "hand rank" is worse than worthless.**

We'll put preflop hands into four broad and flexible categories:

1. Bread and butter hands
2. Often playable hands
3. Sometimes playable hands
4. Rarely playable hands

Bread and Butter Hands

These are the hands that you should most like to see when you first look at your cards. They tend to perform well with deep stacks, and they're usually worth playing. These hands include all pocket pairs, ace-king, suited aces (e.g., A♣6♣), and no gap suited connectors from king-queen suited (e.g., K♥Q♥) down to five-four suited (e.g., 5♠4♠).

Often Playable Hands

These hands are often worth playing, but usually not quite as good as the bread and butter hands. They include ace-queen, king-queen, any two suited cards jack or higher (e.g., K♦J♦), and one gap suited connectors from queen-ten suited (e.g., Q♥T♥) down to five-trey suited (e.g., 5♣3♣) (four-trey suited also).

Sometimes Playable Hands

These hands are sometimes worth playing, particularly in late position or against bad players. They include any two offsuit cards ten or higher (e.g., K♦T♠), suited kings (e.g., K♠7♠), two gap suited connectors from queen-nine suited (e.g., Q♦9♦) down to five-deuce suited (e.g., 5♥2♥) (four-deuce suited and trey-deuce suited also), and no gap offsuit connectors ten-nine offsuit (e.g., T♦9♠) down to five-four offsuit (e.g., 5♣4♥).

Rarely Playable Hands

All other hands are rarely playable. You'd play them against very bad players, as semi-bluffs, or to balance your strategy.

Again, these are fuzzy categories, and we don't mean to imply that one hand is better (in an absolute sense) than another simply because it is "Often Playable" versus "Sometimes Playable." These categories are merely intended to give relatively new players a basic idea of which hands have value and which hands don't have as much.

The Strategy

We have simplified this strategy as much as possible. However, it is still a little complicated, and that complication is more or less unavoidable. You don't need to memorize this strategy; indeed, we recommend that you do not memorize it. If you are a relatively new player, or you are unsure of your preflop play, then use it as a sanity check to make sure you aren't way off base. If you are an experienced, winning player, you can practically ignore it.

We use a few abbreviations. The first three have become relatively standard in the poker literature. LP means late position, and it indicates two seats: the button and one off the button. MP means middle position, and it indicates two seats: two and three off the button. EP means early position, and it indicates the other seats between the big blind and the first MP seat. (In a nine-handed game there will be three such seats, and in a ten-handed game there will be four.)

We also use three more abbreviations that are new with this book. UR means to "usually raise," UL means to "usually limp," and UF means to "usually fold." We introduce these abbreviations to emphasize how important balancing your strategy is in no limit. We don't feel you should make any play *every* time.

If we say a hand is a UR (usually raise), we mean that you should raise with it about 80 percent of the time and limp with it the other 20 percent. You can change that to 70/30 or 85/15 if you'd like; 80 percent isn't a magic number. (Though it's not completely meaningless either; a change to 95/5 or 55/45 would be a deviation from the strategy.)

If we say a hand is a UL (usually limp), we mean that you should limp with it about 80 percent of the time and raise it the other 20 percent. Again, those percentages are somewhat flexible.

If we say a hand is a UF (usually fold), we mean that you should fold it about 80 percent of the time, limp with it about 10 percent, and raise it the other 10 percent. Typically you'll be playing these UF hands for one of three reasons:

1.   Your opponents are particularly bad
2.   You are semi-bluffing
3.   You are balancing your strategy

Now here's the strategy. Hands are listed as UR, UL, or UF. If a hand doesn't appear in any of the three lists, we intend you to fold it. Also, we tell you how often to raise, but we don't tell you how much to raise. We provide that guidance in the chapter "Sizing Your Preflop Raises."

You are First to Enter the Pot

No one, except for the blinds, has entered the pot yet. Everyone has folded to you. If you are in EP:

- UR — Big pairs (AA-QQ) and AK

- UL — Other pairs (JJ-22), AQ, any two suited cards jack or higher (e.g., K♠J♠), no gap suited connectors J♦T♦ down to 5♣4♣, and suited aces (e.g., A♥4♥). You may want to fold some of those hands instead of limp if the game is such that one of your opponents is likely to make a big preflop raise.

- UF — One gap suited connectors queen-ten suited (e.g., Q♥T♥) down to five-trey suited (e.g., 5♣3♣) (and four-trey suited)

In MP, use the requirements for EP, except promote JJ, AQ, and two suited jack or higher to UR and suited one-gappers to UL.

In LP, we unfortunately can't, in good faith, give you any specific guidance. While all deep stack preflop decisions depend on numerous factors, that dependency is enormous when everyone folds to you in LP. Exceptional players against weak blind players might well be able to play virtually any hand in this situation, while weaker players against strong blind players should still play fairly tightly.

We will offer two nuggets of advice, though:

1. If you are new to the game or otherwise don't feel comfortable "going on your own," don't stray too far from the MP guidelines. You'll be folding some profitable hands, but that's the (temporary) price you will pay for your inexperience. Don't worry about it. Play what you're comfortable playing.

2. Limping can definitely be ok. Some macho types will tell you never to limp first in from LP. But that advice belongs to limit games or tournaments. In deep stack cash games, limping, even on the button, will frequently be a fine play.

Exactly One Player
Has Limped in Front of You

In EP and MP, use roughly the same strategy as you would if no one had yet entered the pot.

In LP, play somewhat looser than you would in MP. For instance, you might limp with T♥7♥ or raise with 9♣9♠.

Two or More Players
Have Limped in Front of You

Play roughly the same range of hands in EP, MP, and LP that you would play against one limper, but make the following three adjustments:

1. When you raise, your raise should be significantly bigger. Add at least one big blind to the size of your raise for each limper. See the chapter "Sizing Your Preflop Raises" for more information.

2. Your "usually" plays should become "almost always" plays. That is, instead of an 80/20 ratio, you should adopt a 95/5 ratio.

3. Raise more often (perhaps 20 percent of the time instead of 10 percent) with *the best* of your UF hands (e.g., J♣8♣). These are semi-bluffs.

Someone Has Opened for a Raise, No Callers Yet

In EP and MP:

* UR — Pocket aces and kings

* UC — AK, AQ suited, QQ-99, and occasionally other bread and butter hands

Also reraise occasionally with the best hands not mentioned (that you would otherwise fold). For instance, sometimes reraise with hands like 6♣6♦ and J♠T♠.

In LP, play the same as in EP and MP except add all pocket pairs and no gap suited connectors down to five-four suited (e.g. 5♠4♠) to the UC list.

When the raise is to an amount larger than four times the big blind (i.e., in a $5-$10 game, the raise makes it more than $40 to go), tighten up from these suggestions. The bigger the raise, the more you tighten up. On the other hand, if the raiser is a loose and wild raiser, you can call and reraise more loosely than these suggestions.

Someone Has Opened for a Raise, One or More Callers

Play the same way that you would with no callers with one exception: With ace-king, usually make a big reraise instead of calling.

Someone Has Opened for a Raise, and Another Player Reraised

Move in with pocket aces or kings, and fold everything else.

From the Blinds

In all scenarios, tend to play somewhat tighter than you would in LP. You will be out of position postflop, so most hands won't be worth playing.

In particular, don't worry about "defending" your big blind. The small amount of blind money usually won't provide enough incentive to play a weak hand out of position. You should call raises sparingly from either blind.

But finally, if several players have limped into the pot, make a big raise occasionally as a semi-bluff. When you do this, choose your *worst* hands, stuff like J♣4♠, to do it with. There's no sense in wasting a perfectly good hand like T♥8♥ for a bluff when you can simply check (or throw in one chip) and see a flop. (Of course, raises will more often be made with your legitimate good hands.)

Final Thoughts

We haven't given you a play for every situation, and we don't intend to. We hope that this strategy will serve you well as a guide and sanity check for your own play. And we also hope that your knowledge and judgment will soon be keen enough that you will never need to refer to this strategy again.

Adjusting to
Stack Sizes — An Example

You're playing in a nine-handed $5-$10 game. None of your opponents is either particularly good or particularly bad. The game is somewhat aggressive before the flop; many pots are raised. You have $700, and everyone has you covered. You are three off the button with

Everyone folds to you. What should you do?

Medium pocket pairs are very good hands in no limit, so you obviously shouldn't fold. Your first decision is between open-limping and raising. And then, if you raise, how big should your raise be?

Let's compare limping to raising to $40 in a few scenarios. We'll outline each scenario and decide whether it worked out well for you or whether choosing the other option would have been better.

- **You limp, and everyone folds to the big blind, who checks.** In this scenario, it's unclear whether raising or limping would have been better. If you had raised, you may have won the blinds or been called by the big blind who is out of position with a likely weaker hand. Then again, pocket eights does well heads-up in position after the flop, so you don't particularly want to raise out the big blind. You don't want to miss out on a possible $700 win to lock up a $15 blind steal.

- **You limp, and a few players limp behind you.** In this case limping may have been slightly better, since if you had raised, some (but probably not all) of the limpers may have folded. With a medium pocket pair and a medium-deep stack (70 times the big blind), most of your total win will come those times you flop a set. A set is worth significantly more in a multiway pot than in a heads-up one. So limping turned out well for you.

  On the other hand, if all your opponents would have called your raise anyway, then raising might have been slightly better. You're more likely to stack someone if you flop a set in a raised pot than an unraised one. Then again, if you don't flop a set, raising costs you an extra $30, so it is close.

- **You limp, and someone raises to $40 behind you.** When this happens, you should be very glad you didn't raise. It's true that if you had raised, the player behind you probably would have merely have called your raise. If this would have happened, then raising and limping again are close in value. The money result is the same either way (although the playing dynamics are different).

  But sometimes, especially with big pocket pairs, your opponent will reraise to $120 or more. This is a disaster for you. Depending on the exact size of the reraise, it will either force you to fold or to make a call you wish you didn't have to make. Either way, your raise is bad in light of the Fundamental Theorem of Poker; it encourages your opponent to play correctly given your specific hand.

  Small and medium pairs often perform well against big pairs when the preflop betting remains a small percentage of the stack sizes. But big pairs pull away as the preflop betting gets big. By raising, you encourage players with big pairs to save themselves by making the natural play — a reraise. If you had let the big pair put in the first raise, you could have called and possibly doubled up with small risk. But by allowing the big pair to reraise, your hand has lost all its value.

With this stack size (70 times the big blind) and this particular hand, you're better off limping rather than raising to $40. Raising is perhaps slightly better those times you could have stolen the blinds or played heads-up against the big blind. But limping is certainly better when it encourages others to enter the pot with weak hands. And limping is far, far better when raising would have elicited a reraise from a big pair. Allowing yourself to be reraised turns a good situation (small preflop pot against a big pair) into a total loss.

Raising offers a few marginal (and debatable) upsides, but it can also lead you to disaster. Limping is clearly better.

The Effect of Stack Size

This line of reasoning works when your stack is 70 times the big blind. The analysis changes, however, if your stack is much bigger or much smaller than that.

With a deep stack (say 200 times the big blind) getting reraised isn't such a disaster. For instance, you have a $2,000 stack in a $5-$10 game (everyone has you covered). You raise to $40, and someone with a big pair reraises to $120. It's $80 to you, but there's still almost $1,900 behind. You can still play very profitably against the big pair.

Indeed, with stacks this large, a small to medium raise (e.g., to $30 or $40) may be the best play. The advantages of raising, primarily making the postflop bets larger in size those times you flop a set, outweigh the disadvantages.

With a short stack (say 10 times the big blind), raising also becomes better. Your focus should no longer be on doubling up if you flop a set. Instead, you should concentrate on stealing the blinds or playing heads-up. This is doubly true if your stack is short because you are playing in a tournament with an ante. In that situation, move all-in immediately to maximize your chance to win the blinds and antes.

Final Thoughts

This example demonstrates well how stack sizes can change your decisions dramatically. The same hand, opening with pocket eights in middle position, should be played in three different ways with three different stack sizes.

With a short stack in a tournament, maximizing your chance to steal the blinds and antes is the most important consideration, so you should raise all-in. With very large stacks, increasing your chance to win a huge pot if you flop a set is most important, so you should raise a modest amount.

But with an in-between stack, about 70 times the big blind, the most important consideration is making sure you don't get reraised off your medium pair.[23] A poorly-conceived raise can be a gift to your unwitting opponent with a big pair. Raising puts him in the situation where his natural play works out perfectly for him. Don't do that!

---

[23] This whole analysis breaks down completely if your hand is something like ace-queen. In fact, the arguments go almost exactly the other way for ace-queen. It's a hand that will be happy winning the blinds or getting it heads-up. And it will often welcome a reraise rather than fear it, as the reraise lets ace-queen get away before it gets into trouble on the flop (if it makes top pair, but is still no good).

Blocking Bets

An aggressive player in a $5-$10 game raises to $30 in late position, and only the big blind, holding

calls. The flop comes

giving the big blind the nut flush draw. He checks and calls a $60 bet. The turn is the Jc, giving him a gutshot to go along with his straight draw. The big blind now bets $80, and his opponent calls.

Why would the big blind bet all of a sudden? Is it a semibluff? If so, why would he bet so little? The pot was $180 at the time, and he bet only $80.

While the big blind would have been delighted if his opponent had folded, his bet wasn't intended as a bluff. Sure, the button might fold if he held a weak, but slightly better hand like a pair of sixes. But, while a few better hands might fold, the bet isn't primarily a semibluff. It's a blocking bet.

A *blocking bet* is a small bet made by an out of position player designed to keep the street "cheap." That is, the big blind wants to see the river card with his straight and flush draws, but he doesn't want to have to call a pot-sized bet to do it. He was worried that, if he had checked, his opponent would have made a $180 bet.

By making a blocking bet of $80, he "set the price," not his opponent. That is, against most opponents, he will usually either win immediately, or he will get called and see the river for a total of $80, not $180. That makes his draw far more profitable than it would have been had he checked.

Obviously the downside, however, is that his blocking bet might also get raised, perhaps even pricing him out entirely. If that happened, he'd lose an extra $80.

For the sake of completing the example, let's set some hypothetical percentages for the likelihood of various outcomes. Let's assume that if he had checked, his opponent would have bet $180 80 percent of the time and checked behind 20 percent. And in response to his blocking bet of $80, he'll get a fold 10 percent of the time, a call 70 percent, and raised big (i.e., any amount forcing him to fold) 20 percent of the time.

If he checks, his opponent will	This percent of the time
Bet $180	80%
Check	20%

If he bets $80, his opponent will	This percent of the time
Fold	10%
Call	70%
Raise big	20%

Let's assume his draw is exactly 3-to-1 to come in (which is fair because two of his flush outs pair the board, and he might just lose a bundle if his opponent is lucky enough to make a full house). There is $180 in the pot on the turn. If he bets $80 and his opponent folds, he wins $180. If he bets and is called, then he wins $180 + $80 = $260 one-fourth of the time, and he loses $80 the other three-fourths. Actually, because of implied odds, he will probably win somewhat more than $260 on average when he makes his draw. Let's say he wins an average of $100 more on the river.

So if he bets $80, he wins $360 one-fourth of the time and loses $80 three-fourths of the time. If he bets $80 and gets raised, then he loses $80.

Thus, his EV for the blocking bet is $23.

$$\$23 = (0.10)(\$180) + (0.70)[(0.25)(\$360) + (0.75)(-\$80)]$$
$$+ (0.20)(-\$80)$$

If he had checked and called a $180 bet, then he would be in a roughly break-even situation if, after making his draw, he could expect to win another $180 or so on the river (more than the $100 we assumed last time because the pot is now bigger). That is, he would win $180+$180+$180 = $540 one-fourth of the time, but lose $180 three-fourths of the time, making calling break-even:

$$\$0 = (0.25)(\$540) + (0.75)(-\$180)$$

So all the EV from checking comes from those times his opponent checks behind, and he gets to draw for free. Let's say that he wins an average of $50 on the river when his opponent checks behind and he makes his draw (less than either time before because now his opponent will fold far more frequently since the check behind indicates weakness). So one-fourth of the time, he wins $230.

Thus, the EV of checking is merely $11.

$$\$11 = (0.80)(\$0) + (0.20)(0.25)(\$230)$$

By setting the price at $80 with his blocking bet, he increased his expectation by $12. (Again, we don't expect you to think this precisely at the table. But we do want you to get a feel as to how the various factors of these situations lead to different plays.)

Blocking on the River

In the previous example, we examined a situation where someone used a blocking bet to draw cheaply. But blocking bets can also be useful after all the cards are out. This is most often the case when you have a mediocre hand — perhaps a fairly good one pair hand — that will usually be worth checking and calling with, but just barely. That is, say your opponent likes to bet about half the pot on the river (typical of many players). Betting half the pot offers you 3-to-1, so if you think you will win more often than 25 percent of the time, you should call.

More concretely, say you are heads-up on the river in a $200 pot. If you check, your opponent might check behind or bet $120. When she bets $120, you estimate that you will win 35 percent of the time if you call. Since you are getting 320-to-120 or 8-to-3, you should call, and your EV is $34.

$$\$34 = (0.35)(\$320) + (0.65)(-\$120)$$

But since you are almost a 2-to-1 dog to win *if she bets*, you would have preferred that she bet less than $120. Sometimes you can make that happen by making a blocking bet.

For instance, say you bet $80 preemptively. Now, if you maintain your 35 percent win rate *when called* (assuming you can always be sure that you are beaten if you get raised), your expectation improves.

For simplicity, let's assume that she'll bet 50 percent of the time if you check (and you will always call), and she will call (or raise) 50 percent of the time if you bet. (Also, assume that if you check and she checks, your hand will always be enough to win the pot.)

Now we can compare the expectation of checking and calling versus the blocking bet (and folding if need be). The expectation of checking is $117.

$$\$117 = (0.50)(\$200) + (0.50)(0.35)(\$320) + (0.50)(0.65)(-\$120)$$

The expectation for the blocking bet is $123.

$$\$123 = (0.50)(\$200) + (0.50)(0.35)(\$280) + (0.50)(0.65)(-\$80)$$

The blocking bet nets an extra $6. Of course, we blithely made quite a few assumptions for this example. Most notably, we assumed that the bets were made and called 50 percent of the time in each example. But there's no reason to expect that to be the case. When you check, your opponent will either bet for value or bluff. We assumed she would do one or the other with 50 percent of her hands.

But when you bet, she will fold all the hands she would have bluffed with. On the other hand, she will now call with some weaker bluff-catcher hands she might have checked down. Of course, she will also call with every hand she would have value bet. So we assumed that the number of value betting hands plus the number of bluff-catchers would also amount to 50 percent of her hands.

Thus, the big assumption we made is that she would bluff with roughly the same number of hands she would call (but not bet) with, hoping you are bluffing. There's no reason why this would necessarily be the case other than that we simply stated it to be true. If your opponent is a consummate bluffer, she might bluff with far more hands than she'd call with. Against such an opponent, making blocking bets isn't nearly as attractive, as you preempt your opponent from bluffing off her money.

Likewise, your opponent could call with far more hands than she would bluff with. Against such a "calling station" player, you might want to bet the river, but no longer as a blocking bet; you'd now be betting for value! Since she doesn't bluff often, you might not win the requisite percentage to justify calling a half-pot bet. But since she calls with weak hands often (perhaps too often), you can value bet weaker hands than you normally might.

We also assumed that you could safely assume you were beaten if raised. If you pick good situations for blocking bets and don't overuse the play, this should be roughly true. But if you start to overuse the play, your stronger opponents will begin to catch on to what you are doing, and you will find your blocking bets getting raised far more frequently. (That's bad news for any blocking bet, whether done with a draw or on the river.) If your opponents are savvy enough to detect and raise a blocking bet, obviously that fact makes the play far less attractive.

Downsides to the Blocking Bet

The blocking bet can be a valuable weapon when used sparingly. Generally, it performs better against unaware opponents who won't understand why you are making the play. Against tricky, aggressive players, *use it with great caution*. If they pick up on your intentions, your proverbial goose is cooked.

As we alluded to before in the river example, the main drawback to using a blocking bet on the river (as opposed to with a draw) is that you preempt bluffs. Sophisticated players play aggressively and bluff (or, more generally, bet weak to marginal hands) relatively frequently. To get the best of these players, your strategy must include checking and calling with some fairly strong hands to induce and pick off these bluffs. Like the aikido master, you must use your opponents' strengths against them.

If you tend to use blocking bets with your medium-strength hands, you give your aggressive opponents way too much information with which to beat you. They know that if you make a blocking bet, they can save their bluffing money (and still sometimes move you off your hand with a raise). If you check, you are quite likely to fold to a bet, and their bluffing frequency and profitability will skyrocket. These players force you to "play square," and will largely blunt the effectiveness of your blocking bets.

Another downside, closely related to the last one, is that using blocking bets frequently makes all of your hands easier to read. By its nature, a blocking bet must be smaller than an average bet (or at least smaller than your opponents' average bets). Also, blocking bets are generally made on weak- to medium-strength hands. If your smallish bets tend to be weak- to medium-strength hands, that tells your opponents a lot. It also tells your opponents that when you make larger bets, you are significantly more likely to have a strong hand or a bluff. That is, if you make blocking bets often, the fact that you *haven't* made a blocking bet will betray significant information as well.

Defending Against the Blocking Bet

Raise. The blocking bet hates a raise. Remember, the whole point of the play is to keep the betting cheap. Raising will thwart that plan with certainty, and it will often win you the pot immediately (particularly if your raise is sizable, and your opponents' implied odds for drawing are unfavorable).

In fact, the raise is so devastating to a blocking bet that if you could somehow read your opponent's mind enough to know that he was making a blocking bet (but not know anything else about the nature of his hand), you might be right to raise with 100 percent of your weak hands (provided you could raise enough to force a fold).

So the problem then becomes detecting a blocking bet. Again, remember that blocking bets must be smaller than normal, and they must be made when out of position. If it's before the river, look for possible draws your opponent might want to see cheaply.

Some players are horrendously transparent with their blocking bets. A few try to get greedy by making their blocking bets tiny (e.g., $10 into a $100 pot). Naturally these bets make for an easy raise. Others are less transparent. But in all cases, never act on a bet before you verify the exact size, compare it to the pot size, and determine if it's unusually large or unusually small. Blocking bets will always be smaller than average. If you pay close attention to your opponents' betting tendencies, you'll begin to identify bets that are uncommonly small. These are candidates for blocking bets. (We say "candidates" because good players, including you, will sometimes simulate blocking bets with excellent hands.)

Final Thoughts

A blocking bet is a preemptive bet made by a player first to act. The bettor attempts to "set the price" for the betting round by betting an amount smaller than what he expects his opponent would bet. Blocking bets can be made before the river (usually with draws, but also occasionally with modest made hands) or on the river.

Blocking bets are most effective against unaware or unskilled opponents. Sharp players will seem to read your mind when you make too many of these, and they will raise them again and again. Weaker players, though, will tend to let you get away with setting your price (as long as you don't make it too small). If you are playing against such an opponent, blocking bets are a powerful, but subtle, way to control him from out of position.

The Call Bluff

The call bluff plays an integral role in a well-rounded deep stack strategy against thinking opponents. It's not a play you should make repeatedly; like many daring no limit plays, it plays a balancing role in your strategy. An occasional use of the play prevents your opponents from reading your hands too accurately and forces them to play defensively.

The call bluff, or delayed bluff, is simple. Your opponent bets, and instead of raising immediately as a bluff (or longshot semi-bluff), you just call. Then you bluff bet or raise on the next round.

The call bluff is most effective with position against a single opponent. Being out of position or against two opponents makes it quite risky. Being out of position *and* against two opponents makes it prohibitively risky, except in unusual circumstances.

Here's a basic example. You're playing $10-$20 with $2,000 stacks. A straightforward player opens in middle position for $100. You call on the button with the

The blinds fold. (The pot is $230.)
The flop comes

giving you a gutshot. Your opponent bets $150, and you call, possibly as the first leg of a call bluff. (The pot is $530.)

The turn is the 2♥. Your opponent checks, and you complete the call bluff by betting $400. (The size of the bet depends on how likely you are to follow up with an all-in river bluff if called.)

Unless your opponent happens to have a monster, and there's no reason to think he does, then your bluff will often succeed. You are representing a made flush, among other things, and few players will be happy to risk their remaining $1,750 in a $530 pot with a significant chance of being drawing dead. Your position, the somewhat threatening board, and the deep stacks will force your opponent off many hands, frequently including those as strong as ace-king.

Notice that we said that you called on the flop "possibly" as the first leg of a call bluff. Just because you call on the flop with a call bluff in mind doesn't force you to follow through. If the turn had been the A♣ instead of the 2♥, and your opponent had bet $600 instead of checking, you'd be daft to "follow through" with an all-in raise of $1,150 more.

This flexibility is part of what makes the call bluff so powerful: You stay in the hand with a modest investment and deploy your bluffing capital only when your opponent appears weakest. If you always bluff-raise rather than call bluff, you'll end up with a lot of $500 losses that could have been $150 losses.

Obviously, this flexibility is largely negated when you are out of position. If you check and call on the flop, you must either launch your turn bluff without extra information, or you must check again. If you check again, your opponent can check behind and significantly blunt your bluff. You can still try on the river, but then your opponent can call without fear of a big bet in the future; one call and he gets to showdown. Besides, your opponent might make his hand on the river.

Another advantage of the call bluff is that it turns a passive play, calling, into a weapon. When you combine call bluffs with slowplays or rope-a-dopes (just calling in position with big hands to induce extra action), you freeze your out of position opponents.

A mere flop call becomes scary: Are you drawing? Are you slowplaying? Are you call bluffing?

Our example was really a call semi-bluff since you flopped a gutshot. Indeed, with stacks this deep, you'd likely call with your gutshot even if bluffing later in the hand was only a marginal possibility. With $380 in the pot and another $1,750 behind, the potential reward for catching the nuts on the turn is probably alone worth a $150 call. Add in the chance that your opponent will check the turn, or that you'll catch a pair and win a showdown, and it's an easy call.

As a quick aside, it's perfectly reasonable to call on the flop with two very different hopes: you'll catch your straight and win a big pot or you'll miss your straight, but bluff your opponent out. On the surface, these hopes may seem contradictory, "Well, which is it? Do you think you'll win a big pot, or do you think you can bluff him out?" The wonderful thing about poker, though, is that it can be both.

Say you think you have a 40 percent chance to stack your opponent if you catch your straight and a 60 percent chance to bluff him out if you don't. These possibilities are each independently profitable, and when paired together, their profitability sums.[24] Sometimes you'll make a pot-sized bet and win immediately. Other times, you'll make a pot-sized bet, get raised, and show up with the nuts. Either way you make money.

Remember, your opponents can have a range of hands. You don't know exactly what they have; the best you can do is to assign a probability to each holding. It's perfectly reasonable to play in a way that takes advantage of their best and worst hands simultaneously.

Let's get back to the example. Because of the added gutshot value, this was a "no-brainer" call bluff. Most experts would play

---

[24] The fact that the profitabilities sum, of course, means that the play may be right even if the individual components by themselves were not profitable.

out that example hand by calling the flop and possibly bluffing the turn almost no matter their image or who their opponent is.

Some call bluffs are anything but "no brainers" though. For instance, suppose instead of 7♠6♠ you had Q♠T♠ on the K♥8♥4♠ flop. Usually, of course, you should fold.

But sometimes, depending on your opponent or image, you can try a call bluff. For instance, if your opponent is particularly straightforward or prone to folding good hands, you can try call bluffing with "nothing." The strength of the call bluff as opposed to the raise bluff is that it keeps your options open before you make a risky bet; you get a little more time to gather information before you commit. So the more information your opponents give away, the more profitable the call bluff "on air" can be.

Specifically, some poor players will rarely check any good hand on the turn if they have bet the flop and were called. That's an information leak tailored for call bluffs. You can call the flop and see what they do on the turn. If they bet, you fold. If they check, you know they are probably fairly weak, and you can make a profitable bluff.

Defending Against the Call Bluff

Given the last paragraph, you should see the obvious defense against the call bluff. After you bet the flop and someone behind you calls, you should sometimes check-raise the turn. These check-raises should usually be made with good hands, but also sometimes not.

The primary advantage of the call bluff is an informational one. So to defend against the play, you should make sure the "information" you give off between the flop and turn is of little use. Usually you check bad hands and bet good ones, but sometimes you mix it up. Check those good hands. And occasionally when you check bad hands, check-raise bluff. If you keep your opponents guessing, they'll generally be loathe to play back at you, and they'll save their call bluffs for more readable players. When you're out of position, if you can manipulate your opponents into playing more straightforwardly against you, you usually should.

Final Thoughts

Some people seem to think the call bluff is a particularly clever play. Perhaps it's because calling with "nothing" is counterintuitive. But it's no cleverer really than any other play. Don't be too enamored with yourself when you pull one off successfully. It's all in a day's work.

Use the call bluff as a tool of oppression when you have the button. Positional advantage in deep stack no limit can be crushing, and one major reason is that your out of position opponents have to fear a call almost as much as a raise. Keep your flop calls dangerous with slowplays and call bluffs, and you'll paralyze your opponents.

Check-Raising

Most players love to check-raise. Check-raising is deceptive, and it's always fun to watch your opponents fall into your trap. And, besides being fun, check-raising plays an important role in any no limit strategy.

But many players don't use the check-raise correctly, unleashing it at inappropriate times or not using it when they should. This section will provide a few guidelines about proper check-raising.

Don't Do It
Just Because You Can

In limit poker, with few exceptions, you should check-raise with very good hands whenever you think you can. That is, if you are fairly sure one of your opponents will bet, check-raising will usually be your best play.

This isn't true in no limit; you can be virtually certain one of your opponents will bet, yet you still shouldn't check-raise. Why?

The first reason is that check-raising allows your opponent to set the bet size. Say you have the nuts, first to act, in a heads-up pot on the river. The pot is $200 now, and there is $1,000 left to bet. You expect your opponent to call if you bet $200 or to bet if you check. But your opponent tends to make smallish river bets; perhaps into a $200 pot you would expect him typically to bet about $80.

So, say your choices are between betting $200 or checking, hoping your opponent bets $80, then raising another $200. You should only try the check-raise if you are quite sure both that your opponent will bet and that he'll call your raise. With any major doubt about either of those, you should simply bet $200 yourself.

If you have an 80 percent chance to have your $200 bet called, then your expectation from betting out is $160.

$$\$160 = (0.80)(\$200)$$

If your opponent will bet $80 about 90 percent of the time and call $200 more another 40 percent of the time, then your expectation is $139.20.

$$\$139.20 = (0.90)(0.40)(\$280) + (0.90)(0.60)(\$80)$$

We set the "call the check-raise" percentage to 40 rather than a higher number to reflect the fact that check-raising is a power move. Indeed, if you were almost certain that your opponent was strong enough to call a $200 check-raise, then you should be making a larger bet yourself (either a straight bet or check-raise).

The reason your direct bet made more money than the check-raise in this example was that, by checking, you allowed your opponent to set the bet at a relatively small amount. In essence, by checking you allowed your opponent to make a sort of blocking bet against you.

This brings us to the two major drawbacks of a check-raise in no limit:

1. Check-raising permits your opponent to set the bet size.

2. Check-raising is usually a powerful move. Betting out often gives away less information about the strength of your hand.

When to Check-Raise

So when do you check-raise? With more cards to come or against more than one opponent, this is a very tricky question that is so dependent on stack size, player proclivities, and specific situations that no book can hope to address it fully.

But heads-up situations on the river are easier to analyze. There are basically three situations, heads-up on the river, where you should give serious consideration to going for a check-raise:

1.   You think your opponent will bet with more hands than he will call with.

2.   You have a great hand and you think your opponent will both bet and call a check-raise, but not raise if you bet or call an original bet that is approximately the size of the sum of the bet and check-raise.

3.   You want to bluff.

These are explained in more detail below.

Situation No 1. You think your opponent will bet with more hands than he will call with. The first of these reasons is by far the most important, which is ironic because your check-raise will rarely get called! The only time it will get called is if you have underestimated the strength of your opponent's hand or (rarely) if your check-raise arouses enough suspicions or stubbornness on your opponent's part that he will call with mediocre hands he wouldn't have bet in the first place.

But that doesn't matter. You should still usually go for a check-raise in this situation simply because it makes you more money. You don't make your money so much because of the "raise" part, but more because of the "check" part.

We have discussed elsewhere that it is often right to check (and call with) a good hand on the river as long as you think that your opponent will more likely bet (usually a bluff) a worse hand than yours than call with one. (This condition is met more often in no limit than in limit because the bigger river bet is more likely to get mediocre hands to fold.)

Well the same condition often holds true with a great hand. With a merely good hand your check and call will often induce and win you an extra bet. Don't blow that won bet just because your hand is better than merely good.

Situation No. 2. You have a great hand and you think your opponent will both bet and call a check-raise, but not raise if

you bet or call an original bet that is approximately the size of the sum of the bet and check-raise. This second situation, while logically ironclad, suffers from the fact that in real life it comes up so rarely. You need to be awfully sure that he will bet and call a check-raise that adds up to approximately the original amount you would bet and also be fairly sure that he wouldn't raise a smaller bet on your part. You really have to know your opponents well to pigeonhole them so specifically.

The most likely situation might be where the last card completed a flush, and you have the nut flush.

In theory there could be other situations where a check-raise with a great hand against an opponent's good hand might be better than a simple bet. For instance, you might think that a check will always result in a bet of about $100 and an 80 percent chance that a $300 raise will be called. But a simple bet of $400 is only 70 percent to be called. These situations (as well as the original one specified in situation No. 2) are so rare that you really can't go wrong making a fairly big bet almost every time when your great hand acts first against a likely good hand.

There are, though, a couple of reasons to check the river occasionally with a great hand against an obvious good hand. One reason is that you don't want him to be sure that your check indicates weakness. His uncertainty may, on a future hand, stop him from betting a slightly better hand than yours for value. His fear of a check-raise thus saves you money.

The other reason you might sometimes check a great hand against an apparent good one is to set up a future check-raise bluff.

Situation No. 3. You want to bluff. A check-raise bluff on the river should be tried every once in a while against certain players in certain circumstances. The daring version of this play is doing it when there is little doubt that your opponent has a good hand. This means that you are opting not to come out bluffing with your busted hand, but instead you are trying the more expensive check-raise bluff. It's risky to be sure, but perhaps it's also wiser as well. Because many players are much more likely to fold to a check-raise than to a mere bet.

In fact, I (David) have sometimes seen players go for the check-raise bluff even in situations where they knew that a bet out bluff would probably work. They are so sure that their opponent will probably fold to a check-raise that they greedily choose that option in spite of its greater risk. Notice that this really is a daring play because you not only need to be relatively sure that your opponent will fold, but also that he will bet. Obviously this play requires a very accurate read of your opponent (both his hands and his betting and calling tendencies). In most games you should remove it from your bag of tricks.

It is a different story, though, if you think your opponent will likely bluff the river. If you also have nothing, and he might beat you by accident if you call, a check-raise might be the best play. As far as betting out instead, that might also be a good play, but obviously not if you are quite sure your opponent will bluff if you check.

Even if you aren't sure your opponent will bet, however, a check-raise bluff might be right while a bluff bet would be wrong. This situation arises when it appears that your opponent will often have a decent, but not bettable hand, and less often have a busted draw that he will probably bluff with. You don't come out bluffing because you will be called when he has the decent hand. But when he bets after you check, you get renewed hope.

Final Thoughts

Before the river, check-raising is not that rare a weapon, especially in multiway pots. One reason relates to the fact that betting in early position shows so much strength that you rarely get more than one call. A check-raise can trap people in the middle. But even here the play should be used judiciously and only expert players recognize the best opportunities for the play when they arise. A book really can't do the subject justice.

There is one time, though, where a check-raise is fairly automatic. This situation is when you are heads-up on the flop, and your opponent raised before the flop. Since many players will usually bet the flop when checked to, you should frequently go for a check-raise with any hand you might otherwise bet. (Note that the less likely your opponent is to make a continuation bet after the flop, the less automatic the check-raise play becomes.) The goal of the check-raise is to grab an extra bet when your opponent missed the flop.

When your opponent does bet, you often raise with your good hands, your good draws, and occasionally some semi-junk (always adjusting, of course, for the specific opponent and the specific situation).

In most situations, when to check-raise and when not to check-raise is an extremely complex topic. While we have but scratched the surface in this section, hopefully we've given you some ideas to think about while you play.

Betting Yourself Off a Hand

It's the turn. You have

and position on your lone opponent. The board is

There's $100 in the pot, you have $1,000 in your stack (your opponent has you covered), and it's your turn to act. After a brief stare down, you conclude that your opponent probably has your five-high beaten. So if you bet, it would be as a semi-bluff.

Say you narrow your choices to two: check, hoping to catch a trey, or bet $100, hoping that your opponent folds. And say you are virtually certain that two out of three times, your opponent will fold if you bet. The other time, she'll check-raise all-in (and you'll naturally fold). Should you bet?

The expectation of bluffing is $33.33.

$$\$33.33 = \left(\frac{2}{3}\right)(\$100) - \left(\frac{1}{3}\right)(\$100)$$

Semi-bluffing has a positive expectation. But before you put your chips in the middle, perhaps you should also analyze

154

checking. Assume that, if you check, you will give up if you don't catch a trey. But if you do catch your wheel (giving you the nuts), you'll win your opponent's entire stack ($1,000 plus the $100 in the pot, for $1,100 total) X percent of the time, and win the $100 pot the rest of the time. Your chance to catch a trey is 4/44 or 1 in 11. So, under these assumptions, the EV of checking is:

$$EV = \left(\frac{10}{11}\right)(\$0) + \left(\frac{1}{11}\right)\left[(X)(\$1,100) + (1 - X)(\$100)\right]$$

Note that if X is at least one-third, then the term $(1/11)$ $(X=1/3)$ $(\$1,100)$ is equal to $33.33 by itself. The $(1/11)$ $(2/3)$ $(\$100) = \$6.06$ is gravy.

So if you have one chance in three of stacking your opponent if you catch your straight, you should try to do that *even though semi-bluffing is also quite profitable*. To get an exact value of X at which checking becomes better than betting under these conditions, we have to do a little algebra:

$$\$33.33 = \left(\frac{1}{11}\right)(\$1,100)(X) + \left(\frac{1}{11}\right)(\$100)(1 - X)$$

$$\$33.33 = (\$100)(X) + \frac{\$100}{11} - \frac{\$100}{(11)(X)}$$

$$\$33.33 = \$100X + \$9.09 - \$9.09X$$

$$\$24.24 = \$90.9X$$

$$X = 0.2667 \text{ or about 27 percent}$$

It turns out that if she'll get all-in with you on the river just over a quarter of the time when you make the wheel, it's better to check for the longshot than take the immediate profit of the bluff. On the other hand, if she'll get all-in with you less often than that, take that immediate profit.

Before we continue, you should realize that this simplified exercise shortchanges the value of checking somewhat. We assumed that your hand would be entirely worthless if you checked and didn't catch a trey, but that's not really true. You might catch a four or five, check it down, and find out you have the best hand. You might also have a profitable bluffing opportunity on the river.

This decision appears again and again in no limit hold 'em, and it's a crucial one. You are last to act and have a hand with some value. Should you check it, hoping to score a profit the old fashioned way, or should you take a stab at the pot, risking a check-raise? As you might expect, the answer to this question is complex, but you should learn what considerations go into the decision.

The important factors are:

- The likelihood that your bluff will succeed
- The likelihood that you will be check-raised off your hand
- The value that your hand might have on the river if you miss
- The likelihood that your draw will come in
- Your implied odds if you make your hand

These factors are strongly interrelated, so it doesn't make much sense to analyze them individually. Generally speaking, if you will have to fold to a check-raise, the more value your hand has, the *less likely* you should be to semi-bluff with it. While this conclusion is highly counter intuitive, the explanation is not. The first EV equation (the one that calculates the value of bluffing) doesn't depend on the value of your draw. The second one, however, does. The more valuable your draw, the higher the EV of checking. The higher the second equation goes, the less attractive bluffing becomes.

Some ways your draw can have more value than usual:

- The draw has lots of outs
- The stacks are large
- Your opponent is a "caller"
- The draw is to the nuts

Notice that the final three conditions are all "implied odds" boosters. The more money there is left to bet, and the more likely your opponent is to call a bet after you make your draw, the higher your implied odds.

Your draw being to the nuts is also an implied odds booster. It works for you those times your opponent happens to be on a similar draw to yours. When your draw is to the nuts (and theirs isn't), you will always win the "big hand versus big hand" confrontations, which gives you a major implied odds boost. When you are drawing to less than the nuts, you will sometimes lose your stack rather than win it, and that slashes the value of your draw from both ends (big wins turn into big losses).

For instance you have J♥T♣ with position on a single opponent. The pot is $100, and you have $1,000 left (your opponent has you covered). It's the turn, and your opponent has checked to you. Assuming your bluff is equally likely to succeed in either case, you should often be more willing to semi-bluff if the board is Q♥9♥4♠9♣ than if it is Q♥9♦4♠6♣. In both cases you have an open-ended straight draw, but in the former hand, there is a flush draw and pair on board. Since the straight draw has less value on the former board, checking (playing for the draw) has less value, and bluffing becomes more attractive as an option.

Indeed, the main danger of semi-bluffing, that you will be check-raised off your draw, may not be a danger at all in the former case. For instance, if you are playing against someone who would check-raise only with a full house or better (granted, an uncommon breed), you actually gain from the check-raise! It tells you that you are drawing dead, and it prevents you from losing any money on the river if you make your hand.

Bluffing With
a Fairly Good Hand

Most players learn early on how they should play the river. They should bet their good hands for value, check down their mediocre (or fairly good) hands, and bluff occasionally with their bad hands. Betting the good hands is obvious, as is bluffing occasionally with the bad hands. But why check down mediocre hands?

Generally speaking, mediocre hands are those that are somewhat likely to win a showdown, but that are unlikely to be called by a weaker hand. That is, they're strong enough that few better hands are likely to fold, but they're weak enough that few worse hands are likely to call.

In limit hold 'em, unimproved ace-king is often in such a situation. For instance, if you have

on a

board, and your opponent checks to you in an eight bet pot, you have a decidedly mediocre hand. A bet will offer your opponent 9-to-1. In that situation, you're likely to get called if your

158

opponent holds a pair, but you're unlikely to get called if he doesn't. Now, he may fold a weak pocket pair like 4♥4♠, or he may call with a good ace-high like A♠J♣, but those are fringe cases. Most of the time, if you are called you will lose. And only very rarely will your opponent fold a better hand. In total, a bet fails both as a bluff and as a value bet, so checking is best.[25]

Many players internalize this concept quickly and thoroughly. Bet good hands, check mediocre hands, and occasionally bluff with bad hands. This becomes "automatic" play. In no limit, however, you should be careful with this decision to bet or check, because the good-mediocre-bad lines blur quite a bit.

In particular, you should try bluffing with some "mediocre" hands that would frequently win a showdown. Why? Here's some simple math:

Say you are last to act in a $100 pot. Your opponent checks. If you check it down, you expect to win approximately 30 percent of the showdowns. So checking gives you an expectation of $30 (30 percent of $100).

If you bet $100 as a bluff, however, you expect to win 70 percent of the time — the 30 percent you would have won in a showdown plus an additional 40 percent. These extra hands your opponent holds are decent, but not great hands. In practice, they might be something like top pair with a modest kicker. Now your expectation is $40.

$$\$40 = (0.70)(\$100) - (0.30)(\$100)$$

Even though your hand would frequently win a showdown, bluffing got enough extra hands to fold to make it worthwhile.

---

[25] Mathematically if they both just barely fail, a bet may still be right. This "two-way bet" can also sometimes work in no limit, but it is too tricky to analyze here.

A Wrench in the Works

In the last example, we compared bluffing against checking. We assumed you'd never get check-raised off the best hand, and therefore, if bluffing showed a profit versus not bluffing, then bluffing was the right play.

But you have more options than to bluff or not to bluff. You can also bet for value. For bluffing to be right, it has to be better than both checking and betting for value.

For instance, say the pot is $100. Your opponent checks to you on the river, and you estimate that you have the best hand about 70 percent of the time. You think that if you bet $150, your opponent will call with the best 10 percent of his hands (all better than yours) and fold the other 90 percent. If you bet $50, however, you think he'll call with the best 80 percent of his hands and fold the worst 20 percent. (Thus, you'll usually have him beaten when he calls.)

Checking will net you the $100 pot seventy percent of the time, for an expected win of $70. Betting $150 will win you $100 ninety percent of the time, but lose $150 ten percent. Thus, the expected win for bluffing is $75, a $5 improvement over checking.

$$\$75 = (0.90)(\$100) + (0.10)(-\$150)$$

If you bet $50, then you'll win $100 twenty percent of the time, win $150 fifty percent of the time, and lose $50 thirty percent. The expected win for value betting is $80, a $5 improvement over bluffing.

$$\$80 = (0.20)(\$100) + (0.50)(\$150) - (0.30)(-\$50)$$

Bluffing (with a big bet) is better than checking, but value betting (with a small bet) is better yet.

Hands that work out this way will be somewhat rare. An example might be if you flop top two pair against a preflop raiser and call sizable bets on the flop and turn. The river completes a draw, perhaps an obvious straight draw, and your opponent checks. If you make a big bet, your opponent may fold everything except the straight. If you make a small bet, though, your opponent may look you up with most hands.

Another Angle

Bluffing occasionally on the end with "checking" hands will give you a small extra edge against thinking opponents. Opponents who are adept at hand reading will know that a river bet tends to be for value or as a bluff. They will expect you to check your medium hands. So, as soon as you bet, those opponents will discount the possibility that you hold what you do. Depending on how the hand has played thus far, this may lead them to the conclusion that you "must" either have a monster or have planned an elaborate bluff.

Monsters don't come often, but if you play well, neither do elaborate bluffs. If your opponents don't know that you'll occasionally bluff with a fairly good hand, they may overweight the chance you have a monster and make some very big laydowns.

For instance, say you have

on a

flop and bet approximately the pot on both the flop and turn (the turn is a blank). You should consider yourself a significant dog against most opponents once they call on the turn. If your opponent checks the river and you check behind, you'll win sometimes, but usually you'll lose to ace-king or better.

If you *occasionally* make a big bluff on the river, some players will lay down ace-king or two pair figuring that you must either have flopped a set or (rarely) have been on more or less a total bluff from the start. While they may consider king-queen part of your range of hands on the flop and turn, they'll rule it out once they see the big river bet.

Final Thoughts

Bluffing with a fairly good hand is situational. Usually you should check behind with your "good" hands. But don't do it automatically. Against weak-tight players prone to making ridiculous folds or thinking players unlikely to have a hand that beats your "obvious" monster, sometimes you should bluff.

On the other hand, against calling stations or on boards where your opponents might particularly suspect a bluff, you should often value bet "good" hands you would normally check. Before you act, pause and consider all three options. Sometimes you'll unearth a play that might surprise you.

Playing Strong Draws on the Flop

When you have a strong draw on the flop, and an opponent bets, often you must decide whether to move in or just to call.[26] There's no simple rule; the decision is largely a mathematical one dependant on a few factors. In this section we'll detail the process for making the decision.

You're on the button with

The preflop pot is $200, and you and your opponent each have $1,000 left. The flop is

---

[26] If the stacks are extremely deep, then you might also consider making a big raise that doesn't put you all-in. The downside to that play is that you might get into a tough situation if your opponent reraises you. The upside is that, by leaving some money behind, you're more likely to get your opponent to fold. Also, if you have position, you tend to have an advantage for the remaining money if your opponent flat calls.

giving you a flush draw and a gutshot straight draw (twelve outs). Your opponent bets $200. Should you move in or just call? To simplify the problem, we'll set the following parameters:

- The chance that your opponent will call if you move in is A.

- The chance that he will check the turn if you call is B.

- If you call, and he doesn't check the turn, he'll move in (bet $800).

- If you make your hand, he'll call $800.

With twelve outs twice, you'll make your hand about 45 percent of the time by the river. You won't necessarily win that often, however, because your opponent could be drawing to a bigger flush or fill up. So let's say you'll win about 40 percent of the time if you get all-in on the flop.

Your expectation if you move in and get called is -$120.

$$- \$120 = (0.40)(\$1{,}200) + (0.60)(- \$1{,}000)$$

Your expectation if you move in and your opponent folds is $400 (you win the $200 pot and his $200 bet).

Thus, the total expectation of moving in is given by

$$EV_{allin} = (A)(- \$120) + (1 - A)(\$400)$$

So, for example, if he will call your move in 60 percent of the time, your EV is $88.

$$\$88 = (0.60)(- \$120) + (1 - 0.60)(\$400)$$

If you just call, then you'll make your hand on the turn (and win a showdown) about 22.5 percent of the time.[27] Since your opponent will call $800 if you make your hand, your expectation in that case is $1,200.

The 77.5 percent of the time you miss, your opponent will either check (with probability B) or bet $800 (with probability 1 - B). If he bets $800, you'll have to fold, as you would be getting only 3-to-2, and you are a bigger dog than that to make your hand on the river.

So if you miss, and your opponent bets, your expectation is -$200. If you miss, and your opponent checks, then you have another 22.5 percent chance to make your hand.

Thus, the expectation of calling looks like:

$$EV_{call} = (0.225)(\$1,200) +$$
$$(0.775)\left\{(B)(-\$200) + (1-B)\left[\begin{array}{l}(0.225)(\$1,200) + \\ (0.775)(-\$200)\end{array}\right]\right\}$$
$$= \$270 + (0.775)\left[(B)(-\$200) + (1-B)(\$70)\right]$$
$$= \$324 + (B)(-\$210)$$

Here are the two expectations (in terms of the probabilities A and B):

$$EV_{allin} = \$400 + (A)(-\$520)$$
$$EV_{call} = \$324 + (B)(-\$210)$$

---

[27] This number follows from our 40 percent estimate above.

Moving in is better than calling when $EV_{allin} > EV_{call}$:

$$\$400 + (A)(-\$520) > \$324 + (B)(-\$210)$$
$$A < 0.15 + 0.40B$$

Plugging in some numbers, if your opponent will call your move in about 30 percent of the time (A = 0.30), and will bet the turn if you call 60 percent of the time (B = 0.60), then

$$0.30 < 0.15 + (0.40)(0.60)$$
$$0.30 < 0.15 + 0.24$$
$$0.30 < 0.39$$

which is a true statement, so moving in would be better. The numbers we chose will be representative of many situations, so clearly moving in is often the best play.

It won't always be the best play, though. If you're against a timid player who rarely follows up with turn bets, you might be better off not moving in and trying to see both the turn and river cards for $200. For instance, if your opponent will call your move in about 30 percent of the time, but will bet the turn if you call only 20 percent of the time then

$$0.30 < 0.15 + (0.40)(0.20)$$
$$0.30 < 0.15 + 0.08$$
$$0.30 < 0.23$$

which is false, so calling would be better.

We simplified the problem in a couple of ways, not the least of which is that we assumed that if you call and make your hand, you'll always get paid off for $800. Obviously, this won't happen in real life, and our model overvalues calling accordingly. We also made some approximations throughout the algebra to keep it somewhat easy to follow.

Final Thoughts

As is often the case with our calculations, we don't expect you to play poker by solving equations like this. The point is that if you are familiar with the process to solve the problem, you will know which factors to consider at the table. As we can see, the pertinent factors are how often your move-in will get called, how likely your opponent is to bet the turn if you just call, and how big the stacks are compared to the pot size.

In this case, having your move-in called is (obviously) bad because you are the underdog when called. Getting bet into on the turn is very bad, because it prevents you from seeing the river card. And having a very deep stack will tend to make just calling better.

In a nutshell, moving in is better

- The more outs you have

- The more likely he is to fold

- The more likely he is to make a big bet on the turn if you just call

- The less likely he is to call if the card that makes your hand comes

- When your stacks are not exorbitantly large

Meanwhile remember that in order for these all-in bets with draws to work well, you must sometimes make the same play with big hands when the flop contains a possible draw.

Multiple Level Thinking

Multiple level thinking is largely what separates professionals from amateurs, what separates players who win at the top levels from those who lose. The notion itself is simple enough, but its implications are far-reaching. In deep stack no limit, your success will directly reflect your mastery of this concept.

Multiple level thinking is a fundamental hand-reading technique. Simply put, it's the ability to analyze a series of actions on different levels and to use that analysis to formulate likely ranges of hands for your opponents. What are the different levels?

The first level (we'll actually call it the "zeroth" level to reflect its triviality) is to know what you have, and to know what hands you can beat and what hands beat yours. If you have

on a

board, you have a straight made with your ten. You beat any of the myriad two pair and trips hands, you tie with another stiff ten, and you lose to king-ten, two spades, a full house, quads, or a straight flush.

That's the zeroth level. Almost everyone masters that level.

The next level, the "first" level, is to think about what your opponent has. He made a big bet, so he probably has a good hand. Or his betting pattern was typical of a weak hand or a bluff. These are all first level assessments because they draw conclusions about your opponent's holding without regard for what he's thinking, just by looking at his actions "in a vacuum."

The second level is to think about what your opponent likely thinks you have. Your opponents are thinking people (probably), and they will do some analyses of their own. They will try to put you on a range of hands, and they will choose their moves based on what they think you have.

Thus, it behooves you to consider, based on your actions, what your opponents might think you have. If you raised preflop, your opponents are more likely to think you have ace-king than ten-seven. (Obviously, if you actually have ace-king, this is bad. If you actually have ten-seven, it's good.)[28] If you bet the flop, but checked behind on the turn, your opponents are likely to think you have a weak or marginal hand.

The third level is to think about what your opponent thinks you think he has. That's a bit of a mouthful, but the idea is simple: Thinking opponents will think on the second level. That is, they'll think about how you'll interpret their actions. The third level is to think about how they might assume that you'll interpret their actions.

The fourth level would be to think about what your opponent might think that you think he might think you have. Each successive level is to think about what your opponent might be thinking on the previous level.

If this is the first time you've been exposed to multiple level thinking, at least with regard to poker, you might think this is mumbo jumbo. Who cares what he thinks I think he thinks I think he has? Well, when put that way, it can sound a little silly, but again, this sort of thinking is second-nature to top-notch players.

---

[28] It's good if your opponent thinks you have ace-king and you have ten-seven in one sense. But it's still bad that your cards are weak.

Now that you have a feel for the basic idea, we'll show you, generally speaking, how and when to think on each level.

When Shallow Thinking is Best

Shallow thinking is thinking on the zeroth or first levels: thinking only about what you have and thinking about what your opponents have. Shallow thinking is best when the decisions are simple; simple decisions come when there is little money behind. When the stacks are small compared to the blinds (or the size of the pot later in the hand) decisions can become automatic. For instance, if you are in a no limit tournament with a stack five times the size of the blinds and antes and the prizes far off, in many cases the only information you'll need is a look at your hand. If your hand is better than X, you'll move all-in. If it's worse, you'll fold.

Even if the prizes are upon you, you still often won't have to think past the zeroth level. It's a simpler decision if you don't have to think about prizes, but even with prizes to complicate things, it's a decision you can make without thinking about how your opponents play and think.

Another example of a zeroth-level decision is if you hold the nuts and your lone opponent has moved all-in. You're calling without regard to anything other than what's in your hand. Contrast this to holding the nuts, but having to be the bettor rather than the caller. In that case, especially if the stacks are deep, you might have quite a bit to think about.

Many other decisions are first-level decisions. Say you have a stack twelve times the big blind. Someone opens in front of you, and you're on the button with A♥Q♣ or 8♦8♠. Now you can't just look at your hand to make the decision; the right play depends on what your opponent might have.

But it ends there. If your opponent is a loose raiser and could have a wide range of holdings, you move in. If she's tight, then you fold. That's all the depth you need to explore.

When You
Need to Think More Deeply

Deep stacks require deeper thinking. So do better (and deeper- thinking) opponents. As a quick aside, you can think only one level deeper than your opponent, as, for instance, the third level means thinking about how your opponent may be reasoning on the second level. If your opponent doesn't think on the second level, then your third level won't be applicable.

For instance, if your opponent thinks only about what he has (that is, only on the zeroth level) then you can think on the first level, "What does he have?" But you can't think on the second level, "What does he think I have?" because he doesn't think you have anything. He's not on the first level, so your second level becomes meaningless.

Let's go back to an example of deeper thinking. Say you are playing $5-$10 against a decent, but not excellent, player. He'll think about what his opponents have, but not go deeper than that very often; he's a first level thinker. You both have $2,000 (relatively deep) stacks.

You open one off the button for $40 with

Your opponent calls in the big blind (as he would with a number of hands). The flop comes giving you top pair.

He checks, you bet $80, and he calls. (Pot is $245.) The turn is the K♦. He checks, and you check. The river is the K♣. He thinks and bets $250, the size of the pot. This is a somewhat larger bet than you'd expect from him given his past play. What should you do?

Well, you have a marginal hand, to be sure: a pair of tens with a nine kicker. That's the zeroth level thought.

Your opponent called preflop. He'd do that with a lot of hands, perhaps, but not every one. He's more likely to call with suited or connected hands or pocket pairs than with something like T♦2♠. He checked and called a pot-sized bet on a T♠8♠5♣ flop. Calling a significant bet out of position probably means he caught a sizable chunk of the flop: perhaps a ten or a flush or straight draw or maybe something even better. A turn king came, and he checked again — not surprising given his flop action. You checked.

The river came another king, and he made a relatively big bet. With what hands would he likely make a big bet? Generally, big bets mean big hands: trip kings or a full house, maybe. With a hand like A♥T♦, he might bet, but it would probably be a modest blocking/value bet.[29] Big bets can also mean bluffs: since big bets are less likely to be called than small ones, some players make their bluffs a little on the big side compared to their "normal" bets. That's the first level.

If you stop there, you still don't really know what to do. He might have a big hand, or he might be bluffing. Since you are getting roughly 2-to-1, you have to win about 33 percent of the time to justify calling. You could try to determine the probability of each possibility just by counting the possible hands he might play this way and then determine what percentage you can beat. But that would be both time-consuming and prone to error (not just the calculation, but the assumptions you'd have to make along the way).

---

[29] See the section "Blocking Bets" starting on page 135.

So think a little on the second level. What might he think you have? You opened preflop from late position, something you probably do with a fair range of hands, but one tilted toward the big hands. That is, he'd expect to see pocket aces more often than nine-trey, even though you're dealt nine-trey more than twice as often as pocket aces.

You bet the T♠8♠5♣ flop when checked to. You might do this if you hit the flop, but you also might do this as a continuation bluff. He'd know that. When you check the K♦ on the turn, he will naturally assume you have a marginal or semi-weak hand. Perhaps you have a flush or straight draw, or maybe you have a pair smaller than kings. Or maybe you have ace-queen or another hand that missed entirely.

The river K♣ doesn't help any of those hands. So if you were weak on the turn, you're still probably weak. Given the action throughout the hand, it would be natural to assume that this first-level thinker would "put you on" a modest holding.

Given that knowledge, why would he make an extra large bet? He probably expects you to fold. If he has a big hand himself, surely he'd rather you call $100 than fold to $250. And if he has a decent, but not great, hand like A♥T♦, he'd probably either check or make a modest value bet, as a big bet would rarely get better hands to fold and also rarely get called by a weaker hand. (Remember, he's not stupid, just not a deep thinker.)

So the bigger than average bet here is likely to be a bluff. With big and mediocre hands alike, you'd expect a smallish bet because he probably puts you on a modest hand. The big bet is designed to blow you out. Perhaps he called the flop with Q♠7♠ or 9♣7♣ and now has no chance to win by checking. He's worried you have enough to call a $100 bet, so he makes it big enough to scare you out.

If your assumptions are right, if your opponent is a decent player and first level thinker, you have a clear call. You have second level thinking to thank for making that decision so clear.[30] If your assumptions are wrong, however, and your opponent actually thinks on the third level, then your second level thinking might be your downfall. If he thinks on the third level, then he might realize that you know he would put you on a modest hand due to your turn check. He would also know that sometimes you would check behind on the turn with a king or other hands you might call with on the river.

With a big hand, he might make an extra big bet, knowing that you would interpret it as a sign of weakness in this situation. That way he gets the best of both worlds: a better chance of being paid off and for a larger amount too. In deep stack no limit, the player who thinks on the deepest level and, therefore, has greater hand reading insight, often possesses an insurmountable edge.

Final Thoughts

The key to no limit isn't always thinking on the fourth or fifth level. Usually thinking that deeply is unnecessary and only likely to lead you to absurd conclusions about what's going on. When you are short stacked, as you often are in tournaments, usually the zeroth and first level will suffice: "What do I have, what does he have, am I getting the right odds?"

You can also easily overthink bad and mediocre players. In our example, second level thinking suggested a good call against your regular Joe (first level) opponent, but left you paying off the expert (third level). If you always insist on thinking on the fourth level to thwart the expert (since he must know that I would take his big bet as weakness since I checked behind on the turn), you'll

---

[30] Although as a general rule we do not advocate a strategy of being more likely to call a bigger bet on the river than a smaller one, this hand appears to be an exception.

get exploited by the amateur (I think he's weak, so maybe I'll try a bluff now).

Tailor your thinking to your situation and opponent. If you can reliably figure out how your opponents think and stay one step ahead of them, you'll make a lot of money.

Swapping Mistakes

Somewhere out there in math land, there's probably a perfect no limit hold 'em strategy. It's a strategy that never loses in the long run, no matter how your opponents play against you. If they call a lot, bet a lot, or fold a lot, the perfect strategy wins. If they are tricky or straightforward, the perfect strategy wins. In fact, the perfect strategy beats every opponent except another playing the perfect strategy.

What would this strategy look like? Well, it would exhibit many of the principles we've talked about in this book. It would be aware of implied odds, both the odds it gets and the odds it gives. It would call with draws only when it expected to make more on average than the price of the call. Likewise, with good hands it would bet enough (or refuse to pay off enough) to deny its opponents with draws a profitable call.

It would mix up its play to balance perfectly. Every check, call, bet, and raise would be made with a mix of hands sufficiently diversified to avoid divulging useful information about the nature of any specific holding.

We said that this strategy exists in math land, and, at least for now, that's the only place it exists. No limit hold 'em is complex enough that, while we can posit that such a strategy likely exists, and we can figure out what it would be in many individual cases, deriving a general solution covering every possible scenario is virtually impossible.

We can't know exactly what the strategy is, but perhaps we, as students of poker, should strive to play as closely to that strategy as we can get. If perfection is unattainable, surely near perfection must be the next best thing.

For many non-poker games, that reasoning holds true. In tic-tac-toe, the perfect strategy is fairly obvious, and if you play it, you will never lose. On the other hand, if you refuse to play the perfect strategy, you'll find yourself losing game after game to a player who does play it. Perfection is attainable, and it's virtually always the best way to go.

Chess is far more complex than tic-tac-toe, but the same reasoning likely holds. While no one currently plays perfect chess, it's likely that one *could* play perfect chess. And if you did, you'd never lose.[31]

But poker is a strange bird. If, somehow, you were blessed tomorrow with the knowledge of the perfect strategy (and stripped of all other poker knowledge), then you'd do quite well. Playing your perfect strategy, you'd be guaranteed not to be a long-term loser, and, in today's games with plenty of bad players, you'd likely win a mint.

But you wouldn't be the best player. At least you wouldn't be if you defined "best player" as the one with the highest average win rate in three- or more-handed games. You'd be a big winner, in the top few percent of all players, but a number of other players would win even more.

How can that be? How can someone play better than perfect? The trick is that we've defined the "perfect" strategy to be unbeatable. It's designed so no one can get the best of you. It is, fundamentally, a defensive strategy.

The biggest winners don't play the perfect defense. They go on the attack, even if it means exposing a few vulnerabilities along the way. They know that it's critical to understand the principles behind that unexploitable strategy, and that sometimes they'll need to fall back on it (or something close to it) when their opponents launch a counterattack. But they'll make the most money taking calculated risks to attack and exploit their opponents' errors.

---

[31] Well, you probably would never lose. In chess, the player with the white pieces moves first, and that privilege confers an unbalanced advantage throughout the game. So it's possible that if two "perfect" players played against each other, white would win every time. But more likely, as in tic-tac-toe, they'd draw game after game.

> **The key to no limit hold 'em success isn't to play perfectly. It's to swap mistakes with your opponents. You trade small mistakes to your opponents if they will trade back big ones.**

What does swapping mistakes mean? Say you find yourself heads-up against a particularly pleasant opponent. His "strategy," if you can call it that, is to call every bet. It doesn't matter what he holds or how much you bet. If you bet, he'll call. He'll also never run out of money (and neither will you); if you bust him, he's always got another buy-in ready.

Obviously, anyone could beat this player. But to win the maximum from him, you have to adjust your play to take advantage of his peculiar calling habit.

First, you'd purge bluffing from your strategy entirely. You shouldn't bluff if you're guaranteed to be called. You'd bet all your good hands on the river, never checking them as you occasionally would out of position against a better player. You'd even bet lots of weak hands you wouldn't dream of betting against a normal player.

Somewhat less obviously, you'd check every hand up to the river. Since you're guaranteed a call, you gain no advantage from betting before all the cards are out (though with some very good hands, you could bet earlier and not give up anything because no card could come that would cause you not to bet).[32]

This strange "wait until the river and bet it all" strategy is the right way to play against this opponent; it's the way that generates the maximum profit per hand. It significantly outperforms the "perfect" strategy.

---

[32] Note that you gain nothing from betting early only because it's no limit and because your opponent promises to call every bet. If the game were limit or pot limit, where you couldn't necessarily bet everything on one round, the strategy would be different.

However, it doesn't resemble the perfect strategy at all. If you played that way against typical opponents, you'd get slaughtered. It's tailored to beat this specific opponent and no other.

Your opponent makes huge mistakes; he calls all bets no matter how bad his hand is. If you want to beat him for the maximum, you must be willing to make some "mistakes" of your own: never bluffing, checking good hands on the flop and turn, giving free cards, overbetting marginal hands, etc. You trade your mistakes for your opponent's mistakes, and since his mistakes are bigger than yours, you profit from the trade. If you refused to make mistakes, you'd have none to trade, and you wouldn't make the most of your opponent's willingness to make huge mistakes.[33]

You Can't Win Them All

In this heads-up game, the "swapping mistakes" theory doesn't quite ring true. After all, is a mistake really a mistake if no one exploits it? The mistakes you trade to your opponent are worthless to him because he doesn't do what it takes to profit from them. You capitalize on his mistakes, but he ignores yours.

That's fair enough. But if we extend our discussion to a three-handed game, you'll see that you really are swapping mistakes. Say you're playing in a game with the same "call every bet" opponent and another, savvier one. Your savvy opponent plays like a normal person. When you bet, she'll call only if she thinks she's a favorite. And she'll bet when she thinks it's the right play.

The thing is, she's underbankrolled. While you and the calling station play with $10,000 stacks, she plays with only $100 at a time. With the addition of a tough spot to your game, should you revert to a perfect strategy?

---

[33] This is one time that we use the word "mistake" in a different way than the Fundamental Theorem of Poker way.

No, you shouldn't. You should play almost exactly as you played before; you check every hand to the river and then move in with hands favored over a random holding. The key is that the savvy player has only $100. Your crazy strategy is full of mistakes, and she's going to exploit them for profit. When she actually bets her $100, both you and the other player will, on average, be big underdogs to her. She'll make money from both of you. But she's chipping away at you only $100 at a time, while you're pummeling the other guy for $10,000. You're making mistakes, and someone is now exploiting them, but that doesn't matter. You're trading small, $100-sized mistakes for big, $10,000-sized mistakes.[34] You're much better off doing that than making no mistakes and letting your calling station opponent keep his $10,000 too often.

In practice, your opponents won't be as dense as the "call them all" player described above. Even bad players who frequently make big mistakes will catch on sometimes if they are getting destroyed. If someone keeps calling and losing, after a while he'll start folding a few hands. And if someone folds hand after hand to your bluffs, eventually he'll decide to call.

So you will, in practice, always be swapping mistakes with your opponents. They make mistakes, and you attack them, making theoretical mistakes of your own. Sometimes your opponents will hit the spot you left open. That's fine, as long as you're trading a little for a lot.

Be Vigilant

Making mistakes intentionally to exploit your opponents is the right thing to do. All the best players do it. But such a strategy requires vigilance. You are leaving yourself open to attack, and

---

[34] The mistakes don't actually cost you the full $100 since even bad plays often win.

sooner or later, some shrewd player will come along and start probing your weakness.

Say you play against people who routinely enter too many raised pots out of position. Position is such an important advantage that no one can win consistently playing a great majority of their hands from out of position. Being too willing to play out of position is a big mistake. What mistake should you make to swap for it?

When these players limp in, you should play more loosely and aggressively from late position than the perfect strategy would suggest you should. They like to play raised pots out of position; play with them. When they limp in, raise modest hands such as

By maximizing the number of pots you play in position, you can overcome the slight weakness of your starting hands and make more money. Loosening up is the right adjustment to make, but be aware that it is, in comparison to the perfect strategy, a mistake. Someone who sees what you are doing and has a mind to exploit it can do so. Specifically, they can reraise you with weaker hands than they normally might, knowing that you are less likely to have a hand strong enough to call. (That reraising adjustment, of course, is a "mistake" itself, also exploitable by someone so inclined.)

The point is, always be aware of basic no limit concepts. No matter who you are playing, the fundamentals remain the same. For every play, try to think of what the perfect strategy might be. Then adjust that strategy to capitalize on your opponents' weaknesses. Be aware of how your strategy deviates from an unexploitable one, and watch out for opponents who might be trying to exploit your mistakes.

Poker history is full of hot shot maestros who quickly racked up big wins by making just the right mistakes to exploit their regular opponents. Unfortunately, their egos usually didn't allow them to recognize their deviations from perfect play as theoretical mistakes; in their minds, they were natural talents playing an unbeatable game.

Then, the sober, seasoned players moved in, systematically targeting the maestros and their mistakes. Since the maestros were oblivious to their own mistakes, they lost. And they kept losing, wondering louder with each bad session how they could possibly run so badly against these "unimaginative" players. Their big wins disappeared, and, broke, they slumped out of the poker world none the wiser.

Don't be a sucker. There's a perfect, unbeatable strategy, and it's determined by math, not by talent. Great players don't stick to that strategy; they intentionally deviate from it to take advantage of their opponents. But truly great players also know full well what weaknesses those deviations expose, and if they see someone going after them, they shut down quickly. They're willing to make mistakes, but only when they can swap those mistakes to their opponents for bigger ones. When their mistakes become the big ones, they stop making them.

Learn the fundamental principles of no limit and stay perpetually aware that your goal is to trade small mistakes for big ones.

Adjusting to
Loose Games and Players

Some of your most profitable no limit opponents are the loose players. Loose players play too many hands and go too far with them. Sometimes they don't raise much, but call too often (loose and passive), and sometimes they raise and call too often (loose and aggressive), but their main characteristic is that they put way too much money in the pot with hands that are too weak.

Before we discuss how to beat these players (and it isn't very hard), we want to distinguish truly loose and aggressive players from dangerous seemingly loose and aggressive players.

Some very good players will play a style that, to a lightly trained observer, might appear loose and aggressive. They play lots of hands preflop, and they bet and raise liberally. The difference is that they play recklessly only for the small preflop and flop betting. Once the betting gets big on the turn and river, they play a very tough game, and with superior hand reading and manipulation skills, they trick *others* into playing too loosely against them.

Truly loose and aggressive players aren't so cunning. They simply play too many hands and bet and raise too often with them, both early in the hand and for the big money.

Here's an example of the difference. With $1,000 stacks in a $5-$10 blind game, you open for $40 with from middle position. Everyone folds to the big blind, a truly loose and aggressive player, who calls. The big blind has

The flop comes

giving you a full house and your opponent a flush draw. He checks, you bet $60, and he raises $240 more to $300. You know your opponent is reckless, so you simply move all-in now, $660 more. He calls in an instant.

You roll over your full house, and he realizes he's drawing dead to a runner-runner royal flush. Your opponent's flop play was atrocious, but truly loose and aggressive players periodically make enormous mistakes like this one.

A dangerous loose and aggressive player would never play a hand like that. Instead, they play hands like this one:

With $1,000 stacks in a $5-$10 blind game, you open for $40 with K♥J♥ from middle position. The dangerous player calls on the button, and the blinds fold. You don't know what he has, but he's loose preflop, so he could have a wide range of hands.

The flop comes J♣9♣6♠. You bet $60, and he calls. Again, he's loose for small bets, so he could have a number of hands. And he's tricky, so he might have a draw, he might be slowplaying a strong hand, or he might be calling with very little intending to bluff the turn. (The pot is $205, and you each have $900 left.)

The turn is the 8♠, completing possible straights and putting another possible flush draw on board. You bet $150, and he makes it $300 more or $450 total. Your dangerous opponent has maneuvered you into a tough situation. Sure, he's loose, but when the big money starts going in, he makes sure he has the upper hand.

Until you have experience telling these two player types apart, be extra careful before you start licking your chops over a potential live one. Watch closely and make sure the "mistakes" your opponent is making are for big bets, not small ones.

> **Don't play your loose opponents for live ones until you see them make at least one major error for a large bet.**

If you are somewhat inexperienced, you might want to wait for two major mistakes before you adjust your play, as you might not have analyzed the first mistake carefully enough.

Why so much caution? You must be cautious when making the adjustments we are about to suggest in this chapter because, while they win the most from loose players, they leave you quite vulnerable to tough players. If you accidentally mistake a tough player for a live one, you may end up getting fleeced.

The Adjustments

There are four simple adjustments to make against loose players, both passive and aggressive ones:

1. **Loosen up.** Play looser preflop when the loose opponent has entered already, especially when you have position and the stacks are deep.

2. **Big preflop pots for big pairs.** Seek big preflop pots with big pocket pairs like pocket kings, but avoid them with big unpaired cards like ace-king.

3. **Value bet top pair.** Value bet top pair and overpair hands far more aggressively than you normally would.

4. **Bluff less often.** Don't bluff as often against opponents who call a lot. When you do bluff, do it most often on the flop with strong draws, so if you get called you aren't taking much the worst of it.

Loosen Up

If a loose player has entered the pot in front of you, then you should seek to play sort of like the dangerous player described earlier (although for a different reason). You too should play a lot of pots *while the bets are still small,* hoping to catch the advantage later in the hand and win big on the turn and river.

For instance, say you are playing with at least relatively deep stacks (more than 100 times the big blind), and a loose player (passive or aggressive) limps in from early position. If everyone folds to you on or near the button, you can play a wide array of hands, including holdings as weak as: 2♣2♥, 9♣8♠, T♠7♠, A♣5♥.

The better you play after the flop, the wider the range of hands you can play. Raise your better hands for value as well as sometimes the weak ones to balance. If the blinds are somewhat tough, raise a little more often to isolate the bad player.

For example, say you are playing $1-$2 with $300 stacks, and a loose and passive player limps in. Everyone folds to you one off the button with the

You should definitely play, and sometimes you should raise to about $8 or $10, particularly when the blinds play fairly well and are likely to fold.

Your goal is to see the flop relatively cheaply (though not necessarily as cheaply as possible) and hope a profitable scenario arises after the flop.

If the loose player raises preflop, particularly if the player is loose and aggressive (raising with a wide range of hands), you can call on the button with a similarly wide range of hands, though you should fold some of the weakest hands you would play against a limper.

For example, you are playing $1-$2 with $300 stacks, and a loose and aggressive player makes it $10 to go. If you are on the button, you should consider calling with hands like Q♥T♥, K♠8♠, A♦J♣, and 5♦3♦.

Big Preflop Pots for Big Pairs

When you have a big pair before the flop, usually you should be happy to get all-in preflop against a weaker hand. If you have

and your opponent will call an all-in bet with hands like 8♦8♣, A♣T♣, or J♠T♠, you should virtually always try to get the money in as soon as possible.[35]

---

[35] We say "virtually always" because it's theoretically possible that you'd be better off waiting to see the flop (or even turn or river) before you get the money in. It's really only theoretically possible, though; in practice, if you can get all-in preflop against a likely weaker hand, do so.

With deep stacks against a tough player, however, you shouldn't just move in with pocket queens. Why? Tough players usually won't call you without at least pocket kings.

For instance, you are playing $5-$10 with $3,000 stacks. A tough opponent opens for $30, and you reraise to $100. He reraises to $300. You would be daft to move in for $2,700 more. You'll get called only by pocket aces (or maybe kings), and your opponent will have one of those hands quite often after putting in the third raise.

Against a loose and aggressive player, however, moving in might be right. It would definitely be right if the stacks were shorter, and your move-in was the third raise. For instance, you are playing $5-$10 with $600 stacks. You open for $40 with pocket queens, and the loose-aggressive player makes it $150 to go. Move in.

The same advice applies if you have pocket aces, but for a slightly different reason. Obviously, you aren't worried about getting called by a better hand, but you are worried about not getting action. If you make big all-in raises against tough players, you give them easy laydowns (possibly even if they have pocket kings). To make the most out of the hand, you often must play somewhat deceptively by calling preflop and taking your chances after the flop.

Against loose and aggressive players, though, you can frequently move in preflop with pocket aces, as loose players tend to call big raises with hands that are too weak.

If you have ace-king, however, you don't necessarily want to get all-in against a loose player before the flop. This is especially true when you are in position. You may be better off just calling preflop and seeing if you flop a pair. If you don't flop a pair, you can save some money. If you do, you can hope your opponent flopped a weaker pair or a marginal draw and bet your top pair for value. This leads us to the next adjustment.

Value Bet Top Pair

Against tough players, you typically can't win a whole lot by value betting with top pair. Say you flop top pair, bet the size of the pot on the flop, and get called. On the turn you don't improve, you bet two-thirds the size of the pot, and you get called. On the river you don't improve, you bet half the pot, and you get called again. Against tough players, you'll usually lose in this scenario. If they didn't outflop you, they likely outdrew you either on the turn or river. Unless you've shown some reckless play lately, tough players usually won't call three significant bets without being able to beat top pair.

Loose players will. Obviously, it depends on exactly how loosely your loose opponent plays, but top pair with a good kicker can be a big moneymaker against some players. Your loose opponents might call you down with top pair and a weaker kicker, or they might flop a draw and miss, but catch a weaker pair and pay you off.

In situations where you might check top pair against a tough player, you should consider betting it for value against a loose player.

Bluff Less Often

In light of the last three adjustments, hopefully this one is obvious. Loose players call too often. While that tendency makes value betting more profitable, it tends to negate bluffing.

Note that we don't say "never bluff." If you never bluff, you'll be easy to read (even by loose players), and you'll miss out on some profitable opportunities. Loose players call too often, but they don't call with *everything*. You can keep making many of your "routine" bluffs; just make them somewhat less frequently and generally avoid big or daring bluffs.

Final Thoughts

Much of the cautious advice in this book is intended for play against tough players. If we recommend that you check a good hand or play passively against a calling opponent, usually we're advocating a defensive play to prevent a tough player from getting the best of you.

Loose players, both passive and aggressive ones, are entirely different animals. They are your ideal opponents, the ones you make your money from, and you should attack them. Don't play overly defensively against them. Isolate them with raises before the flop. Play lots of hands (in position) against them. Try to get them all-in before the flop if you think you have the better hand. If they will call you down with weak hands, value bet ferociously. Don't sit around waiting to flop a set to try to get their money; bet weaker hands for value.

But be careful. Some wolves put their "loose player" sheep's clothing on when they play. Make sure your opponent isn't playing loosely only for small bets. Wait until you see them make a big mistake or two before you adjust fully to take advantage of them.

Finally, if you have a really loose and bad player at your table, they should usually become your top priority. Move to the seat on their left (unless they are habitual preflop raisers). Buy enough chips to have them covered. Play many pots against them. Isolate them. It's often only a matter of time before loose players go broke. Maximize the chance that they go broke to you.

Adjusting to Weak Tight Games

Note: The players described in this section can be found in small stakes games in Las Vegas cardrooms. Obviously, they may also play in many other places, but they are quite common in Las Vegas. Ed wrote this section because he's most familiar with these games.

A deep stack weak-tight no limit game may be the second-most profitable style of poker game regularly available.[36] But it's only ultra-profitable if you make the right adjustments. If you just play your "normal" no limit game, you'll largely miss out on the bonanza.

Defining the Game

What makes a no limit game weak-tight? Well, it's populated principally by players who fold too frequently, particularly to big bets on the turn and river. Whenever the big bets come out, they always seem to fear you have the nuts, and their excellent hands don't seem quite good enough.

While the ability to make "big laydowns" is critical to deep stack no limit success, weak-tight players tend to make absurd laydowns just because a lot of money will be at risk. They'll keep folding even when it's entirely clear to them and everyone else that they aren't always against the nuts.

They tend to misevaluate pot odds-based decisions with a bias toward folding. For instance, say they have

---

[36] Second only to loose-passive.

on a

flop, giving them a twelve out monster draw against most hands. The pot is $200, and they bet $50 (weak-tight players tend to underbet significantly any time they are worried about their hand). Someone raises them $200 more (for a total of $250). A weak-tight player might fold, not wanting to risk $200 on "just a draw." The pot contains $500, though, and they'd have to call only $200, so they'd be getting 5-to-2 on a call. But they won't take it.

Weak-tight players generally don't think about overlays and odds. (And when they do think about them, their thought process is generally excruciatingly pessimistic toward their chances.) They think in absolute dollar figures. In a $2-$5 game, a $20 bet is ok to call with a draw. A $200 bet isn't. They won't look at what they stand to win if they call, or how often they will win. They'll just decide they don't have a $200 hand and wait 'til next time.

As we mentioned earlier, weak-tight players tend to underbet whenever they are worried about their hands. For instance, they might bet $20 or $30 with top pair in a $100 pot. If someone calls, they might bet the same amount, $20 or $30, on the turn. Or they might get spooked and check.

Some weak-tight players also *overbet* their big hands. For instance, if they flop the nut straight, they might automatically make a huge bet or raise immediately to make people "pay to draw out."

Overall, this strategy is incredibly unbalanced. They wear their fear on their sleeves: small bets mean moderate hands and worry about being behind, and huge bets mean very strong hands and worry about being outdrawn. Needless to say, this strategy is heavily exploitable, but we'll save that for later.

Weak-tight players may bluff, but they'll usually do it only with small sums. In a $5-$10 game, they might make a $50 flop bet as a bluff. Or they might even make a $150 flop raise. But they won't ever try the big $800 river bluff. And if they do bluff, it's usually a single shot affair. Expect them to cry uncle usually after getting only a single call.

You may also hear weak-tight players complain about the big bets and raises other players make. They'll say stuff like, "Can you believe it, $300 on just a pair of queens?" or "Boy, I can't wait until they actually deal me a hand; I'll gut these guys."

So, the weak-tight player exhibits the following general characteristics:

- Folds too often, particularly to big turn and river bets

- Bets too little with mediocre hands

- Bets too much early in the hand with excellent hands

- Bets too little on bluffs, and doesn't follow up with a "second barrel" often enough

- May complain about never getting a hand or always being blown out by "garbage"

A player can obviously be generally weak-tight without exhibiting each of these characteristics perfectly. Just because you see a player bet too much with excellent hands, don't, for instance, assume necessarily that he won't try a multi-street bluff. Each player is different, and these are just general characteristics that tend to coexist in some players.

Also, the whole game needn't be composed of weak-tight players to be great; one weak-tight player with deep pockets and a proclivity for calling raises preflop can be all that's needed to make a game terrific.

In any event, players that fit the weak-tight model are somewhat common. They tend to be particularly common in live (as opposed to online) games, and particularly at small stakes. For example, in many $2-$5 games in Las Vegas it's not unusual for almost all the players to be weak-tight to some degree or another.

The Adjustments

These guys make two broad mistakes: they tip the quality of their hands too early, and they allow themselves to get blown out of big pots too frequently. The adjustments to beat them exploit these errors.

The general idea is to build fairly big pots early, then take them away with big bets on later streets. By betting big with strong hands and small with weak ones, they'll essentially tell you when it's safe to bring out the big guns. Obviously, if they bet big, they get the pot. Otherwise, you put in the big raise and watch them fold.

Specifically, when a weak-tight player or two has limped in, play extremely loosely on the button (and somewhat loosely one off the button). Against some really terrible players, 100 percent of hands might be profitable. If your opponents have some clue, you might want to avoid the very worst trash — stuff like T♥5♣, for instance.

But many hands that you might be used to tossing automatically like J♣4♣, 9♣7♠, or A♥5♦ can be profitable. Why?

Simply put, weak-tight players don't see the showdown very often. You don't need a good hand if they fold. If your control over them is less than totally complete, then you might want a little hand value to fall back on if things go awry. But you won't need much.

So the first adjustment is to play most of your hands when you are in late position. The second is to raise with a lot of those extra late position hands. For example, say you are playing $1-$2 with $200 stacks. A weak-tight player limps in middle position. You have 9♥7♥ on the button. You might want to raise to about $10. This is particularly true if the players in the blinds are either unlikely to call or are weak-tight themselves.

Weak-tight players fold too often. Folding the best hand in a small pot is no big deal. Folding the best hand in a big pot is a big deal. According to Fundamental Theorem of Poker, you want to create situations where your opponents make the biggest errors possible. Bad folds are big mistakes in big pots. So build a big pot.

You want to raise the biggest amount you can that they are likely to call and that won't tie them to the pot. That is, you want them to call the preflop raise, but you still want them to fold bottom and middle pair to a pot-sized bet on the flop. And you want them to fold top pair and most draws to a follow-up pot-sized bet on the turn. Don't raise so much preflop (compared to your stack sizes) that it will make them feel "pot committed."

If you follow this advice, you'll play lots of raised, heads-up and three-handed pots in position. That's a terrific start. Typically your opponents will check the flop. Usually you should make a continuation bet about three-quarters the size of the pot. The bet should be reasonably big for two reasons:

1. Weak-tight players evaluate hands by first thinking about what they could lose. While they tend to fold too often to all bets, they fold especially too often to big bets. That is, they tend to make bigger mistakes against bigger bets.

2. A bigger bet will give you a lot of information. A weak-tight player might call $20 with any flopped pair or reasonable draw, but $40 only with top pair or better or a strong draw. Weak-tight players tend to give away too much information about their hands on the flop. A generously-sized continuation bet entices them to do just that.

Weak-tight players will often fold immediately. When they call, you must rely on hand-reading to decide whether to follow up with a bluff on fourth street. Pay attention to your specific opponents, and judge both their likely hand ranges and how they'll react with those hands to bets of various sizes.

But don't necessarily take a flop call as a sign to give up. Remember, your opponent will fold too often to big turn bets, and the pot will be fairly large. Here's a hand I played against a weak-tight player to show how perseverance can pay off.

I was playing $5-$10 with a $1,200 stack. My opponents had me covered. One player limped to me in the small blind, and my hand was

I raised to $40. A weak-tight player in the big blind called, and the limper folded. (The pot is $90.)

The flop came

I bet $100, and my opponent thought for a while before calling. I thought he likely had a queen, but he also possibly had a five, a flush draw, or a medium-sized pocket pair like nines. (The pot is $290, and we each have $1,060 left.)

The turn was the 2♣. If I bet about $300 (leaving $760 for a river bluff), I figured he'd fold the pocket pairs and flush draws. I also figured he'd fold any queen except ace-queen and possibly king-queen. With a five or a full house, I expected him to raise.

(This isn't to say that he *should* play this way, just that I thought he would.)

So I bet $300. He thought for about a minute and then called. I put him on exactly ace-queen or king-queen. (The pot is $890, and we each have $760 left). The river was the 7♥, so the flush came in.

I bluffed my remaining $760. Despite getting better than 2-to-1 on a call, I thought he was almost certain to fold. The bet was far bigger than any he had been faced with thus far. I figured he was almost certain to have just two pair, probably queens up, and didn't figure that he'd call with it.

He groaned when I moved in and thought for about another minute. Then he turned his hand face-up —

— and folded.

So the specific read was off. He had flopped trips instead of top pair. But my general read was right on target. He was going to fold when the big bets came out unless he had a virtual lock. By all rights, he should have beaten me into the pot, but he didn't. His weak-tight tendencies took over, and he feared the worst. His "monsters under the bed" thinking caused him to build and then abandon a large pot.

Some of you may feel that this example is too results-oriented. We're not recommending that you routinely try to bluff players off big hands like his. It was definitely lucky that the flush card came and that the bluff worked in this instance. However, weak-tight players will sometimes surprise you by making folds that, to you, seem ridiculous. They spend so much effort trying to trap people and avoid being trapped themselves that sometimes they make very silly laydowns.

Final Thoughts

Here's one final tidbit about weak-tight players. They sometimes tend to tilt more violently than other player types. They spend the whole night throwing away hand after hand to aggressive players. Then, they finally flop a set and get it all-in on the flop against a flush draw. And the flush draw comes in. If they don't leave immediately, watch out: They may go on mega-tilt for the next few hands. This is particularly true if the devastating beat just took most of their money, but not all of it.

I was playing a $2-$5 game in Las Vegas. The player directly on my left was extremely weak-tight; his play strongly fit each of the five criteria. He had been sitting around getting blown off hands for several hours, and he was stuck a couple hundred dollars. With $700 left, he got his opponent's $450 stack all-in on the flop with a set against top pair. The turn paired the top card, and the river paired the kicker, giving the player originally with top pair a very unlikely winner with a runner-runner full house.

The weak-tight player turned bright red. But he still had about $250 left. Two hands later, he limped in from the button in a five-handed pot. The flop came A♥9♣6♠. One player bet about the pot, $25, and the weak-tight player moved all-in for $220 more. The bettor called instantly and showed A♣Q♣. The weak-tight player had pocket kings.

When his "ace magnets" indeed did flop an ace, he blew a gasket. He had a "this isn't my day" reaction and made a (normally uncharacteristic) reckless all-in raise. Be on the lookout.

Weak-tight players are both fairly common and extremely profitable opponents. Wait until you have position, and build a pot with a preflop raise. Then use their predictable postflop behaviors to read their hands. When they seem unwilling to commit their stack, force them to with big bets and bluffs. They may pick up on your strategy, but usually they won't change gears to compensate. (Though be careful, some might switch up their play.) They'll resign themselves to standing up to you, "Once I finally get a hand," but meanwhile, feel free to help yourself to pot after pot.

The Advantage
to Being Short Stacked

Many no limit players will tell you that playing with a stack significantly shorter than the table average will make it hard to win. In tournaments that idea is obviously in one sense true (it's harder to come in first place with a short stack), but in cash games it is total baloney. In fact, playing a short stack provides you two major intrinsic advantages over your deep-stacked opponents.

Definition of a Short Stack

For the purpose of this section, a short stack is simply a stack that is significantly smaller than those of at least several of your opponents. For instance, if half or more of the players in your game have $200 stacks, and you have a $50 stack, you have a short stack.

Dispelling the Myths

Most people seem to think that playing a short stack cripples you for one major reason: Your opponents can "hurt" you, but you can't "hurt" them. That is, with your $50 against their $200, they have to risk only a quarter of their stack to win your whole stack. That idea is completely true and also completely irrelevant. If you win a quarter of their stack, you've won $50. If they win your whole stack, they've won $50.

Fifty dollars is fifty dollars. When you buy a new shirt with your fifty dollars, the clerk won't ask you what percentage of a stack that fifty represents. Win the hand and you win a shirt. Lose the hand and you lose your shirt. As long as you have plenty more fifties in your pocket, losing your whole $50 stack hurts you no more than your opponent losing a quarter of their $200 stack hurts them.

Some other people think playing a short stack hurts you because you can't "push anyone off a hand." With short money, people will just look you up because being wrong doesn't cost them much. Again, that criticism is true, and this time it's slightly more relevant.

Playing a short stack definitely changes the dynamics of the game. In particular, you'll usually get your stack in either preflop or on the flop. You won't often have much left to do any betting on the turn and river. Calling you is "cheap" relatively speaking, that is, opponents don't have to worry about getting themselves into a reverse implied odds situation where they are risking a lot to win a little. So bluffing won't be successful nearly as often as it would be if it came with the threat of bigger bets later in the hand.

Nevertheless, these handicaps go both ways. You can't bluff your opponents as well, but they can't bluff you either. Short stacks change the game, but they change the game for everyone, so it doesn't put you at any intrinsic disadvantage.

The Advantages

There are two major advantages to being short stacked. Both of these advantages apply only when your opponents have much deeper stacks. These are not advantages of playing a small amount of money; they are advantages of playing a small amount of money when your opponents have much more.

1. Deep stacks tend to play more loosely against one another (often correctly so) than they should against a short stack. So when you enter the pot, you'll find your money in against weaker-than-average hands.

2. After you are all-in, your opponents will keep betting, sometimes forcing players to fold. Whenever someone folds

a hand that has a chance to outdraw you, you gain; and in this case, you gain without having to risk anything further.

Here's an example to illustrate the first reason — that your opponents play more loosely against each other than they would against just you. You have $400 in a $10-$20 blind game. A very loose and bad player with a $4,000 stack limps first in. You make it $120 to go with a good hand, pocket queens perhaps. An expert player on the button with $4,000 picks up pocket fours. The expert player knows that, as a short stack, your raise likely represents a strong hand. With a small pocket pair, she's either a significant dog against a big pocket pair or a minor favorite against two big cards. Overall, pocket fours are a definite dog against your range of hands, and since you have so little behind, she won't have the implied odds to call trying to flop a set against you.

However, the presence of the very bad player makes this an easy call for the expert. Sure, she's taking somewhat the worst of it against you, but with a pocket pair on the button and $4,000 stacks, she stands to make that negative expectation back and more against the very bad player. She wishes you hadn't entered the pot, but your presence isn't enough to deter her from playing against the bad player.

Having a short stack has allowed you to get the best of both the bad player *and* the expert. Because of the differences in money involved, the expert should tailor her strategy to the poorly-played deep stack, not the well-played (and annoying) short stack. That means both players are playing incorrectly against you, while you play almost perfectly against them.

The second reason, that your opponents keep betting after you are all-in, also helps you significantly. Tournament players know this concept well: When a short-stacked player goes all-in, they often have a "gentleman's agreement" to check the hand down, even if they would usually have bet without the all-in player. They do this to avoid giving the short-stack player a benefit at both of their expenses.

In cash games, you won't see this behavior very often; your opponents will continue to bet against one another after you are all-in. The incentive to check a hand down is stronger in a tournament than in a cash game (because the prize structure rewards survival, not chip accumulation). But in cash games players often bet and build side pots, forcing some players to fold.

Every time a player folds without you having to bet any further, you have an advantage. You have reduced your chances of being outdrawn (or increased your chances of outdrawing, whatever the case may be) at no cost whatsoever. It's literally like free money. But you can't get this free money without being all-in with a short stack.

Why Play Deep Then?

Short stacks have structural advantages that deep stacks don't have. If that's the case, why would anyone play deep? Why not simply play short and let your natural advantage grind away at your opponents?

Actually, many players would be better off if they did play short rather than deep. They would simplify their decision-making, make fewer errors, and harness the advantage of being short stacked.

Many of these players don't play short either because they believe the myths about the perils of being short-stacked or because they don't find short stack poker very engaging. When you play short-stacked, mostly only preflop decisions matter. "Should I play my pocket eights against that raiser or not?" There's no big river bluffing, there's no setting players up for future falls, there are no big wins or losses.

Playing short-stacked also requires you to play more tightly preflop than deep stack play does. The larger a percentage of your stack you bet preflop, the more your hand strength matters. If you play short, you have to wait for good hands. If you play deep, you can play loosely and still be a winner.

Bad and mediocre players play deep stacked when they'd probably do better with a short stack because they find short stack poker boring. Good players play deep stacked because the bad players do. A good player can make far more money playing against deep stacked bad players than they can playing short stacked, despite the intrinsic advantage of being short stacked.

Bad players lose a lot more money playing deep stacked than they would if they played a short stack. They lose that money primarily to deep stacked good players. Good players have to buy in big to get a shot at that extra profit.

When Should You Play Short?

If you are reading this book, presumably you wish to be a good player. If that's the case, you'll have to spend most of your time playing deep. That's the only way you'll develop the skills necessary to win the most in your games. But there are two times you might consider buying in short to harness the natural advantage:

1. When you move up in stakes
2. When you have just joined the game

When you move up in stakes, your opponents will generally play a somewhat different style than what you're used to. They'll also generally play better. It makes some sense to buy in short for your first few sessions just to get a feel for your new situation. For instance, if you are a big winner at $2-$5 moving up to $5-$10, and your standard $2-$5 buy-in is $500, you might want to keep that same buy-in for your first few $5-$10 sessions. That will help you overcome the intimidation of playing bigger (because you aren't risking as much and because you are keeping things simpler), and it will allow you to use the short stack to your advantage. Once you get better and are sure you can win playing deep at the new level, start buying in bigger.

Similarly, some players always buy-in short when they first enter a game. They aren't familiar yet with the players, or even if they are, sometimes games play differently than what they might be used to. Playing short for the first few hands allows you to minimize your chance of making a mistake due to your newness to the game, and it affords you the natural advantage of playing short.

Then, when you've played a bit, you can buy more chips if you think it serves you best. Remember, you can't take chips off the table, but you can always buy more. It's much better to buy $200 and then buy $300 more than to buy $500, but soon wish you'd only bought $200.

Playing a Short Stack

Since most of the money gets bet early in the hand, and being all-in necessitates a showdown, short stacks should concentrate on playing premium hands and generally avoid bluffing. Play tightly preflop and try to get your money in when you likely have the edge against the hands your opponents might have.

Indeed, a totally algorithmic strategy of playing only premium preflop hands (say AA-77, AK and AQ) will beat almost any no limit game when you have a short stack of approximately twenty times the big blind. Ed suggests just such a strategy to beginners, in more detail, in his book, *Getting Started in Hold 'em*.

That's not to say that such a strategy is optimal. For expert players, playing short routinely is a sure way to slash win rates. But it is remarkable that a robot playing a short stack can beat even relatively tough no limit games. Don't underestimate the intrinsic advantages of playing a short stack.

For more tips on playing short stacked, read the no limit section of *Getting Started in Hold 'em* as well as the relevant sections of this book (soon to come).

Final Thoughts

Playing short-stacked has acquired a stigma in the no limit community. Short stack players are "fish" or "weak" or "annoying." That stigma doesn't translate to reality, though. Short stacks hold an intrinsic advantage over deep stacks at the table, and there are situations where the smart player should buy in short. Don't let misinformation or ego make your buy-in decisions for you. Short stacks are sometimes best, and you'll improve your win rate if you understand that.

Calling Preflop All-in Raises

While no limit hold 'em can be a complex game requiring sensitivity to a dozen or more factors in each decision, it can also be a frighteningly simple game. When the stacks are small compared to the big blind, the game often devolves into a "preflop all-in and call" game, where one player moves all-in, and one other player calls.

These situations are most common in tournaments where the stacks are often small compared to the size of the blinds. They can also occur in cash games, particularly for those players who intentionally seek them out by limiting their buy-ins.[37]

No matter how you play, or what you like to buy in for, though, you will occasionally play a "preflop all-in and call" pot. Since the strategy for playing such pots is remarkably simple (at least compared to the rest of the ideas in this book), all aspiring no limit experts should know it cold.

Yet few players do. Many players have a rough, intuitive understanding of what hands are worth playing and what hands aren't, but this understanding usually is rough indeed. Furthermore, some of the calls can be quite counterintuitive, particularly when the pot offers attractive 2-to-1 pot odds, and many players flub these.

"Preflop all-in and call" situations are simple enough that the correct plays can be memorized. For anyone who plays no limit tournaments seriously, correct strategy for these situations is low hanging fruit; learn it now and you'll fix some leaks easily.

This section presents strategies for calling all-in raises. The archetypal scenario pits you in the big blind against a single all-in raiser. Other scenarios occur also. You limp, someone raises all-in,

---

[37] For those who still haven't read it, we recommend that you read the discussion of small versus large stack no limit play in *Getting Started in Hold 'em* by Ed Miller.

and it's folded to you. Or you raise, someone reraises all-in, and it's folded to you. If you call, you turn your cards over, and the race is on. Should you call the raise or fold? Obviously, it depends on the quality of your hand, the size of the raise, and the range of hands your opponent will raise with.

Later in the chapter is a table listing all the hands with which you can profitably call given a raise size and range of opponent hands. The raise sizes are divided into three categories by the pot odds you see with your call: 2-to-1, 3-to-2, and 6-to-5.

Let's assume we are playing a no limit game with blinds of $10 and $10. (No limit games sometimes feature two equally-sized blinds.) A 2-to-1 raise would be to $40 (since you are calling $30 to win $60). A 3-to-2 raise would be to $70 (calling $60 to win $90). A 6-to-5 raise would be to $160 (calling $150 to win $180). These represent raises of 3x, 6x, and 15x the big blind, respectively. Most preflop raises you see will fit relatively closely to one of those categories. If you are faced with an in-between raise, like, say, 10x the big blind, you can interpolate between the 6x and 15x ranges by playing tighter than the 6x range, but looser than the 15x one.

If the raise represents most, but not all, of your stack, then pretend the raise is for your entire stack. If you call a raise for most of your stack, you've almost always committed to betting the remainder of your stack on a future round. (If you have $50 remaining and call a $40 raise getting a bit better than even money, you should almost always call a future $10 bet also, getting over 8-to-1.) Since calling for most of your stack is essentially a commitment for your whole stack, you should treat it that way in the calculation.

Next, we divide the range of hands your opponent might have into six categories: Very tight, Tight, Average, Loose, Very loose, and Any two. Our "Very tight" raiser plays only 3 percent of his hands. Our "Tight" raiser plays 5 percent. Our "Average" raiser 10 percent, our "Loose" raiser 25 percent, and our "Very loose" raiser plays 50 percent. Our "Any two" raiser plays 100 percent of his hands.

The specific ranges of hands we chose to fit these percentages are listed in following table.

Table I: The Hand Range Categories

Very tight (3%)	AA-JJ and AK
Tight (5%)	AA-99 and AK-AQ
Average (10%)	AA-77, AK-AT, and KQ
Loose (25%)	AA-22, AK-A5, Any two cards T or higher (e.g., QT), and K9s-T9s
Very loose (50%)	AA-22, AK-A2, Any two cards 7 or higher (e.g., T7), K6-K4, and K3s-K2s
Any two (100%)	Everything

Obviously, some players might not adhere to these ranges exactly. They might raise 18 percent of their hands, between the "Average" and "Loose" ranges. Or, they might raise 25 percent of their hands, but choose a slightly different set of hands.

Regardless, these categories provide enough resolution that you should be able to interpolate well between them. If you familiarize yourself with these 18 hand ranges for calling, your decisions in these situations should improve significantly.

Table II: The Hand Ranges for Calling

	6-to-5 (15x)	3-to-2 (6x)	2-to-1 (3x)
Very Tight (3%)	AA-QQ	AA-QQ, AKs	AA-TT, AK
Tight (5%)	AA-JJ, AK	AA-TT, AK	AA-22, AK-AQ, AJs, KJs-KTs (not KQs), QJs-JTs
Average (10%)	AA-99, AK-AQ, AJs	AA-55, AK-AJ, ATs	AA-22, AK-AT, A9s-A2s, KQ, KJs-K9s, QJs-Q9s, JTs-54s, J9s-97s, J8s
Loose (25%)	AA-44, AK-A8, A7s, KQ, KJs-KTs	AA-22, AK-A2, KQ-KT, K9s-K6s, QJ, QTs-Q9s, JTs	AA-22, AK-A2, KQ-K2, QJ-Q6, Q5s-Q2s, JT-J8, J7s-J2s, T9-T8, T7s-T3s, 98-97, 96s-93s, 87-86, 85s-84s, 76, 75s-73s, 65, 64s-63s, 54s-52s, 43s-42s
Very loose (50%)	AA-22, AK-A2, KQ-K7, K6s-K5s, QJ-QT, Q9s-Q8s, JT, J9s	AA-22, AK-A2, KQ-K2, QJ-Q7, Q6s-Q2s, JT-J8, J7s-J6s, T9, T8s-T7s, 98s	AA-22, AK-A2, KQ-K2, QJ-Q2, JT-J2, T9-T3, 98-95, 87-85, 76-75, 65-64, 54-53, Any two suited except 72s
Any two (100%)	AA-22, AK-A2, KQ-K2, QJ-Q2, JT-J4, J3s-J2s, T9-T7, T6s-T3s, 98-97, 96s-95s, 87s-86s	AA-22, AK-A2, KQ-K2, QJ-Q2, JT-J2, T9-T2, 98-93, 92s, 87-85, 84s-82s, 76-75, 74s-73s, 65s-64s, 54s	Everything except 42o-32o

While committing these ranges to memory entirely might be an overly daunting task, you should at least find the patterns in the ranges. That way, even though you don't know by rote which hands are profitable, you'll be able to figure it out from your knowledge.

The most important pattern is that, at 2-to-1, generally you should call more loosely than the range of hands you expect from the raiser, at 3-to-2, you should call slightly more tightly than the raiser, and at 6-to-5, you should call significantly more tightly.

That is, at 6-to-5 odds, you generally need at least a hand that is *better* than the worst hand your opponent would raise with. At 3-to-2, you need at least the worst hand your opponent would raise with (and usually one notch better than that). And at 2-to-1, you can call with some hands that are significantly worse than even the weakest hands your opponent might raise with.

The "Tight" raiser (AA-99 and AK-AQ) shows a great example of this pattern. Getting 6-to-5 odds you can call only with AA-JJ and AK. Getting 3-to-2, you can call with TT also, but still not 99 or AQ (not even AQs). But getting 2-to-1, you can profitably call with *any pocket pair* as well as AK-AQ, and a number of big suited hands, some of which might be dominated by either AK or AQ.[38]

The "Average" raiser category (AA-77, AK-AT, and KQ) also shows how loosely you can call getting 2-to-1. At 6-to-5 against the average raiser, you can play only AA-99, AK-AQ, and AJs. But at 2-to-1, you can play a wide range of hands: any pocket pair, any suited ace, and many suited connectors, including those

---

[38] KQs just misses the cut here, probably because it is dominated against AA, KK, AK, and AQ. AJs is slightly better and barely makes the cut because, while it too is dominated by AA, AK, and AQ, it does better against KK. Paradoxically, against the tight raiser, KJs is better than KQs because KQs is dominated by both AK and AQ, but KJs is ok against AQ. These idiosyncrasies disappear as the raiser opens up and raises more hands. Against an "Average" or looser raiser, the bigger the hand is, the better.

as weak as 54s. Not many players would instinctively call with five-high against someone raising 3x the blind. They would especially not call against a raiser as tight as our "Average" raiser. But it's a profitable call nonetheless.

Some Qualifications

The results of these charts are merely raw expected value computations. That is, getting 2-to-1, if the hand will win more than one-third of the time against the proposed range of hands, it's listed as a call.

While a raw expected value computation is usually all you need to determine a call, sometimes other factors can swing a close call to a pass. These situations often arise in tournaments. For instance, say you are playing a sit 'n go tournament with a $50-$30-$20 payout structure, and there are four players left. (Fourth place gets zero.) If you are third in chips, and the fourth place player is getting the big blind next hand, you'd be nuts to call a raise for all your chips with Q♣J♠ even if you thought the raiser was "Loose" and you were getting 3-to-2 pot odds.

Since queen-jack is a borderline hand for that situation, you could expect to win roughly 40 percent of the time. You'd bust out with no prize the other 60 percent of the time. Assume that if you folded and let the fourth place player take the blinds, he would be a 70 percent favorite to bust in the next two hands. That would make you 70 percent to win at least $20, and some percent to win more.

Let's just assume very conservatively that you'd win first place 10 percent, second place 20 percent, third place 40 percent, and fourth place 30 percent. By folding, your real expectation would then be $19.

$$\$19 = (0.10)(\$50) + (0.20)(\$30) + (0.40)(\$20) + (0.30)(\$0)$$

By calling, your real expectation can't be any higher than (0.40) ($50) = $20, and that's if you won the tournament every time you called. If you won only 75 percent of the time, and came in second the other 25 percent (still optimistic) you'd get $18,

$$\$18 = (0.40)\big[(0.75)(\$50) + (0.25)(\$30)\big] + (0.60)(\$0)$$

making the marginal call with queen-jack clearly wrong. Fold, and hope the fourth place player busts out.

While this isn't a tournament book, this is a good time to discuss briefly an often misunderstood tournament principle. People often say, "You have to play extra tightly in a tournament because you're playing on a short bankroll."

But that isn't right. The times you play extra tightly are like those in the above situation, namely, when the prizes are very near or already on top of you, and when calling the raise drastically increases your chance of getting a small prize or no prize at all.

If you are nearly a chip leader, then you needn't play extra tightly when calling an all-in raise from a smaller stack. And if you are early in a large, multiday tournament, you needn't play extra tightly either. At that point, the tournament chip values still correspond closely to their nominal cash values.

Close all-in calls can also be wrong if the call constitutes a large percentage of your bankroll. The call will still be +EV, but it can slow the average growth of your bankroll all the same because you have far fewer chips to work with if you lose.[39] So if your goal is to grow a bankroll as quickly as possible, you may have to call somewhat more tightly than what this chart recommends *when the call represents a significant percentage of your total bankroll.*

---

[39] If you want to learn more about this idea, research the Kelly Criterion.

Final Thoughts

For most people, learning correct "preflop all-in and call" strategy is not fun. It's not why we play poker. But, fun or not, it's an important aspect of no limit hold 'em, particularly in tournaments. And it's also simple. While you may get away without knowing proper calling strategy against bad players, against good players it will eat significantly at your earn.

Think of learning these charts like practicing scales for a musician or running sprints for an athlete: It's not fun, and it's not why you are passionate about your field. But it's fundamental, and if you don't have this bedrock strategy right, it will show through in your overall results.

The Sklansky-Chubukov Rankings

You are in the small blind in a $1-$2 blind game. Everyone folds to you. You have

but you accidentally flip your cards over for your opponent to see. (Assume your hand is not ruled dead at that point.) Unfortunately, your opponent is a computer that can instantly and flawlessly determine its best play now that it knows your hand.

After posting your small blind, you have $X in your stack. You decide that you will either move all-in or you'll fold. For what values of $X is it better to move all-in, and for what values is it better to fold?

Clearly, for small values of $X, you should just move in and hope your computer opponent doesn't have a pocket pair. Most of the time it won't, and you'll win $3. When it does, you'll be a dog, but that will happen only a small percentage of the time.

Specifically, your opponent is slightly worse than 16-to-1 against to have a pair. So with a stack of 16 x $3 = $48, moving in would show an immediate profit. Since you win immediately 16 out of 17 times, you could lose 100 percent of the time when you're called and still make a slight profit. And you won't lose anywhere close to 100 percent of the time (after all, you're a "coin flip" against queens through deuces).

But for very large values of $X, you won't win $3 often enough to make up for those times the computer happens to get lucky and catch a pair (particularly aces or kings). For instance, if you had $10,000, moving all-in would be very stupid. Every once in a while, your opponent will have pocket aces or kings and have a giant edge. You won't win enough blinds to compensate.

So the question is, what's the break-even value of $X? If your stack is below that value, you should move in. And if it's above it, you should fold.

After you are dealt A♥K♦, there are 50 cards remaining in the deck. That allows your opponent 1,225 possible hand combinations:

$$1,225 = \frac{(50)(49)}{2}$$

Since the computer knows what you have, it will never call you as an underdog.[40] Every non-pair hand except another ace-king is an underdog, so the computer will fold all of those hands. In addition, of the nine possible ace-king combinations remaining, two of them are underdogs against your hand: A♠K♥ and A♣K♥. Your hand can beat those hands by making a heart or diamond flush, but those hands can beat you only with one flush, a spade or club flush respectively. The K♥ being under your A♥ is a liability.

Seven ace-king combinations will call your all-in raise, and that's it for the non-pair hands. Every pocket pair will call you also. Your opponent can make pocket aces or kings three ways

---

[40] Strictly speaking, it won't call you when the call would be negative expectation. Since the pot lays odds because of the blind money, it will still call even if it's a very slight underdog. After you move all-in for $X, the pot will be laying ($X+$3)-to-($X-1). For the actual value of $X for A♥K♦ (we'll soon calculate it), the computer could win as little as 49.7 percent of the time and still call. As it turns out, no hands exist that are between 49.7 and 50 percent against ace-king. The closest hand is 49.6 percent.

each, and it can make queens through deuces six ways each. So that makes 72 pocket pairs.

$$72 = (3)(2) + (6)(11)$$

Seventy-nine hands out of the 1,225 possible call you if you move in with ace-king. When you are called, you will win about 43.3 percent of the time. This number is relatively close to 50 percent, because most of the times you are called will be a "coin flip" situation. The only times you are a big underdog are when you are up against pocket aces or kings.

To find out what $X is, we should write an EV equation for moving in, then set it equal to zero and solve for X. You'll be called 6.45 percent of the time (79/1,225), which means the computer will fold the other 93.55 percent. When the computer folds, you win $3. When it calls, you win $X + 3 about 43.3 percent of the time, and you lose $X the other 56.7 percent. Thus, the EV equation is:

$$0 = (0.935)(\$3) + (0.0645)[(0.433)(\$X + 3) + (0.567)((-\$X)]$$
$$0 = 2.81 + 0.079X + 0.0838 - 0.0366X$$
$$2.89 = 0.0087X$$
$$X = \$332$$

The break-even point is $332. We call this the Sklansky-Chubukov (S-C) number for A♥K♦ (or any unsuited ace-king).[41] If you have less than $332 in your stack in a $1-$2 game, it's better to move in *even if you have to turn your hand face-up.*

---

[41] The numbers are named for David Sklansky, who posited that calculating these numbers could help solve preflop problems, and Victor Chubukov, a games theorist from Berkeley, who calculated the values for every possible hand. Chubukov's calculated values appear in this book.

That's right, if you have $300 and ace-king, you should bet $300 to pick up the $3 in blind money rather than fold.[42]

Hopefully, that's a startling conclusion for you. Very few people's instincts would tell them to move in for over 150 times the big blind playing with their hands face-up with anything less than aces or maybe kings.

The reason this conclusion is hard to "get" is that most people generally dislike laying odds. Ask someone to lay you $100 to win $1, and you'll get turned down virtually every time, no matter what the bet. "It just isn't worth it to risk $100 to win one measly dollar," is the thinking. But it is worth it, at least in terms of expectation.

Furthermore, in real poker you try not to show your hand to your opponents. When your opponent doesn't know that you have ace-king, it's even better for you, and you can move in profitably with a somewhat bigger stack than $332. After all, pocket deuces is a favorite against you, but who is going to call $300 with that hand? In reality, a player might call you only with pocket aces, kings, or queens and fold everything else. Since they are folding so many profitable hands, you can move in profitably with stacks even greater than $332.

Now, before you get too excited, realize that we've shown only that moving in is better than folding if you have less than $332. We're not saying that moving in is the best possible play; raising a smaller amount or even just calling could be better than moving in. But you'd better not fold.

So you may say, "Great, so now I know not to open-fold ace-king heads-up. Thanks, I really needed to read a book and wade through calculations to find that out." But you'll be glad you did,

---

[42] This statement assumes that you can't derive useful information from the other players' folds. In practice, if seven or eight players fold, they will each have been slightly less likely than random chance would suggest to have been dealt an ace. This means that your opponent in the big blind will be somewhat more likely than 3/1,225 to have pocket aces.

as this method of calculation can be used for any hand, not just ace-king. And the conclusions for some hands are quite surprising. The precise definition of a Sklansky-Chubukov number is this: If you have a face-up hand and a $1 blind, and your sole opponent has a $2 blind, how big does your stack have to be (in dollars, not counting your $1 blind) such that it would be better to fold rather than move in, assuming your opponent calls or folds perfectly.

Here is a list of a few representative hands and their corresponding Sklansky-Chubukov numbers. You can find the entire list of hands in the "Sklansky-Chubukov Rankings," starting on p. 299.

Table I: Sklansky-Chubukov Numbers for Selected Hands

Hand	S-C #
KK	$954
AKo	$332
88	$159
A9s	$104
A8o	$71
A3o	$48
22	$48
K8s	$40
JTs	$36
K8o	$30
Q5s	$20
Q6o	$16
T8o	$12
87s	$11
J5o	$10
96o	$7
74s	$5

With some qualification and adjustment, you can use the Sklansky-Chubukov number for a hand to help you decide how good a "move-in" hand you have. You do have to make a few adjustments, however.

Remember, the S-C numbers are calculated with the assumption that your opponent knows your hand and will play perfectly against it. This assumption makes the S-C number a bit of a worst-case estimate. You can't possibly go wrong (have a negative expectation) moving in with less than the S-C number (as opposed to folding), but you may well be right to move in even with a significantly bigger stack.

How much bigger, however, depends on how the S-C number is calculated. There are two major types of hands, robust and vulnerable hands. Robust hands can be called profitably by a large number of hands, but they don't fare too badly against those hands on the whole. Vulnerable hands can't be called very often, but when they are called, they are significant underdogs.

For instance, pocket deuces is a prototypical robust hand. More than half the time, the big blind will have a hand that can call it profitably: 709 out of 1,225 hands (57.9 percent). But when it is called, deuces will win 46.8 percent of the time, almost half the time.

Ace-trey offsuit is a vulnerable hand. Only 220 out of 1,005 hands can call it profitably (18.0 percent), but when called it wins only 35.1 percent of the time.

Both pocket deuces and ace-trey offsuit have an S-C number of $48. The robust hand, deuces, is in some ways the better move-in hand, though. That's because your opponents will tend to make more calling *mistakes* when you have deuces than when you have ace-trey.

Say you move in for $40. Most players will call that raise relatively tightly. Even if they know that you might move in with a "weak" hand, they still probably won't call without a pocket pair or an ace. For instance, most players will almost certainly fold T♥7♥ to a $39 raise.

That fold is correct if you have ace-trey, but it's a mistake if you have deuces: ten-seven suited is actually a favorite over pocket deuces. So your opponents' tendency to fold too many hands to big all-in raises will hurt them more when you hold a robust hand than when you hold a vulnerable one.

> **Sklansky-Chubukov numbers always underestimate the real move-in power of a hand. But they underestimate the power of robust hands more than vulnerable ones.**

Suited connectors are also robust hands, and so they too have more move-in power than their Sklansky-Chubukov numbers might suggest. For instance, 8♥7♥ has a relatively small S-C number of $11. But it is a strongly robust hand: it can be called profitably by 945 out of 1,225 hands (77 percent), but it wins 42.2 percent of the time when called. Since many hands that could call profitably will fold instead (e.g., J♥3♣), you can move-in profitably with eight-seven suited with significantly more than $11.

The scenario we used to derive the S-C numbers involved everyone folding to you in the small blind. But you can also use these numbers when you are on the button. Since there are two possible callers remaining rather than one, your chance to be called roughly doubles. As a rough approximation, you can halve the S-C number for a hand and determine if it's profitable to move in from the button.[43]

As you may have surmised by now, these S-C numbers are most useful when you are playing in no limit tournaments. Despite their shortcomings, they can help you decide whether it's right to move in or fold when you have a mediocre hand.

---

[43] To be sure, this is a very rough approximation. We're ignoring the chance that you could be called in two places. We're ignoring the fact that you don't already have a dollar in when you're on the button. We're ignoring the fact that the small blind should generally call more tightly than the big blind. We're ignoring some other things also. If you aren't comfortable ignoring all those things, don't make the approximation. *Caveat emptor.*

For instance, say the blinds are $100-$200, and you have $1,300 on the button. The prizes are still a long way off, and your stack is significantly shorter than average. Everyone folds to you. You look down and see K♥8♦. Should you move in, or should you fold? The S-C number for king-eight offsuit is $30. You are on the button, not in the small blind, so halve it to $15. Your $1,300 stack with $100-$200 blinds is equivalent to a $13 stack with $1-$2 blinds. Since your $13 is less than $15, you should move in.

The S-C numbers tend to underestimate the move-in power of a hand, so the decision isn't really even as close as it might seem. (In the previous example, for instance, many opponents would incorrectly fold ace-eight through ace-deuce.) Add in a $25 ante, and it's an absolutely automatic move-in.

Final Thoughts

It's automatic to move in on the button with king-eight offsuit with a stack of six and a half times the big blind. You should move in just as automatically with J♦9♦ (S-C number of $26). Does that surprise you? If so, study the Sklansky-Chubukov numbers starting on page 299 and give yourself some quizzes.

Any ace tends to be a powerful move-in hand. Ace-eight offsuit has an S-C number of $71, and even the lowly ace-trey is $48. They are vulnerable, not robust, hands which hurts them. But remember, S-C numbers underestimate the move-in power for all hands. They just don't underestimate vulnerable hands as much. When everyone folds to you on or near the button in a tournament, and you have an ace, you often have an easy move-in even when your stack is more than ten times the big blind.

Tournament pros know that these "loose" move-ins are correct; in fact, that knowledge is the main reason many of them win money at all playing tournaments. This secret is what separates tourney pros from amateurs. Use the tables starting on page 299 to help you decide when to move in, and you'll find that your tournament results improve very quickly.

When to (and When Not to)
Use the Sklansky-Chubukov Rankings

In the last section, we explained what Sklansky-Chubukov (S-C) numbers are, and we gave you a basic idea of how you might use them to make decisions. But we gave you only a basic idea, and we would be remiss if we left things there, as there are right and wrong ways to interpret the S-C numbers.

We offer you extra guidance in this section to help you make the most of this tool.

Adjusting for an Ante

Although the precise S-C numbers apply to a precise situation — you have a $1 small blind, and your lone opponent has the $2 big blind — it is only slightly inaccurate to look at it in terms of the odds you are laying.

In other words, if a hand has an S-C number of 30, it basically means that you have a positive EV if you lay 10-to-1 or less (30-to-1). Thinking of it this way is very useful if there is an ante. When there is, you should divide the S-C number by three to see what odds you can lay.

For example, say the blinds are $300 and $600 with a $50 ante. The game is ten-handed, so there is $1,400 in the initial pot. You have

in the small blind, and your stack is $9,000.

222

If everyone folds to you, and you move in, you are laying about 6.5-to-1. The S-C number for king-four offsuit is 22.8, so divided by three, you can profitably lay up to about 7.5-to-1. Thus, moving in is profitable, but only because of the ante. Without it, you would be laying 10-to-1.

The Best Hands for Moving In

As useful a guideline as the S-C numbers are, especially when heads-up (or perhaps three-handed where you would roughly divide the S-C number by two), there are many times you should not blindly follow its "advice." Sometimes you should move in even though the S-C number suggests not to, and sometimes you should not move in even if doing so is profitable (according to the S-C number).

As a general principle, the times that moving in is most attractive is when S-C proves that doing so can't be a negative EV play, and you don't have a good reason to play your hand another way.

This situation is most likely to occur when you are out of position, you are facing a good, aggressive opponent, and you are looking at a hand that is weak except for its showdown value. The king-four offsuit previously mentioned is a good example of such a hand.

With a $200 stack in a $10-$20 game, the natural inclination would be to fold K♥4♠ in the small blind if everyone else has folded. This inclination is particularly strong if your opponent in the big blind is a good player.

A limp is likely to induce a raise (that you don't want to call). And a small raise is likely to get called. Neither option is attractive.

Yet, folding can't be right because the S-C number for king-four offsuit (22.8) is greater than your stack size. (We'll discuss a single exception shortly.) Moving in *and showing your cards* is profitable, so moving in without showing your cards must be at least as profitable. In fact, not showing will likely make your hand

even more profitable, as your opponent is likely to fold hands like
K♠6♣ and A♥2♦ that he'd call with if he saw your hand.

Generally speaking, the best hands to move in with are those
that don't "play well," but that have some showdown value (i.e.,
that have one high or medium-high card). You should love to be
all-in with hands like A♣4♦ and Q♠7♦ as long as you don't have
more chips than the S-C number.

An Exception to Moving In

If the Sklansky-Chubukov number suggests that you should
move in with hands that you would have otherwise folded, you
should listen and move in instead. But there is one exception: If
you're in a tournament with a very weak hand and a very short
stack, sometimes you should simply fold to ensure that you get to
see some free hands.

For instance, say you have $500 in the small blind at a ten-
handed table with $100-$200 blinds and no antes. You hold

and everyone folds to you. The S-C number for ten-trey offsuit is
5.5, which suggests that you should move in.

Moving in does have a positive expectation, but folding has
an even more positive expectation, as it ensures that you get to see
up to eight free hands due you. If you move in, you're likely to get
called, and if you get called, you'll probably lose and get knocked
out. Ensuring that you see the free hands will be worth more to
you than the slightly positive expectation you gain by moving in.

Moving In
With "Too Many" Chips

Often you should move in even if you have more chips than the S-C number. That's because the S-C numbers were calculated assuming that your opponent would play perfectly against your hand, and in practice that assumption will rarely hold.

Take a hand like

The S-C number for ten-five suited is 10. But the number is only that low because your opponent is assumed to call (correctly) with about 72 percent of his hands. This set of hands includes many really ugly ones like J♥3♠ and T♦6♥.

In practice, most players would fold hands like these to a significant all-in raise without thinking. Instead of calling with 72 percent of their hands, they may call with about 30 percent. Because they will fold so many hands that you want them to fold, you can get away with raising with a larger stack than the S-C number. Because of this effect, the true "move-in number" for ten-five suited is approximately 20. A move in with, for instance, 13 small blinds almost has to be right (even though that's more than the S-C number of 10). This reasoning also holds for lots of other mediocre hands with S-C numbers below 20 or so.

Moving In May Not Be Best with Hands that Play Well

Remember, though, that we have been talking about hands that don't "play well," especially out of position. These are hands that you look at and probably feel like folding.

If your hand is more "playable," or if you are in position (for instance, in the small blind on the button in a heads-up match), you should often not move in even if the S-C numbers suggest that you do so. You should limp or make a small raise instead. (But you should never fold, and you should almost never make a large raise of a significant chunk of your stack — you're almost always better off moving in than making a raise of more than 25 percent of your stack.)

The main time you should ignore the S-C "advice" to move in is when you have a fairly big stack, and the S-C number is bigger still (perhaps when the S-C number is above 30 or so). The only really good move-in hands at the high levels are offsuit aces and kings with weak kickers (e.g., A♣3♠ or K♥7♦).

Certainly you are wasting the value of a hand like jack-ten suited if you move in with it with 20 or 30 small blinds. Whether you should just call or make a small raise is highly related to the playing style of your opponent. But a move in, though profitable, is almost certainly less profitable than other options as long as your stack is decently-sized. (Of course, if your stack is relatively short, move in with jack-ten suited — as well as nine-eight suited, eight-seven suited, or any other hand with an appropriate S-C number.)

Small pairs are a little different. Pocket deuces has about the same S-C number as queen-jack suited (48 vs. 49.5), but the two hands should be played differently.

The main difference is that deuces will so frequently lose if you make a small raise and get played with. (Queen-jack suited will win more often in that situation.)

This reasoning would tend to suggest that you should make a small raise with queen-jack suited, but move in with deuces. But against most players, we don't think moving in with deuces is the best play with about 20 or more small blinds. Rather, we think the counterintuitive play of limping is best, but by only a little bit.

When in doubt, though, never be afraid to fall back on Sklansky-Chubukov and just move in.

Some Preflop
Heads-Up All-In Matchups

You should be familiar with how a few hands play against one another heads-up and all-in before the flop. This is especially important knowledge if you play a lot of tournaments, since these scenarios come up over and over in tournament play.

A♥A♠ vs. K♦K♣

81.25% | 18.75%

When a pocket pair is pitted against a lower pair, the bigger pair is about a 4.5-to-1 favorite.

5♥5♠ vs. A♣K♣

51.78% | 48.22%

When a pocket pair is pitted against two overcards, the hands are about even money against one another. The pair gains a slight advantage when the overcards are unsuited and unconnected.

5♥5♠ vs. A♣2♠

70.59% | 29.41%

When a pocket pair is pitted against one overcard and an undercard, the pair is about a 2.5-to-1 favorite.

8♣8♦ vs. 4♥3♣

84.01% | 15.99%

When a pocket pair is pitted against two undercards, the pair is about a 5.5-to-1 favorite.

8♣8♦ vs. A♥8♥
70.08% | 29.92%

When a pocket pair is pitted against an overcard and a card of its rank, the pair is about a 2.5-to-1 favorite.

8♣8♦ vs. 8♥5♣
89.89% | 10.11%

When a pocket pair is pitted against an undercard and a card of its rank, the pair is about a 9-to-1 favorite.

A♣K♠ vs. J♥9♦
63.92% | 36.08%

When a non-pair hand is pitted against two undercards, the bigger hand is about a 9-to-5 favorite.

A♣J♠ vs. K♥9♥
59.84% | 40.16%

When a non-pair hand is pitted against an in-between card and an undercard, the bigger hand is about a 3-to-2 favorite.

A♣T♠ vs. K♥Q♥
55.93% | 44.07%

When a non-pair hand is pitted against two in-between cards, the bigger hand is about a 6-to-5 favorite.

A♣K♠ vs. A♥Q♣
74.75% | 25.25%

When a non-pair hand is pitted against an undercard and a card matching one of its ranks, the bigger hand is about a 3-to-1 favorite.

Final Thoughts

These are the basic matchups. The numbers change some depending on which hands are suited versus unsuited, connected versus unconnected, and sharing suits versus not sharing them. They also change quite a bit if the cards are high (A♣K♠ vs. A♥Q♣) versus low (A♣7♠ vs. A♥4♣) due to counterfeiting.

Nevertheless, if you play a lot of tournaments, you might want to commit these approximate odds to memory. This knowledge should help you with your raising and calling decisions.

Manipulating
Your Opponents

Learning to manipulate your opponents is a skill of marginal importance in many forms of poker, but in no limit hold 'em it's very important. If you play at medium stakes or higher, most of your opponents will be at least somewhat competent, and it may sometimes be hard to get their money. Particularly, it can sometimes be difficult to make a lot off your big hands: Flopping a big hand is fun, but if you can't convince someone else to lose their stack to you when you do, it isn't worth all that much.

To win the most on your big hands (and other hands too), you need to concentrate actively on manipulating your opponents. Trick their hand-reading processes into thinking you have the wrong hand at just the right time. Or cloud their judgment so they'll make the wrong play even if they do read your hand correctly.

This section is by no means a complete exposure to the topic. Indeed, one could easily write ten times this amount on the topic and still not cover every technique available for manipulating your opponents. Consider this section an introduction, and allow it to pique your imagination.

Get Pigeonholed

Being pigeonholed is usually bad, but it's definitely not in poker; that is, as long as you *don't fit* well into the perceived hole. Poker players of all skill levels love to categorize their opponents: "He's weak, she's a bluffer, he's wild, and she always has the nuts."

Some players play so one-dimensionally that a few words can describe their play almost entirely. Not you![44] Your play is complex, and you are capable of incorporating a number of factors into your decision-making, making your plays difficult to read. But that won't stop your opponents from trying to sum your play up glibly. Raise a few hands in a row, and you "play fast." Fold for a long period of time, and you're "squeaky tight." People like labels, stereotypes, and neat categories. That tendency doesn't change at the poker table.

You can use your opponents' pigeonholing tendencies against them. Encourage your opponents to stick a label on you, then surprise them at just the right moment.

There are several ways to do this. The first (and cheapest) is simply to use the randomness of the cards to shape your image. This method works great against people you haven't played with often — those who don't already have a conception of your general style.

Say you sit down, and you happen to fold your first twenty or thirty hands. Maybe you see a flop or two, but you fold quietly to the first bet after missing. Oftentimes none of your opponents will pay this fact much mind (either because they don't notice or because they know that a cold run could happen easily to anyone).

But some people will make a lot more of this "information." They will assume you are tight and a "folder" (on all streets, not just preflop). An aggressive player might use this notion as an impetus to run an extra bluff or two at you. Others may decide that if you bet big, "you must really have it."

You can use these ill-informed conclusions against your opponents. Against aggressive players, you might call with some slightly weaker hands hoping to snap off some of the extra bluffs they will try. And you can run those extra bluffs yourself against the players who assume that you "must have it."

This idea, to use to your advantage the image your natural play may have formed, is certainly not new. Indeed, even

---

[44] Unless, of course, you are in a game that calls for it.

unskilled players sometimes realize this. So don't get carried away.

Many players won't drastically change the way they play against you no matter how they perceive you. Even if they just saw you get caught bluffing ten times in a row, they still won't call a big bet with ace-high hoping to catch you an eleventh time. So don't overestimate the impact that your "accidental" image might have. Don't think, "I haven't played a hand in a while; it's time to try a bluff." That's too general. You should think specifically that *this* player is likely to change their play *this* hand because of something you've done in the recent past.

Make Obvious Errors to Induce Costly Errors

There is a big difference between obvious errors and costly errors. An obvious error is a play that most players will instantly identify as wrong. Raising preflop with 8♣5♣ is usually an example of an obvious error. Even people who have only watched poker on television know that playing such "trash" hands is usually a mistake. Calling with a weak draw without getting sufficient implied odds is another example. Even bad players are familiar with the idea that longshot draws are usually not worth playing for.

The thing is, just because a play is an obvious error doesn't make it an expensive error. Some obvious errors are actually, mathematically speaking, only very slight errors. Say you have

and the flop comes

The preflop raiser (a player very likely to have aces, kings, or ace-king in this situation) bets an amount that offers you about 8-to-1 implied odds. Your chance to make the gutshot on the next card is 4/45 (assuming your opponent doesn't have a queen), or 10.25-to-1 against. Calling is an error (unless you expect you might get a free card on the turn).

But it's a small one. Your implied odds come up only slightly short of break-even. If you make this call again and again, on average you'll lose only a small percentage of your stack each time.[45]

But if you catch a queen and bust a flopped set, your opponent isn't likely to see it that way. He may call you all sorts of names like "fish" and "chaser." He'll do the math in his head, and every time he'll come to the conclusion that your call was wrong. Except he won't see it as slightly wrong; he'll see it as horribly wrong. (Getting stacked tends to mess with some people's sense of magnitude. Nondescript beats turn into whoppers.)

More importantly, he's likely to remember that you're a "chaser" the next time he plays a hand with you. Call another flop bet, and he'll wonder what kind of stupid and crazy draw you have this time. This attitude will make it a lot easier for you to win a big pot if you happen to flop a big hand. Your opponent is likely to take your calls less seriously than he normally might, and he's also

---

[45] To be fair, we've simplified the math. If your opponent has aces, kings, or ace-king, then you won't win 4 out of 45 times because sometimes your opponent will fill up on the river. The point is that the decision is close; if you don't like our numbers, choose ones you do like.

likely to bet more with weaker hands to "make you pay to draw." Both adjustments will allow you to slowplay, just calling on the flop and turn, without arousing suspicions.

Furthermore, you can sometimes use this flawed perception to run an extra river bluff or two. If an unlikely straight or backdoor flush comes in on the river, often it's hopeless to try to represent it because your opponent will think, "There's no way you called the flop with that draw." But if your opponent thinks you are a crazy "chaser," he's more likely to give you credit for having some very unlikely hands. After all, if you're stupid enough to call with a gutshot against an obvious flopped set, you must be stupid enough to do anything.

The key to using this concept for profit is to identify situations where you can make an obvious, but relatively inexpensive, error that may induce your opponent to make not as obvious, but far more costly errors later on (either on that hand or on future ones). Thus, you're trading small loses for hopefully big gains.

Indeed, this tactic is powerful enough that some successful players have built their entire style around it. One such style is known variously as "loose-aggressive" or "hyper-aggressive." These players raise frequently on the cheap streets, preflop and the flop, with marginal and weak hands. But when the betting gets big on the turn and river, their play becomes fairly orthodox. They get a little out of line with the small money, but play straight when it gets big.

This style seeks to unsettle tight players by peppering them with frequent, annoying raises. The tight players start by folding, but soon they realize they are being taken advantage of. They resolve to "take a stand" by lowering their standards somewhat and calling or raising these light bets.

They flop top pair, and they aren't going to be pushed off it this time. They call a $100 flop bet, confident they should let this wild player bluff off his cash. Then they call a $400 turn bet. When the river $1,500 bet comes, they get a sinking feeling. "Maybe he really has a big hand this time?" But this is the "taking a stand" hand, and that means calling the $1,500 also. Sure enough, the loose-aggressive shows down a big hand.

The loose-aggressive style works because the frequent early bets and raises are clearly wrong, but they tend not to be very costly. 8♣5♣ isn't a good hand, but if you play it with position and against the weak players at the table, it will mostly hold its own.

But constantly attacking your opponents with raises with hands like 8♣5♣ can have a profound effect on their decision-making. They may begin to consider you a truly wild player, and some may even feel like they need to "teach you a lesson" for getting out of line so willingly. You know there's a big difference between making a slightly wrong $50 raise preflop and a hopelessly wild $2,000 bluff on the river, but they don't know you know that. They may assume you are just as crazy with your big bets as you are with your small ones. That mistaken assumption will make you lots of money over time.

The loose-aggressive style is quite popular now, however, so many of your opponents will be wise to it. (Many will try it on you as well.) Please don't read this example and conclude that all you have to do to be a big winner is to start raising all your trashy hands preflop. No matter what style you choose, you have to apply it with sophistication, or you won't win.

Nevertheless, making obvious errors to induce costly errors (either later on in that hand or in a future hand) is a valuable no limit tactic.[46] Look for opportunities to befuddle your opponents without giving up much; those small investments can pay big dividends down the road.

---

[46] The obvious errors may be of the "too tight" variety as well. This would be the mirror image of the loose-aggressive style; you use obvious "tight" errors to set up bluffing opportunities. In fact, in limit games this style may be the better way to go. But it's probably not in no limit.

Final Thoughts

There are many more ways besides just these to manipulate your opponents. Some players are very good at putting their opponents on tilt by saying annoying or obnoxious things. Others can influence their opponents' thought process by asking pointed questions during a long thinking period. Again, we don't aim to cover all the possibilities in this book. Just be on the lookout for new techniques. Many good no limit players use some very devious tricks indeed.

Tells

While this isn't a book on tells, we have a few brief ideas to share with you regarding tells and no limit.

It's OK to Pretend

Bridge (the card game) players feel that it's unethical to pretend to think about a decision. If you spend time "thinking" about an "automatic" play to mislead your opponents about what's in your hand, you may be penalized.

Poker isn't bridge. In poker, it's just fine to pretend to think to mislead your opponents. Indeed, if you spend time thinking only when your decision is genuinely tough, you'll be revealing information to your opponent. If you're thinking about calling a river bet, giving away your hand is no big deal. But earlier in the hand, allowing your opponents to "decode" your thoughts will hurt your results.

The solution is simple. Occasionally pretend to think when you have an automatic play. (Don't do it too often, though, or you'll unnecessarily slow the game down.)

Think

As we just said, you can avoid giving off "thinking tells" if you occasionally think when you have nothing to think about. So don't hesitate to think when you need to. No limit is a complex game that requires you to process myriad factors for each decision. And, unlike limit, a single error can be extremely costly. If you need to take some time to think about your play, feel free to do so. No limit etiquette permits you to spend some time to think about big decisions.

Don't agonize over every preflop hand, though. You'll look silly.

Throw Off Fake Tells

This ploy falls under the umbrella of manipulating your opponents. Most competent players will be familiar with the basic poker tells: "Weak means strong," "Bluffers stay stiff and quiet," "Nervous behavior often means a strong hand," and more.[47] If you choose your spots wisely, you can make some extra money in no limit by faking one of these well-known tells to induce a mistake.

In limit poker, faking tells doesn't have much value. That's because, as we said before, no single play will make or break you. To make real money faking tells you'd have to fake them repeatedly. Eventually, your opponents would notice that you were a habitual faker, and they might even use that information against you.

In no limit, however, one or two really big decisions will often dominate a session. If you fake a tell occasionally during big decisions only, your opponents may never pick up that you're doing it, and you may sometimes be able to swing the situation to your favor.

For instance, suppose you suspect that your opponent is familiar with the canonical tell "strong means weak." (This means that if you behave in a confident or aggressive way, you are likely compensating for a weak holding.) You have the nuts and want your opponent to call a big bet. If you behave in a strong way (without overdoing it) you might improve your chances to get called.

Be Aware

Most players (probably including you) give off some accurate tells. Some people start talking (or say certain things) in specific situations. Many players show a particular lack of interest in the

---

[47] The most popular repository of basic poker tells is *Caro's Book of Poker Tells* by Mike Caro.

hand sometimes when they plan to fold. You probably do something that could give your opponents information about your hand that they shouldn't have.

It's impossible to be human and to stamp out every possible behavior or mannerism that could betray information about your hand. It's not particularly fun to try either. So don't. Instead, simply be aware of your behaviors and try to figure out what your tells might be. Then reverse them sometimes.

If you start talking every time you want a call, then talk sometimes when you want a fold as well. If you take the chip off your cards when you plan to fold, then do it occasionally when you plan to raise. As long as you reverse your tells sometimes, the information your opponents might get from them will be so tainted that it's likely to be worthless.

Spotting and Using a Tell

As a devoted reader of this book, no doubt you will be throwing off fake tells and reversing your own tells in the future. You won't be the only one practicing such chicanery. If you spot a tell, or at least if you think you do, use it responsibly. It should represent merely one of many factors that you use to make your decisions.

Don't take so much stock in a tell that you drastically change your play. You might end up being duped horribly by a fake tell. (Or, somewhat less dramatically, you may simply misinterpret a tell or catch a tell that's only semi-reliable.)

In any event, it's generally fairly safe to use a tell to break the tie in a close decision. But the more significantly an accurate tell would change what you would normally do without the tell, the more sure you have to be that the tell is reliable.

Part Two

Concepts and Weapons

Quick Comment

This section is faster paced than the previous one. It consists of a series of brief ideas to improve your no limit play. Some of these ideas are restatements of concepts introduced earlier in the book. This repetition is intentional; important ideas are more likely to sink in if you read them more than once.

As we stated in the Introduction, don't ignore or skim this section simply because it comes second; it contains some of the most important information in the book.

Also, keep in mind that many of the ideas presented in "Part One: Fundamentals" reappear here. And as stated earlier, this repetition is intentional since we present particularly important ideas in both formats.

The concepts are also listed in no particular order. However, we did number them so that if anyone wants to discuss the concepts on our Two Plus Two Forums or elsewhere, they will be easy to refer to. With no further ado, here they are.

The Concepts

Concept No. 1: When in doubt, bet more. This book shows you how to size your bets correctly in many different situations. You'll never be able to calculate your bets exactly, though, so you'll have to err in one direction or the other. Try to err on the big side. This is best almost regardless of the circumstances.

If you are bluffing, that extra amount just might be what was necessary to get the job done. If you are betting an excellent hand, it is unlikely that you have significantly hurt your chances of getting a call (and you might even help your chances). Finally, if your hand is merely good, an overbet with more cards to come, even if it usually wins the pot right away (unless you are beaten), has merits. First, it makes your decision on the next round easier since you will usually either win immediately or know you are in trouble. Second, if your opponents know that you will sometimes overbet medium-strength hands on the flop, you can also overbet more often with big hands.

In general, you're better off betting a bit too much than you are betting a bit too little.

Concept No. 2: Don't give action to tight and trapping players. Know who not to play big pots against. Some no limit players will play a tight and conservative game no matter what. You could make huge raises ten hands in a row and show bluffs each time, and on the eleventh hand they still won't call you without a premium hand. They simply don't play for big money without the nuts (or close to it). Ever.

Identify these players and do not play big pots against them — not unless you have a very big hand yourself. We don't mean a bigger hand than you've shown recently. We don't mean a hand near the top of your range. We mean a big hand in an absolute sense — the nuts (or very close to it).

It's easy to overestimate your ability to put players on tilt. Sure, the tight player might grumble about your wild play. He may grumble a lot, but that doesn't mean he'll start loosening up.

Do not imagine that he's thinking, "Wow, that punk plays all sorts of trash. I think I'll play ace-jack against him for all my chips." He isn't. He's thinking, "I can't wait until I pick up aces so I can bust this maniac."

If you've been splashing around a lot, it can be easy to convince yourself that the nut-peddler has lowered his standards to "take a stand" against you. You may see

preflop or

on a

flop and think to yourself, "There's no way he'll expect my hand to be this good. I got him this time."

But when all the money goes in, he'll still have pocket aces or a set, just like he always does. Don't try to outthink these players. Steal all the small pots and refuse to play big pots against them, and you'll be fine.

Concept No. 3: Most of your actions should include an inherent randomness against perceptive opponents. Avoid making virtually any play 100 percent of the time against good players. Even if you think one play is clearly the best, every once in a while (5 or 10 percent of the time) switch it up. You might sacrifice a little bit of profit in this hand, but by doing so you make all your future hands more profitable.

Concept No. 4: Sometimes you should bluff to stop a bluff. It sounds strange, but when you are heads-up and out of position on the river, sometimes you should bluff to prevent your opponent from bluffing. Generally, you should do this when you have a hand that is just barely (or just barely not) worth a check and call, and you expect your opponent to bet often (sometimes as a bluff).

Say you're heads-up on the river. The pot is $100. You think that if you bet $30, your opponent will call you 50 percent of the time and have you beaten. He'll fold a hand that beats you 10 percent of the time, and the other 40 percent of the time he'll fold a hand that you already had beaten.

If you bet, your EV is $35.

$$\$35 = (0.50)(-\$30) + (0.10 + 0.40)(\$100)$$

If you check, and your opponent either always checks or bets only his good hands (so you can safely fold), your EV is $40.

$$\$40 = (0.50 + 0.10)(\$0) + (0.40)(\$100)$$

But if you check, and your opponent bets $50 with all the hands he'd call you with plus a few of his very worst hands (10 percent of his total hands), your EV is $30.

$$\$30 = (0.50 + 0.10 + 0.10)(\$0) + (0.30)(\$100)$$

Note that the EV equation above reflects the fact that you should fold to the $50 bet, as you're getting 3-to-1 pot odds, but you're 5-to-1 to win.

So if your opponent will never bluff, then in this scenario you shouldn't bluff either. But if your opponent will sometimes bluff, then you do better by bluffing first to stop him from bluffing.

This concept is a little tricky, so take some time to digest it. To summarize, you have a mediocre hand, and you are first to act. Your opponent could have anything from a good hand to a bad hand, and you expect him sometimes to bluff with his bad hands. Even though you will sometimes win in a showdown if you check, often you should bet instead to stop your opponent from bluffing.

Concept No. 5: When you first sit down, evaluate your game and decide whether your profit should come more from big pots or small pots. When you enter a game, your first priority should be to figure out where your money will come from. Who are the worst players, how big are their stacks, and what sort of mistakes do they make?

If the worst players have big stacks and play too loosely, then your profit should come from big pots. Buy in enough to have them covered (or at least enough so you can win a good chunk of their money) and concentrate on setting up the "big one" — the hand where you flop a great hand, make a couple big bets, and get paid off by one of your targets.

If the worst players play too weak-tight, try to win lots of small pots. You'll take advantage of their tendency to fold too much by making frequent small bets and raises and by avoiding big pots. You may even want to limit your buy-in. (Though don't buy in so little that the weak-tight players won't be scared of losing to you.)

After your first few hands, develop a plan, and tailor your plays to help you execute it.

Concept No. 6: It can be right to call with decent hands that have little chance of improving even if you plan to fold if there is a bet on the next round. Many players will call a flop or turn bet for one of two reasons: they are drawing, or they have a made hand and plan to call to showdown. But in no limit, there's another very important reason to call on the flop or turn: calling to see if your opponent will "fire another barrel."

As we've shown throughout the book, there are plenty of reasons to bet the flop, but check the turn if called (or to bet the turn, but check the river if called). You'll do it, and so will your opponents.

Because that check-bet-call/check-check pattern is so common, it can become correct to call a bet just to see if your opponent will bet again on the next round. If they do bet, you plan to fold. But if they check, you expect to win your share of the pots.

For instance, say you have

in the big blind. One player limps, the small blind calls, and you check. The flop comes

The small blind checks, you check, and the other player bets. The small blind folds, and you call.

Hopefully you aren't calling because you plan to call any and all bets to get to the showdown. Automatically calling big turn and river bets in this scenario is a recipe to go broke quickly. And obviously you aren't calling to draw to a better hand. You're calling to see if your opponent will bet again.

If you check the turn, and your opponent follows up with a regularly-sized bet, you'll typically fold. But often he won't bet; he'll check behind. Then you're in position either to make a river value bet or to check and now often call on the river (hoping to induce a bluff).[48]

There's another important reason to make these flop call/turn fold (or turn call/river fold) plays: They set up slowplays and induce bluffs on future hands. If your opponents notice that you'll call on a flop like K♦9♣9♠, but fold to a turn bet, then they may try to bluff more often in the future in similar situations when you hold A♦9♦. Making these "weak" calls helps to disguise your big hands.

Finally, against some players you should play this way even with some very good hands. For instance, say you are playing $5-$10 with $1,500 stacks. You have Q♣J♦ in the big blind. A tight and conservative, but observant player limps in from early position. Everyone folds to you, and you check.

The flop comes Q♥Q♠4♦. You check, and your opponent bets $20. You call. The turn is the 7♣. You check, and your opponent bets $60. You call. The river is the 2♥. You check, and your opponent bets $150. You should strongly consider folding.

What does your opponent put you on? You called twice on an extremely ragged board, so he can't possibly think you have a draw. He may think that you could have an unimproved pocket pair, but he wouldn't necessarily expect you to call $150 on the river with that hand. The fact is that it's obvious to him that you might well have trips, yet he's made a large bet anyway.

He's quite likely to have one of three hands: ace-queen, pocket fours, or pocket sevens. It's very unlikely that he'd bluff three times on this ragged board. And if he had a good, but easily

---

[48] Note that we say you'd "typically" fold. Against some habitual bluffers, you would call again on the turn and possibly the river as well.

beaten hand like pocket aces, he'd probably have checked the river.

It's a shame to call two bets only to find out that your hand is probably beaten, but you had to call those bets to find it out. Don't feel like you must go to showdown just because you called an earlier bet.

Concept No. 7: Don't telegraph that you have one pair unless you can profitably call big bets. One pair can be a very tricky hand to play in deep stack no limit. If you resolve to fold it every time someone makes a big bet, then you'll find your opponents bluffing you out of pot after pot. If you plan to go to showdown with it every time, you'll play lots of big pots against better hands, and you'll find yourself often getting stacked.

So you have to "play poker" with it, identifying situations when you should fold it to pressure and others when you should call with it. If you welcome a big bet with one pair because you expect that bet to be a bluff, then it's ok to telegraph your hand by playing in a way that makes it obvious what you hold. Doing so might help to induce a big bluff.

But if you plan to fold your pair to a big bet or raise, you should make an effort to disguise your hand to discourage a big bluff. You can choose either to make it look weaker or stronger than one pair.

If you make it look weaker, you may still induce a bluff, but a bluffing opponent probably won't bet nearly as much. They might feel that, whereas they need to bet a lot to get you off top pair, they need only a small amount to get you off your "weak" hand. You can then fold to a big bet, but call a small one.

If you make it look stronger, then obviously you decrease the overall chances of getting bluffed at all.

It's not always obvious how to disguise your hand in the way you want to, but it's definitely something you should think about whenever you have one pair and fear a big bluff.

Concept No. 8: Other things being equal, when you're in one of the blinds your preflop raises should generally be a little

larger than normal. There are three reasons why you should usually raise larger amounts from the blinds:[49]

1. Since you'll have to play the rest of the hand out of position, you don't mind winning the pot immediately as much as you might if you could play in position. Put another way, when you raise in position, often you'll want your opponents to call you. When you raise from the blinds, you'll want calls less often, and when you do want calls, you won't want them as strongly.

2. When your opponents call your raise with position and a weaker hand, often they'll be relying on implied odds to make their calls profitable. Big raises cut down your opponents' implied odds.

3. Out of position it is more important that you can narrow down your opponents' possible hands. You can't do that with a small raise.

Concept No. 9: Bets are usually more important than pots.
This concept is so fundamental, we almost didn't include it. But then we remembered how many of you might be reading this with an exclusively limit background: a background that (rightfully) places winning pots before saving bets. But deep stack no limit is a whole new ballgame.

When the stacks are deep, the money in the pot is typically far less than the money remaining to be bet. Your focus usually shouldn't be on protecting the money that's already in the pot. Your focus should be on winning (and making sure you don't lose) more and bigger bets from (or to) your opponents.

---

[49] The exception is pot-sweetener raises that you expect will be called by everyone who limped.

Concept No. 10: Sometimes you should go for a check-raise bluff on the river when a bluff bet would be unprofitable. You're playing $5-$10 with $1,000 stacks. You have

in the big blind. One player limps, the small blind completes, and you check. The flop comes

giving you a flush draw. The small blind checks, and you bet $30. The limper calls, and the small blind folds. The pot is $90.

The turn is the A♣. You check, and your opponent checks. The river is the 2♦.

Since your opponent called on the flop, she probably had at least something at that point. She may have flopped a pair, or she could have flopped one of several possible draws. It's also possible either that she flopped nothing or that she slowplayed two pair or a set.

When you checked the turn, and she checked behind when an ace came, that sequence supported the possibility that your opponent held either a draw or a modest pair.

The river obviously didn't complete any draws, so if she held a draw on the turn, her hand is now busted (though likely still better than yours). But it's also quite likely that she holds a modest pair (now two pair). Let's say, for the sake of argument, that she has a 60 percent chance of having a modest two pair, a 20 percent chance of having a busted draw, a 10 percent chance of having "nothing," and a 10 percent chance of having trip deuces or better.

If you bet, you think she'll call roughly 70 percent of the time (when she has a modest two pair and when she has trips or better). You also think she'll bluff-raise occasionally with her "nothing" hands and busted draws. Given these percentages, you decide that a bluff bet wouldn't be profitable.

So you check. She bets $50 (into the $90 pot). Now the scene has changed completely. The fact that she bet helps you narrow down her hand range considerably.

Specifically, she would be far more likely to check her modest two pair hands, hoping to win a showdown, rather than bet them. So the fact that she bet means that she probably either has trips or better (10 percent overall) or she has "nothing" (30 percent overall). If she's a frequent bluffer, she could easily have nothing now the majority of the time!

A small check-raise (say $70 more to $120) will leave you betting $120 to win $140. If you're right, and she's bluffing the majority of the time that she bets, then your check-raise bluff is profitable while a bet-out bluff wouldn't have been. In fact, even if our assumption that she'd rarely bet modest two pair hands is somewhat wrong, she'll often fold those hands anyway to the check-raise. It's counterintuitive, but true: Sometimes a check-raise bluff will be profitable when a bet bluff isn't.

Concept No. 11: A big bet is the most relevant and accurate information available. When reasonable players make extremely big bets on the turn or river, and you're trying to figure out what they have, all information from the past takes a backseat to the fact that they've made a big bet.

That is, don't think along the lines of, "There's no way he could have seven-four. After all, he raised preflop, and he's as tight a player as they come." Once the big bet comes out, if seven-four makes a big hand, then he very possibly could have seven-four. It doesn't matter that he'd "never" play that hand, because all the information you'd use to come to that conclusion is now less important than the fact that you're facing a big bet, and seven-four is the hand you're worried about.

This isn't to say that your opponent will always have the hand you fear when the big bets come out. Of course not — but even unlikely hands should merit serious consideration.

Concept No. 12: Be wary of overcallers. When someone makes a substantially-sized bet, and there's a call and an overcall, often the overcaller almost has to have a very strong hand (assuming the overcaller is a competent player).

For instance, say the flop is J♥J♦4♠. Someone bets two-thirds the pot, someone calls, and someone else overcalls. If there's some money behind, and the overcaller is a decent player, he almost has to have at least a jack.

Don't discount overcallers just because they didn't raise. Think about the board and how your opponents play, and you can often narrow down the overcaller to a few likely holdings.

Concept No. 13: If you're thinking about raising, but you wouldn't know how to respond to an all-in reraise, usually you should either move in yourself or raise a smaller amount (that would allow you to fold easily to a reraise). We offered an example of this concept in the "Sizing Your Raises" chapter. To recap that example, the blinds are $100-$200, and you have $2,400. You raise $700 with A♥J♠, and an opponent (who has you covered) moves in. Everyone folds back to you. You're getting $3,400-to-$1,700 (or 2-to-1) to call, but you suspect that you're approximately a 2-to-1 dog, so you don't know how to respond.

Your opponent could have some hands that you'd fold to (pocket aces or ace-king, for instance), and he could have some you'd call (pocket sevens). Since you're getting 2-to-1 to call, but you're roughly a 2-to-1 dog, you should be about indifferent between calling and folding. So calling is an ok play.

But if calling is ok, then raising all-in must have been better than raising just to $700. That's because it encourages hands like pocket sevens to fold (incorrectly) rather than to reraise you (which they can't do if you move in first). We repeat the concept and example here because it's an important one, particularly in tournament play.

An interesting exception arises, however, when you have two opponents with different stack sizes (one significantly shorter than yours). Say you have $7,500 with $100-$200 blinds and are dealt A♥J♠ on the button. The small blind has $15,000, and the big blind has $1,400. If there were no small blind, a raise that puts the big blind all-in is clearly the right play.

But in this situation there is a reason to raise a bit less. If the small blind makes a big reraise, you probably can't call. If you raise to $800 or so, that will get the small blind to fold his weak hands and almost certainly result in an all-in move from the big blind with about the same hands he would have called $1,400 with. So why not save some money when the small blind wakes up with a hand?

By the way, the examples we've used for the main concept — if you don't know how to handle a reraise, either bet a smaller amount or move in yourself — have all been preflop examples. And that's not without good reason; chances to apply this concept occur most frequently in tournaments before the flop. But this isn't just a preflop concept. It applies on every street.

Concept No. 14: Raise less often than you would in limit, because raising reopens the betting, and that's riskier to do in no limit. In limit hold 'em, the punishment for getting caught raising with a second-best hand that has outs is a reraise that costs you at most a fraction of a bet. In no limit, the punishment can be a reraise that forces you off your hand, costing you all of your pot equity (and possibly a chance to win future bets as well) or costing you expectation when you decide to call. Raising in no limit is riskier, so you must be more judicious with your raises.

Concept No. 15: Bet more than usual when your opponent likely has a hand that he thinks might be good. Earlier we discussed how to size your bets given the likely number of "outs" your opponent has to beat you. But this assumes that he knows he is drawing. The formula goes out the window if he thinks he may not have to improve to win. In that case, you can bet much more than what the "outs" formula would indicate and still expect to get called.

Concept No. 16: Occasionally overbet with moderate hands to disguise your overbets with excellent hands. When you have an excellent hand, and you suspect your opponent has a good, but second-best hand, you want to make big overbets to win the maximum from the situation. But if you make big overbets only in that situation, astute players will realize what you are doing. So disguise these big bets with overbets *early in the hand* with moderate hands like top pair.

For instance, say you have

on a

flop in a $100 pot. In situations you'd normally make a bet of $80 or so, occasionally make a big bet of $150 to $200. If everyone folds, you can show the hand. As long as you don't do it too often, these overbets won't cost you too much, and they will support you those times you make big bets with excellent hands.

In no limit, there is a multiplier effect on all actions that take place early in the hand. Since bets tend to be sized in proportion to the size of the pot, an extra $100 in flop action could translate into turn bets that are $200 bigger and river bets that are $600 bigger (or more). So your big hands could become far more profitable overall if you can successfully make $150 flop bets with them rather than $100 bets.

Concept No. 17: If your preflop raise is called behind you, check a lot of flops. Unlike limit hold 'em where you usually bet the flop after your raise is called, in no limit you should often check to those callers. That's true even if there is only one caller. You should usually check if you don't have very much, and you should check a lot of your good hands as well. What you do after you check is dependant on your hand and your opponents, and don't be afraid every once in a while to check-raise bluff.

Concept No. 18: Don't get trapped with a fourth street top pair in multiway checked pots. Say you happen to be in a multiway limped pot, and you limped along with nothing great. You missed the flop, and it got checked around. The turn gives you top pair. Unless you have an ace kicker, you should often fold if someone bets more than half the pot.

Specifically, you are playing $10-$20 with $2,000 stacks. You have Q♥J♥ in middle position. Two players limp, and you also limp. Two more players limp behind you, the small blind folds, and the big blind checks. The pot is $130, and there are six active players.

The flop comes 7♠5♠4♣. Everyone checks. The turn is the Q♦, giving you top pair. It's checked to the first limper who bets $100. You should often fold despite having caught top pair.

There's a decent chance you have the best hand, yet that isn't reason enough to call. You are calling $100 to win $230, but reverse implied odds will haunt you. If you are ahead, then likely $230 is all you'll win. But if you're behind, you'll probably have to face another bet and possibly a tough decision.

There are three ways the hand could go wrong:

1. You could be behind already (to the bettor or someone else).
2. You could get outdrawn on the river.
3. You could get bluffed out either now or on the river.

With so many opponents yet to speak, everything has to go right for you to win. It usually won't happen often enough for you to show a profit.

Concept No. 19: Don't call in protected pots without a very good hand. A protected pot is one where anyone who bets should reasonably expect at least one player to call. If many players are still in the pot, it's protected. If someone is all-in or close to it, the pot is protected. And if a player known to be very loose is still in the pot, it is protected.

If one of your thinking opponents bets in a protected pot, that bet carries a lot more weight that it would if the pot weren't protected. Namely, the bet is far less likely to be a bluff. If someone expects to be called, yet bets anyway, you should give them credit for a strong hand. Don't call such a bet without a very good hand yourself.

Concept No. 20: Sometimes you should limp behind limpers with pocket aces. In limit hold 'em, you'd never want to limp behind other limpers holding pocket aces, but in no limit (with deep stacks) it can sometimes be a good play. You'd do this if you have opponents yet to act who like to raise a series of limpers with weak hands.

"Deep limping" with aces balances your play and traps overzealous preflop stealers. You can reraise the raise (even better if someone calls the raise before you act), and you may even get more action than usual because no one will expect that you limped behind limpers with pocket aces.

Just make sure that if no one raises, and you see a flop in a limped pot, you don't trap yourself by losing a lot with an overpair against someone who outdrew you. If you think you'll have trouble getting away from aces if they are beaten, then you should raise to protect yourself. But if you can play them well after the flop in a limped pot, occasionally "deep limping" with aces can be a solid weapon.

Concept No. 21: Sometimes you can try for a deep check-raise with the nuts (or close to it). Similar to the deep limp with aces, you can sometimes try a deep check-raise with the nuts (or close to it) after the flop in a limped pot. For instance, you flop a small set in a multiway pot, and several players check to you. You can sometimes check as well, hoping someone behind you bets and gets a call or two.

Concept No. 22: Ace-king is a powerful "move-in" hand, and frequently moving in preflop is by far the best play with it. Ace-king has some peculiar properties that make it particularly well-suited to all-in moves preflop. Ace-king is the favorite against any non-pair hand, only a slight dog against all pairs through queens, a moderate dog against kings, and a huge dog only against aces. Thus, the only hand it truly "fears" is pocket aces, and the fact that you hold one ace cuts the chances an opponent has pocket aces roughly in half.

Also, ace-king doesn't play particularly well out of position after the flop with deep stacks, especially in multiway pots. In a multiway pot, it's almost a total loss if it misses the flop. And even if it spikes a pair, it can be a tricky hand to play correctly out of position against several players, any of whom could either have a solid draw or have flopped big.

Because ace-king is unlikely to be in big trouble preflop, but often has limited value after the flop, it's often best by far to make a big preflop reraise with it.

For instance, say you are playing $2-$5 with $400 stacks. An early position player makes it $25, and three players call. You have in the big blind. There's $105 in the pot, and you have $395 left. Your best play is likely to move in, all $395.

You are betting $395 to win $105, so you are laying slightly less than 4-to-1. Most of the time, you'll pick up the pot. The original raiser, especially if she's somewhat aggressive, is a significant underdog to have pocket aces or kings. Each successive caller is even more unlikely to have either of those hands.

Sometimes you'll get called by a hand weaker than aces or kings, but that isn't so bad. You'll be, at worst, a small underdog, and the $100 in the pot will more than compensate you for taking slightly the worst of it for your stack. You'll win the $100 in the pot (or your share of it if you get called) often enough to risk running into aces or kings.

Against observant, thinking opponents, however, you might have a problem. The problem is that ace-king is usually the *only* hand that's correct to move in with in that situation. With a weaker hand, you'd either be in trouble too often to risk your whole stack or you'd make more by waiting to see the flop (e.g., with a pocket pair). And with pocket aces or kings, you usually do better by making a smaller raise, one that's more likely to get called.

So if you make the big all-in play, some opponents will be smart enough to realize that you almost certainly have ace-king. Such players may call your big raise with small pocket pairs, knowing that, despite the big bet, they must be the favorite.

If you think you may be against players who would reason that way, you might also want to make the big all-in play occasionally with a big pocket pair. The optimal balancing strategy is complicated, but a simple approximation such as moving in half the time with pocket kings should suffice. (Pocket aces would work also, but moving in frequently with them might "waste" your aces too often, sacrificing more in value than you gain in balancing for the ace-king raises. At least with kings your move in prevents the not unlikely scenario that an ace beats you.)

Concept No. 23: It's ok to limp in, planning to fold to a raise. It's sometimes ok even when you think a raise is likely. For those familiar with limit hold 'em, you may abhor the idea of limping in, then folding to a raise. That's because in limit, it's virtually never a good play.

In no limit, however, it can be just fine to limp, planning to fold to a decent-sized raise. Typically you'd do this with a weak preflop hand that has a chance to win a big pot, but that won't get the right implied odds to play for a bigger preflop bet.

For instance, you're playing $1-$2 with a $500 stack. A loose, bad player limps with $300 limps in middle position. You have 8♣7♠ one off the button and limp. The button, a decent player with a $60 stack, raises to $10. The bad player folds. You should fold as well.

Even though your hand was weak, with position against a bad player it certainly expected to show a profit. So it was worth a limp. But when the good player made it $8 more with the button and only $50 more behind, and the bad player folded, you no longer had the implied odds to play. Both your limp and your fold were correct.

Indeed, sometimes you should limp-fold even when a raise is likely. Say your loose opponent is bad enough that you expect your $2 limp to turn into an average of $6 if you get to see the flop unraised. You'd be right to limp even if you expected someone to raise 60 percent of the time. You'd lose your $2 investment 60 percent of the time, but you'd win $4 forty percent, so your total expectation would be $0.40.

$$\$0.40 = (0.60)(-\$2) + (0.40)(\$4)$$

Deep stack no limit against bad players can afford some extremely high implied odds situations. Don't make hasty decisions without weighing both the pros and the cons. Sometimes it's worth risking a likely small loss to take a shot at an unlikely big win.

There's another important reason to limp-fold sometimes that you shouldn't overlook. Limping and folding to a raise can play a role in your overall strategy as well. If some aggressive opponents see you do it several times in a row, that history could entice them to raise your next limp with a weak hand.

If you suspect a player may be looking to take a shot at your limps, you can limp with a strong hand and get some extra action you might not otherwise get.

Concept No. 24: If you have a hand that you'd limp with in a passive game, consider making a small raise (two to three times the big blind) in an aggressive game instead of limping. Setting the bet size by putting in the first bet or raise is often a useful play. If you'd like to see the flop cheaply in an aggressive game, sometimes you should, somewhat counter intuitively, make a small raise. Doing so encourages your opponents to call your small raise rather than make a big raise themselves.

Specifically, say you'd like to limp in with the A♥9♥ in a $5-$10 game. But you fear that one of your opponents will make a raise to $60 or more if you limp. Consider raising to $30 to set the bet size. Usually your opponents will just call, and you'll get to see the flop for $30.

The downside to the play is that you lose more if you are forced to fold to a reraise. But reraising is a risky play on their part, and most of the time they won't do it without a strong hand. If you balance correctly, sometimes raising small with big hands, people won't take shots at your small raises very often.

Concept No. 25: The button is the true bread and butter position in no limit. In many games you can play an extremely wide range of hands from the button, even for a raise. The deeper the stacks are, the less important preflop hand strength becomes and the more important position becomes. Throw in some weak opponents, and preflop hand strength becomes even less important, while position retains its value.

As a result, you can often profitably limp on the button with an extremely wide range of holdings. Say you are playing $2-$5 with $1,000 stacks. A player who bets and calls after the flop too often with weak holdings (sometimes including pairs smaller than top pair) limps in. You can call $5 with most of your hands: any pocket pair, probably any two suited cards, any big offsuit cards, any ace, and any offsuit connector down to at least five-four. Indeed, if the lowly seven-deuce is a bad call in this situation, it is only very marginally so.

Why can you play so many hands? Implied odds. You are betting $5 for a chance to win $1,000. Any hand, no matter how bad, can flop two pair or trips. Against someone who habitually loses too much with one pair, two pair and trips gain a lot of value. Feel free to play for the longshots if you'll be adequately compensated when you get there.

But when we say the button, we mean the button, not one or two off the button. When you're licking your chops in a good game, it's easy to say, "Well I'm close enough to the button," and throw in your $5 with total trash. Reserve total trash for the button only.

You can still play loosely on the button even when someone has already raised. As a rule of thumb, if the raise represents only a few percent of the stacks (e.g., no more than maybe $50 with $1,000 stacks) you can call with many hands: all pocket pairs, any suited ace or king, two big suited cards, suited connectors (even with a gap), offsuit connectors and, if you're careful not to lose too much if you flop top pair and appear to be beaten, two big offsuit cards like K♥T♠.

In good games, don't waste your button! Many hands will be profitable from that position. Don't throw away all your $5 hands waiting for a $25 hand.

Concept No. 26: When there's an ante, your opening raises should be larger than if there were no ante. But they shouldn't be larger in the same proportion that the size of the initial pot increases; they should be somewhat smaller than that. Say you are playing eight-handed with $100-$200 blinds. Everyone folds to you one off the button, and you raise to $600 as a semi-bluff. You are *laying* 2-to-1 (betting $600 to win $300). You are *offering* the button 3-to-2 pot odds (calling $600 to win $900) and *offering* the big blind 9-to-4 odds (calling $400 to win $900).

Now say you are playing the same eight-handed game with $100-$200 blinds, but also with a $25 ante. The initial pot is $500 instead of $300. Everyone folds to you one off the button, and you raise to $1,000 (again, twice the size of the pot). You still lay 2-to-1 (betting $1,000 to win $500) and offer the button pot odds of 3-to-2 (calling $1,000 to win $1,500). But you are offering the big blind significantly worse pot odds, 13-to-8, than before.

Since the big blind is the player most likely to call you, if your $600 bet is correctly-sized without an ante, then your $1,000 bet with an ante must be oversized. That is, you don't need to risk as much to get the big blind to fold.

All other things being equal, the correct raise size should offer the big blind roughly similar (though not necessarily identical) pot odds both with and without the ante. If you were to raise to $800 instead of $1,000, you would be offering the big blind 13-to-6, which is relatively close to the 9-to-4 from before.

With an $800 raise, you (and the button) now get more favorable odds: You are laying only 8-to-5, and the button is getting 13-to-8. Thus, if a $600 raise was "correct" without an ante, then an $800 raise is close to correct with one.

Notice that the size of the raise increased by adding the extra ante money, $200, to the bet size. A quick rule of thumb that works in unraised pots: when adjusting your bet size for extra money, simply add the extra amount to the bet you would normally make. If there's an extra $300 in the pot, add $300 to your bet.

Notice also that when you raise this amount your semi-bluffing opportunities will be more profitable.

Concept No. 27: When semi-bluffing before the flop, usually do it those times you have one of the *best* hands that you'd otherwise fold. However, when you are in the blinds in an unraised pot, you should usually do it when you have one of your *worst* hands. You are playing $5-$10 with $1,000 stacks. A middle position player opens for $30, and two players call. You are on the button. Your preflop strategy dictates that you usually reraise with your excellent hands (e.g., A♥K♣), call with many good hands (e.g., 3♥3♦ or 9♠8♠), and fold the rest. But you occasionally also reraise as a bluff.

When choosing the times you occasionally bluff, try to pick those times you have a fairly good hand, but one that you'd usually fold. For instance, say you'd generally call with K♠T♠, but fold K♠7♠. The latter hand is a good one to semi-bluff with. It's much better than a truly terrible hand like J♣3♦: If you happen to get action on your reraise, you're more likely to get lucky and actually make a good hand with K♠7♠.

Since you'd normally fold both K♠7♠ and J♣3♦, you typically lose nothing by waiting for the better hand to make your randomizing bluffs.

If you are in the blind in an unraised pot, however, things change significantly. For instance, say you are playing $5-$10 with $1,000 stacks. Five players limp to you in the big blind. Your preflop strategy dictates that you raise your excellent hands and check everything else.[50] (These raises in multiway pots are usually large in size, and your opponents will infrequently flat-call them.) But, again, you occasionally also raise as a bluff.

Now you are better off waiting for your truly terrible hands, J♣3♦ for example, than choosing a hand like K♠7♠. If you check, you get to see the flop for free, and with K♠7♠ you might well flop a strong hand or draw. You could also flop something with J♣3♦, but it's much less likely.

Since your raises in this situation are usually either reraised or (more often) folded to, you are wasting the value of decent hands when you make this balancing play. You should revert back to better hands for small reraises or when your opponents are more likely to just call.[51]

---

[50] You also should make small pot-sweetener raises with some non-excellent hands.

[51] For those who have read *Tournament Poker for Advanced Players* by David Sklansky, this concept is expressed on p. 113 as "Don't turn good hands into seven-deuce." It's okay, however, to turn

Concept No. 28: With strong hands, generally raise either a small, pot-building amount or a large, hand-defining amount. Don't raise an amount in the middle that both tells your opponent that you have a good hand and offers them the right implied odds to try to beat you. Say you are playing a $5-$10 game with an $800 stack. Two good players limp in, and you have K♥K♣ on the button. Raising to $30 or so would constitute a pot-building raise. The raise is small enough that your opponents will all tend to call it. You would raise that amount with a wide array of hands, hoping to build a pot with your positional advantage. So making the raise doesn't give away the fact that you have an extraordinary hand.

Raising to $120 would constitute a hand-defining raise. You'd usually make a raise that big only with good hands, and your opponents will know it. You're unlikely to get action unless one of your opponents also happens to have an excellent hand.

The size of the raise gives away the strength of your hand, but your opponents can't do anything with the information. Even if you always committed the rest of your stack on the flop, you don't offer them enough compensation to call. It's $110 more to them, but they can win only $845. Getting less than 8-to-1 maximum implied odds, they can't call profitably with a pocket pair, let alone any unpaired hand.

If you raised to $80, however, you'd have the worst of both worlds. It's an uncommonly large size, so your opponents would expect an excellent hand. But now the implied odds math works out very differently: It's $70 more to them, and they can still potentially win $845. Now they may have implied odds of slightly more than 12-to-1, allowing them to call profitably with some hands.

Usually you should just make the modest, pot-building raise and hope to win a big one. Occasionally you might want to make the large hand-defining raise. But don't make a raise in the middle.

---

jack-trey into seven-deuce.

Don't tell your opponents what you have and then turn around and give them the right price to try to beat it.

Concept No. 29: It's ok to make small raises (2-3x the big blind) to build the pot or to set up future plays. For some reason, making small raises has acquired a stigma in the no limit community. By small raises, we mean the minimum raise (to twice the big blind) or slightly larger.

While there are right and wrong times to make any play, there's nothing inherently bad about making a small raise. As we discussed in the "Sizing Your Raises" section, there are a number of factors you should consider when you decide what size raise you want to make. The nature of your hand, the way your opponents play, the stack sizes, your past plays, your image, and more go into each decision.

Many preflop raises are primarily intended to elevate the stakes of the game. These raises are based on preflop hand strength or intended as a semi-bluff. You make them only because you prefer the postflop bets to be larger than they would be in an unraised pot. (If you double the size of the preflop pot, you'll more or less double the size of the postflop bets as well.)

Often you should make this sort of raise with "brave" hands — pocket pairs, suited connectors, and suited aces — hands that play well after the flop. The goal is to turn your $5-$10 game (or whatever limit you're playing) into a $10-$20 or $15-$30 game *for this hand only.*

Say you have A♥T♥ in early position in a nine-handed $5-$10 game. You've been playing mostly with an $800 stack, but you just won a big pot and now you have $1,500 in front of you. With the smaller, $800 stack, you would usually limp in with the hand. But now that your stack has doubled, you might be better off min-raising: making it $20 to go.

Mostly your opponents will react to your min-raise exactly as if you had limped. They're not likely to fold their "limping" hands just because you raised. Some players may get scared and just call with a hand they would have raised if you had limped. Others might raise a little more often to challenge your "weak" raise. But usually you'll simply have doubled the stakes. If that's what you want, don't let any know-it-all tell you that it's a bad play. Min-raise away.

Concept No. 30: Implied odds are a critically important decision-making tool, but always be aware that different opponents offer different odds. Overly aggressive (especially on the turn and river) players and overly loose, wild players tend to offer larger implied odds than "typical" players. Weak-tight players and tough players tend to offer lower odds. Whenever you estimate your implied odds, think about what *this* player is likely to lose, not what an average player or, worse, what an ideal opponent would lose. (But also be aware that those who offer smaller implied odds also offer you more bluffing opportunities.)

Concept No. 31: Your implied odds with any draw will be better the less obvious the draw is. For instance, your implied odds will be far better with

on a

board than with

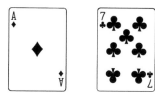

on a

board (as long as there was a bet on the flop). In the former case, your draw is a backdoor flush draw, and many opponents wouldn't expect you to have it. In the latter, you have the ace-high one-card draw on a monotone flop. Everyone is worried about your hand.

The same reasoning applies to straight draws. Gutshots, especially those made with small cards, are a lot stealthier (and therefore offer higher implied odds) than obvious draws made with big cards (e.g., 7♣4♣ on a K♣8♣5♦Q♥6♠ board).

Concept No. 32: It can be correct to fold a hand before the river that has a better than 50 percent chance of being the best hand. Being out of position against a good player with deep stacks is a huge disadvantage in no limit. The disadvantage is so large that, even with the pot laying you odds, you might have to fold a hand that is mathematically favored. (That is, if you were all-in, turned the hands over, and ran out the board, you'd win more than half the time.)

This happens most often when your hand is vulnerable, and your opponent is likely to know it (or at least suspect it). For instance, you have

on a

board. You bet the flop and your opponent, a tough, but aggressive player, raises.

Your options are to call or reraise, and neither is good. If you call, your opponent will push you around on the turn and river, mixing value bets with strong hands and bluffs on scary cards. If you call these down, you'll get value bet to death. If you fold to them, you'll get pushed off the best hand too often, changing you from the "theoretical" favorite to the actual underdog.

If you reraise instead, you more or less stop the bluffs, but you lay too much, winning small pots when you have the best hand, but going for big losses those times you are beaten.

This isn't to say that no merely decent hand is worth playing deep-stacked and out of position, but it is to say that simply having the "best" hand on average isn't reason enough to continue in a no limit pot. There's a lot more to consider.

Concept No. 33: Be willing to risk free cards to manage the pot size and induce bluffs. The free card is the bane of every *limit* hold 'em player. You check, and your opponent checks also. At the moment your opponent checks, you know you have him beaten, and you usually hate yourself for giving him a free shot to outdraw you.

In no limit, however, against good players with deep stacks you have to be prepared to give quite a few free cards when you have just one pair. Out of position, you may have to check the turn a lot. And in position, you should frequently check behind either on the flop or the turn.

There are three major reasons checking pairs is often best:

1. It keeps the pot small. One pair is generally not a "big pot" hand. If you end up in a big pot without improving, more often than not you'll be taking the worst of it.

2. When you're in position, you will sometimes be taking a free card rather than giving one. That is, if you had bet, you would have been check-raised, but now you get to see another card. This aspect is particularly valuable when your opponent has two pair, and you improve to a better hand on the river.

3. It induces bluffs. The structure of no limit forces you usually to show weakness when you are weak. If you frequently use a three-barrel bluff (bluff bets on the flop, turn, and river) you'll bluff away your whole bankroll. To win you have to check most of your weak hands at some point, usually fairly early in the hand. Good players know this fact full well, and they meet your weak checks with bets that are often bluffs. To counter these bluffs, you have to check some fairly good hands also, planning to call with them. Good one pair hands are perfect hands to induce bluffs with.

For instance, say you have the A♠A♣ with $500 stacks in a $2-$5 game. Your opponent limps in early position, and you raise to $20 in middle position. Everyone folds to the limper who calls. The flop comes Q♥7♥3♠. Your opponent checks.

Usually you should bet, but sometimes you should check. And sometimes if you bet and your opponent calls and checks the turn, you should check then. Checking will induce turn bluffs from aggressive players (which, depending on the exact situation, you will either call or raise). Also, occasionally checking will balance your play so your opponents won't be so quick to steal from you when you check behind with A♦J♦ instead (or at least they'll be wrong to steal from you automatically when you check).

No limit, played against good opponents, should not be a bet-and-raise-fest. You have to play a little cautiously, and the price you pay for that caution is giving some free cards away.

Concept No. 34: If you have a close decision between semi-bluffing with a draw or checking it, be more inclined to check if you could make your draw with an overcard to the board. The higher implied odds your draw has, the less attractive semi-bluffing with it becomes. If you can make your draw with an overcard to the board, you tend to have higher implied odds because someone could make top pair or two pair at the same time you make your draw.

For instance, compare A♣6♣ on a K♣9♠5♣ board to A♣6♣ on a 9♠5♣3♣ board. On the former board, no club can come that is also an overcard (since you hold the A♣). On the latter, however, the K♣, Q♣, J♣, and T♣ all make your flush and also put an overcard on board. If your opponent happens to make top pair (or a big two pair) at the same time you make your flush, he's likely to lose more money than he otherwise would. Therefore, the latter offers better implied odds, and you should be inclined to check it.

Concept No. 35: Unusually small bets tend to be made either with a big hand (a suck-in bet) or with a bluff (a cheap stab at the pot). With one pair, your opponents will usually either check or bet a larger amount. As with any hand-reading principle, this one is opponent-dependent. You will run across players of all types, and some of them will make small bets with one pair. But, generally speaking, unusually small bets are either really big or really small hands. (Note: By "unusually" small we mean unusual for a given player. If a player always makes small bets, then obviously a small bet isn't very telling.)

Concept No. 36: Be more apt to slowplay very good hands that aren't quite the nuts than the nuts itself. When you slowplay, you check or call rather than bet or raise with a very good hand in order to deceive your opponents about the strength of your hand and to allow them an extra card to make a good, but second-best hand.

Slowplaying usually requires a strong hand, but you should be more inclined to play fast if you have the absolute nuts (or sometimes the top full house). For instance, if the flop comes J♥6♣6♦, it may make sense to slowplay K♥6♥, but not J♣J♠. Slowplaying K♥6♥ does three good things for you:

1. It may induce an opponent to try a bluff on a future betting round.

2. It may allow someone who would have folded to make a pair on the next card and give you action.

3. It may limit your losses somewhat if one of your opponents happens to have ace-six or a full house. You'll lose a lot no matter what if you are second-best, but if you slowplay for a round or two, you may be able to just call a river bet, saving at least some of your stack; whereas, if you get the money in early, you're almost certain to get stacked.

With J♣J♠, however, item no. 3 works against you. Now instead of saving money against a full house, you have the full house. Slowplaying for a round or two might prevent you from stacking someone who was slowplaying a six (particularly if they have a weak kicker).

Likewise, you should be more inclined to slowplay A♠2♠ on a 5♣4♠3♣ flop than 7♠6♠ on the same flop. With A♠2♠, you're happy to give a free card to someone who might make a big pair on the turn or river. But with 7♠6♠, you don't want to lose your action if someone made a smaller straight against you or is drawing to something like a pair and a straight draw, e.g., 6♦4♦.

Concept No. 37: Bets on the turn should, on average, constitute a smaller percentage of the pot size than flop bets. Say you took an average of the size of every flop bet you ever made, and you found that it was (picking an arbitrary number) about 75 percent of the flop pot size. The equivalent average for your turn bets should be significantly less than 75 percent of the turn pot size.

In general, turn bets should be smaller fractions of the pot than flop bets.

Primarily, the pot odds and implied odds you offer your opponents determine your bet sizes. You should bet enough with your good hands so that you don't offer your opponents enough odds to call profitably with their most likely hands and draws.

With two cards and two betting rounds to come, the flop is a good round for drawing hands. Made hands have to bet a relatively large amount to make it unprofitable for draws to call.

With only one card and betting round to come, however, the turn is a good round for made hands. Bets don't need to be nearly as large in relation to the size of the pot to make draws unprofitable. Thus, flop bets should generally be larger as a percentage of the pot than turn bets. (Remember, though, that this principle does not hold if you think your opponent believes that he is likely to have the best hand. In that case your turn bets can be big.)

Concept No. 38: Be more apt to semi-bluff when your draw isn't to the nuts than when it is. When you contemplate a semi-bluff with a drawing hand, you have to compare the expectation of betting against the expectation of checking.

Say you estimate that the expectation of semi-bluffing is some positive amount $X. Knowing that bluffing has a positive expectation shouldn't necessarily convince you to bet, however, as checking could still be better for one of a couple reasons:

1. You might hit your draw and win money from someone who would have folded to your bluff. For instance, if you have 9♠8♠ on a 7♣6♠2♦ board, and a T♥ comes on the turn, you could win money from someone with T♦6♦ who would have folded to your flop bet.

2. Checking, especially when last to act, could allow you to see an extra card those times your opponent already has a strong hand and would have raised you out had you bluffed. If you check and catch your draw, sometimes you'll win your opponent's entire stack. Thus, occasionally checking will turn a loss (of your bluff bet) into a huge win (of the pot plus your opponent's stack).

Both of these effects are stronger (favoring checking) when you have a nut draw than when you don't. And if you not only don't have a nut draw, but you could even be drawing dead because the board is paired, the effect is stronger still.

For instance, compare 9♠8♠ on a 7♣6♠2♦ board to 9♠8♠ on a T♣T♦7♦ board. On the former board, all eight of your outs give you the nuts. On the latter, you have no outs to the nuts, and you could already be drawing dead to a full house (or to an expensive second-best against jack-ten or ten-six).

The former hand offers you a decent chance of making your draw, catching someone with a second-best hand, and doubling up. The latter hand offers very little chance to double up: If you were to get all-in against someone, chances are better than not that you'd be on the losing end.

With limited implied odds, semi-bluffing becomes more attractive on the paired board. Your best hope is that no one flopped much and that you can pick up the pot immediately. With the nut draw, however, you have higher hopes: stacking someone.

(Note: The above concept applies only when the stacks are big. With small stacks the reverse concept is usually true.)

Concept No. 39: You must adapt your play to different-sized bets. If you will call a twice-pot bet as often as you call a half-

pot bet, you're in trouble. Some no limit players tend to pay too little attention to the size of their opponents' bets. In $5-$10, for instance, they may call a preflop raise to $40 with roughly the same number of hands as a raise to $60. Or they may react approximately the same way with the same hands to a half-pot flop bet as they would to a one-and-a-half pot bet.

Different bet sizes offer significantly different pot and implied odds. To treat a half-pot bet offering 3-to-1 the same way you treat a one-and-a-half pot bet offering 5-to-3 will leave you making lots of mistakes.

Don't think in binary, bet or no bet, terms. Every bet size is different and offers different odds. Always think about these odds while you play.

Concept No. 40: Certain flops require certain-sized bets. No matter what hand you hold, your flop bets, on average, should be smaller on flops like

than they are on flops like

From a mathematical perspective, the "correct" bet sizes in no limit derive primarily from the implied odds they offer. You should size your bets so that your opponents don't get enough odds to call profitably. But you usually shouldn't make your bets so large that it's obvious that they aren't getting the right odds to call. These considerations set upper and lower boundaries on the amount you should bet.

When the flop is something like A♥K♦K♠, your opponents, if behind, will tend to have little chance to catch up. And even if they do "catch up," they'll often discover that they were drawing dead. Since your opponents would need far greater implied odds than normal to justify calling, your bets should be relatively small on such flops. (Small bets offer larger implied odds.)

Your bets should be small no matter what you hold. If you flopped a full house, you'll want to bet a small amount, hoping a loose opponent will be tempted to call with an ace or a gutshot. If you flopped trip kings, you'll want to bet a small amount both to entice a call from a weaker hand and to limit your losses when you are behind. If you flopped a weaker hand, you'll still want to bet a small amount. You do this both to mimic a strong hand and to limit your losses if you are called or raised by a better hand.

On the other hand, your bets should tend to be larger than average on flops like J♥9♣7♥. On such a flop, many draws are possible, and your opponents won't need as high implied odds to consider calling. This is especially true because tough opponents will bet sometimes when an obvious draw comes in, whether they held the draw or not. These bluffs add "outs" to drawing hands and allow them to call larger bets profitably.

Made hands should bet larger amounts to compensate for the attractive implied odds. Doing so will deny many draws profitable calls and will make the hand easier to play on later streets. Bluffs should also bet larger amounts, again to mimic the made hands and to discourage calls with weak draws.

Don't be rigid when you size your flop bets. Some players think things like, "I always bet the pot on the flop. Anything smaller just looks weak." Don't think that way. Among other factors, the texture of the flop dictates how big or small your flop bets should be. Be flexible and adjust your bets and bluffs accordingly.

Concept No. 41: When holding a mediocre hand, usually bet enough (but not more) so that a raise means you are almost

certainly beaten. Good no limit play means maneuvering your opponents into situations where their decisions will be tough. When you make things hard for them, they'll make mistakes, and the more mistakes they make, the more money you make.

Likewise, you should seek to avoid tough decisions as much as possible. Often you should risk a little bit extra now to avoid a tough decision later in the hand (or even sometimes on future hands).

One difficult situation often arises when you get raised holding a mediocre hand. Is your opponent raising with a weaker hand or as a bluff because your bet appeared weak? Or are they raising because they have a better hand?

By betting too little, you may unwittingly stumble into a difficult decision that could have been avoided for just a somewhat larger bet.

For instance, say you are playing against an aggressive opponent who takes particular pride in "making reads and acting on them." That is, he's the sort that's likely to decide you are bluffing and raise with nothing.

You are playing $10-$20 with $2,000 stacks. Everyone folds to you on the button, and you raise to $60 with

The big blind (the player previously described) calls. The flop comes

Your opponent checks.

You likely have the best hand, but you also could easily be beaten. Since you don't have much of a draw if behind, your goal should be to clarify whether your hand is best or not as early as possible.

Since the board is fairly ragged, you don't have to worry much about your opponent drawing against you. That fact would suggest that you should tend to make a smallish bet. If you have the best hand, a small bet should be enough to ensure that your opponent doesn't have the implied odds to draw against you. And if you are behind, a small bet saves you some money.

The problem is that a small bet may embolden your opponent to check-raise bluff when a somewhat larger bet might get an immediate fold. Since you won't call a check-raise, you should bet an amount that discourages a bluff. That way, if you get check-raised, you'll know that you were drawing thin, and you can fold without giving anything away.

The pot contains $130. Your mediocre hand and the ragged board both suggest that you should against many types of players make a small bet, perhaps $60. But instead you should make a bigger bet, perhaps $100 or $120, to discourage a check-raise bluff. If you can make your opponent's actions significantly more "pure" by making a larger bet, usually you should do it.

(Note: Similar reasoning sometimes justifies a bit larger bet to make sure your opponent's calls aren't with weak hands that might throw you off.)

Concept No. 42: If you check the river, most players will bet only with very good hands and with bluffs. They'll check down hands that could win a showdown, but that are unlikely to be called by worse hands. It's heads-up on the end. You check, and your opponent makes a significant bet. Significant, in this case, depends somewhat on your opponent, but it's at least about one-third of the pot. If there's money behind, so your opponent risks a check-raise, that fact makes the bet even more "significant."

Usually your opponent will have either a bluff or a very good hand; it's quite unlikely that he'll have a modest hand (one with a decent, but not great, chance to win a showdown). He'll bet good hands for value, hoping you'll call. He'll bluff hopeless hands, hoping you'll fold. With medium-strength hands, he'll usually check, hoping that his hand is best.

In light of this tendency, you should evaluate your hand on the river somewhat differently than you normally might. In particular, a lot of your medium-strength hands become only "bluff-catchers." For example, if you have top pair with a good kicker, but your opponent bets on the end, there's very little chance he holds specifically top pair with a weaker kicker. He probably would have checked that hand down.

Instead, he has either a hand that has top pair solidly beaten (and he's betting, hoping you'll call with it), or he has a total bust. So it doesn't really matter that you have top pair with a good kicker. You could have top pair with a bad kicker. Or you could have second pair or even third pair. In this circumstance, faced with a sizable bet on the end, all those hands have similar value: they beat a bluff, and that's about it.

Concept No. 43: Big bets mean big hands. Don't make or call big river bets often with weak hands. Big bets are for big hands. Don't forget that. Obviously, the occasional big bluff should be part of your strategy, but it should be occasional. If you get too excited about making big bluffs, or if you convince yourself that your opponents are always trying to execute big bluffs on you, you'll get into big trouble.

Concept No. 44: The bigger a bet your opponent makes, the more of your hands that turn into bluff catchers. This idea is related to the two previous concepts. Top pair may be a "good" hand, but when your opponents make big river bets, they are representing something better. They either have what they represent or they are bluffing; hence, your top pair turns into a bluff catcher because it beats only the bluffs.

In some situations, a big bet can turn even the second nuts into a bluff catcher. For instance, say you are heads-up with position and have K♣T♣. It's the turn, and the board is

9♣7♣3♣Q♠. You checked behind on the flop, your opponent bet the turn, you made a substantial raise, and your opponent called. The pot is $1,500, and you each have $4,000 left. The river is the J♣, putting a four flush on board. Your opponent moves in.

Your second nut flush is now a bluff catcher. Your opponent's bet represents a single card: the A♣. If you call, it can't reasonably be with the hope that your opponent has the Q♣. Why would he bet so much with that hand? He would likely either check it or bet a much smaller amount, hoping that you would be tempted to call with a weaker hand.

The big all-in bet unmistakably says, "I have it... do you believe me?" The strength of your own hand should have little effect on whether you call.

Concept No. 45: Know when a hand (even a good one) has more value as a bluff catcher. When you're first to act on the river, it can be tempting to check your "bad" hands and to bet your "good" ones. Resist the urge to automatically bet all your good hands; your hand might have more value as a bluff catcher.

There are two ways to make money with a good hand: bet it and get called by a weaker hand, and check it and get your opponent to bet a weaker hand. Often you should bet your good hands as instinct would tell you to, but sometimes you shouldn't.

When you value bet, you can profit only when your opponent calls. If he folds, you win nothing. In some situations, it will be relatively unlikely that your opponent has a hand that you can beat *and that he'll call with*. So even though you probably have the best hand, value betting won't make you much money.

Instead, you might want to check, hoping to induce a bluff.[52] Indeed, if you think that it's unlikely that your opponent has a

---

[52] In limit hold 'em this play is only occasionally right. That's because, getting high pot odds, he will often call your river bet with weak hands. Plus if you do induce a bluff, it's a small fraction of the pot. Contrast this with no limit. It's exactly the opposite.

hand good enough to call, he might think the same of you. He might be itching to try a bluff. Think before you bet.

There's another reason to turn some of your good hands into bluff catchers. If your opponents see you check and call with "obviously" good hands, they will be less likely both to bluff and to value bet against you in the future. They know that you check the river with good hands, so they'll tend to check behind you more often. By doing so, your opponents will be less able to use their positional advantage against you, and you'll make more money on your out of position hands.

Concept No. 46: Don't just think about what you put your opponents on. Think about what they put you on also. Think on the second level. What might your opponents put you on? Say, based on your play so far, your lone opponent is likely to think you have a weak hand. Perhaps you checked behind on the turn rather than betting a decent made hand. He makes a big bet on the river. What might he have?

If he thinks you're weak and makes a big bet, the bet is more likely than usual to be a bluff. Most players won't bet big with good hands into likely weak ones. They'll bet small, hoping you'll be enticed by pot odds to make a loose call.

On the other hand, if you have played strongly, and your opponent bets big on the end, look out! Think about what your opponent might put you on, and you'll turn some tough decisions into easy ones.

Concept No. 47: If it's clear your opponent has a hand at least worth a call, but he raises instead, it's almost never a bluff. Say you have on the button in a nine-handed $5-$10 game with $4,000 stacks. A player in early position raises to $30. You call, and the big blind calls. The flop comes

The big blind checks, and the preflop raiser bets $100 into the $95 pot. You raise to $400. The big blind folds, and the flop bettor calls. The pot is $895.

The turn is the 2♣. The big blind checks, and you bet $500. He calls. You think his most likely hand is ace-king or pocket aces. The pot is $1,895.

The river is the T♦. The big blind checks. You think he's likely to call a smallish river bet with ace-king or aces, but that he'd fold those hands to an all-in bet. You decide to bet $600, offering your opponent about 4-to-1 and leaving you with $2,470 behind.

Instead of calling, however, your opponent moves in: $2,470 more in what is now a $5,565 pot. You still have the two pair you flopped, and you're getting 2.25-to-1 to call.

Don't take it. There is little chance your opponent has a busted draw, which means he probably has been calling with a made hand. If that hand isn't at least king-ten, he probably would simply have called your river bet.

Concept No. 48: Often make small bluffs (about one-third the size of the pot) in multiway pots when it appears no one has hit the flop. Balance those bluffs by also sometimes making small bets with good hands. Say you have J♠9♠ two off the button in a $5-$10 game. Everyone has at least $800. One player limps, and you limp. The button limps, the small blind folds, and the big blind checks. Four players see the flop in a $45 pot.

It comes K♥6♠3♣. The first two players check. Consider betting $15 or $20 as a bluff. You're hoping that everyone missed this ragged flop. And, of course, you're also hoping that no one will see this as an "obvious" bluffing situation and challenge you with a resteal raise.

Your bet size should be somewhat smaller than your "typical" bet because this is really an either/or bluff. Either your opponents hit the flop, or they didn't. If they missed, they'll likely fold to your small bet. If they hit, they'd likely call or raise even a pot-sized bet. On more coordinated boards, your opponents could flop marginal draws or other "in between" hands that would call a small bet, but fold to a large one. On this flop, such hands are unlikely, so a small bet should be enough to get the job done. (Any flop with a pair is also a good candidate.)

But if you make small flop bets only with bluffs, your opponents will begin to catch on and raise your small bets to resteal. So also make small bets sometimes with good hands.

Concept No. 49: If someone makes a big bet on the flop into multiple players, typically he will have a good, but not great, hand. This idea should be obvious if you think about it, but it's still a powerful hand-reading trick. A big bet says three things, "I'm not particularly afraid of one or two players calling," "I don't want all of you to call," and "I wouldn't mind winning the pot right now." Only a player with a good, but not great, hand would say all of these things.

Obviously, a player with a great hand wouldn't want most or all the field to fold. They would generally choose either to check or to make a small bet to encourage action.

And bluffing with a big bet into multiple players is dangerous. When several people see the flop, it's quite likely someone caught something decent. A pot-sized (or bigger) bluff offers you even money (or less) on your play. For the bluff to be profitable, all your opponents have to fold a large percentage of the time. Most players intuitively realize that the bluff won't work often enough to be profitable.

So bluffers will likely choose a smaller bet size. That way they don't have to succeed as often to make money. That leaves hands in the middle — good, but not great hands — like top pair. Usually a big bet into multiple players will come from just this sort of hand.

Concept No. 50: If someone bets the flop and gets two or more calls, anyone who bets a significant amount on the turn should get respect. Betting the turn after the flop was bet and called in several places is a powerful move. Anyone who makes such a bet is essentially saying, "I'm prepared to play a large pot, and the threat of someone with a deep stack calling or raising doesn't worry me."

Usually in these situations, someone willing to make such a bet either has a strong hand or is (rarely) bluffing. With a mediocre hand in a big pot, most players would check, hoping that their hand is strong enough to win the pot in a showdown.

In this scenario, however, a bluff is relatively unlikely. After a bet and two or more calls on the flop, the pot is protected. Enough players still remain that no one player could expect a bluff to succeed often enough to be profitable. So the bet is likely to be what it represents, a strong hand.

For example, say you are playing $10-$20 with $4,000 stacks and have

in middle position. Someone limps in early position, and you also limp. Two players limp behind you, the small blind calls, and the big blind checks. Six players are active in a $120 pot.

The flop comes

Everyone checks to you, and you bet $100. The two players behind you call, as does the big blind. There are still four active players, and the pot is $520.

The turn is the 5♥. The big blind checks, and you also check. The next player bets $400. The other two players fold. You too should frequently fold.

You are out of position with a hand that's unlikely to improve against someone who has made a very powerful turn bet. The pot is now $920 and you're getting $920-to-$400 odds to call, but if you call, you and your opponent will both have over $3,400 left. If you call now, your opponent may well bet $1,000 or more on the river. Despite having top pair, you likely can't continue profitably.

Concept No. 51: In tournaments, other things being relatively equal, prefer small river value bets that will often be called to large river value bets that will seldom be called. Put another way, if a smaller bet has a bit less EV, it is still right to make it in most tournament situations. Earlier we discussed how to size river value bets correctly by maximizing your expectation. We came to the somewhat surprising conclusion that you should sometimes make a huge bet with the nuts, even though you won't often be called. In those situations, it's better to win huge every once in a while than win a small amount more frequently.

In tournaments, however, you should usually prefer smaller, more consistent wins to big, infrequent ones. That's because chips change value in tournaments: $100,000 in tournament chips is worth less than twice as much as $50,000.

In tournaments, since mere survival has value, each chip you win is worth less than the last. That is, your last remaining chip is worth a lot more to you than your second-to-last. Similarly, you'd usually prefer winning $1,000 eighty percent of the time to $8,500 ten percent of the time. For more on this concept, see pages 44-45 of *Tournament Poker for Advanced Players* by David Sklansky.

Concept No. 52: The play of check-raising to knock people out, an important tool in limit, should rarely be used in no limit. In limit, since the bet size is restricted, sometimes you have to check vulnerable hands and hope someone else bets. Then you can raise and use the double-sized bet to protect your hand.

In no limit, this tactic is no longer worth it. The cost versus gain is too high.

Concept No. 53: In heads-up pots, whether you are first or second to act is more likely to affect your decision in no limit than it is in limit. In limit, you usually should make the same play whether you are first to act or second. For instance, if you would bet a hand, first to act, you'd bet the same hand second to act after a check. And if you'd check, first to act, you'd often check behind, second to act, as well.

Sure, there are plenty of exceptions. Sometimes you'll go for a check-raise first when you would bet second. Sometimes you'll bet a hand on the river first to act that you would check down second to act, *et cetera*. But the rule in limit is that you usually should make the same play whether you are first or second to act.

That rule doesn't hold in no limit. There are far more situations in no limit than in limit where you'd do something different in first position than in second.

For instance, with a draw to the nuts, often you'll bet when first to act, but check if checked to. First to act, you bet because, by doing so, you set the bet size and give your opponent a chance to fold. Checking will often elicit a bet anyway, and sometimes you won't like the size your opponent chooses.

When you are second to act, there's no longer any value to setting the bet size. A bet would still give your opponent a chance to fold, but with a draw to the nuts, you may not want him to do that. You may prefer trying for a huge win when you make the nuts and your opponent makes a second-best hand.

In limit, you'd generally bet a good nut draw from either position.

Concept No. 54: Checking to induce a bluff is a significantly stronger play in no limit than it is in limit. In limit, you should sometimes check behind on the turn with a decent hand to induce a bluff. This can be an important play in limit, but it is far more important in no limit. In deep stack no limit, reasons to check behind become more compelling.

For instance, say you have K♥T♥ on a K♠7♣6♦8♦ board against an aggressive opponent. He checks. There are two major reasons why you might want to check behind:

1. **Checking behind avoids a check-raise.** If you bet, you will often get check-raised. Since you have a gutshot straight draw with your top pair, both calling and folding to the check-raise cost you considerably. If you call, you do so as a likely significant underdog, but if you fold, you miss out on your chance to draw.

2. **Checking behind might induce a bluff from a busted draw.** If your opponent has a hand like Q♠J♠ and misses on the river, he may view your turn check as a sign of weakness and launch a bluff. You can then call it and make an extra bet.

Generally speaking, getting check-raised is worse for you in no limit than in limit, as it puts you to a tough decision in many more situations. In limit, often your hand will be plenty good enough to call down after a turn check-raise. In no limit, however, you'll often wish very much that you hadn't bet.

Inducing a bluff is also much more valuable in no limit than in limit, as the bluff bet will usually constitute a significantly larger percentage of the pot. In limit, the river bet will often be only one-sixth to one-tenth (or less even) of the pot. In no limit, though, it will typically be at least one-fourth, and it may be more than that. So successfully inducing a bluff is worth more in no limit than in limit.

Since checking behind is better in no limit, you should try the play with a wider array of hands than you would in limit. For instance, in limit you would virtually always bet a hand like A♥Q♥ on a Q♦T♦7♥8♥ board. While you may get check-raised, you have so many outs if behind that you can happily call.

In no limit, however, your opponent could check-raise so much that you may not be able to call. Or even if you can call, it may cost you so much to do so that your great draw loses almost all of its profitability.

Furthermore, your check might induce a bluff from one of the many possible busted draws on the river. And if you happen to catch a heart on the river and make the nuts, you might win your opponent's whole stack in a flurry of river betting.

The upsides of betting a hand like A♥Q♥ on a Q♦T♦7♥8♥ (protecting your hand) are less important in no limit, and the downsides (getting check-raised, stopping a bluff, and losing your chance to make the nuts and win a big pot) are more prominent.

> **With made hands on the turn, many auto-bets in limit turn into checks in no limit. Make sure you evaluate carefully before you act.**

Concept No. 55: Unlike limit, limping first in on the button is frequently correct. Every limit player is familiar with blind stealing — open-raising from late position with a weak hand in an attempt to win the blinds. In limit, it's almost never right to limp in when you could attempt a blind steal instead, since the blind money represents a large percentage of your total expected win. For instance, in a game with $10 and $20 blinds ($20-$40 limit), you might expect a big final pot in the vicinity of $300, and typical pots will be smaller. The $30 in blind money is 10 percent of the final pot and almost 20 percent of your total win.

Since blind stealing works fairly often, you should almost never forgo a chance to try it if you plan to play. After all, even if you get lucky and win a nice pot, you'll probably win only four or five times the blinds.

In no limit, however, the equation changes a lot. Blind stealing becomes far less important in general. Because instead of being 10 percent of a big pot, blinds can be 1 percent or less of the big ones. It doesn't make much sense to forgo a shot to win the blinds when the best you can hope for is a win of ten times more. But when you can hope to win 50 or 100 times more, you might not want to steal the blinds at all.

Indeed, raising in deep stack no limit is rarely intended to steal the blinds.[53] It's used to get value for good hands, manipulate the pot size, semi-bluff, and for other reasons. If everyone folds to you on the button, and you raise, usually you're doing it because you want to build a pot while you have position, not because you want to win the paltry blind money.[54]

Depending on the stack sizes and the skill levels of your opponents, you can often get the most from some hands if you limp with them. An example would be a hand like

with a stack of $600 in a $5-$10 game. If you raise to $30, you cut your potential implied odds roughly by a factor of three (from $600-to-$10 to $600-to-$30). By bloating the pot preflop, you

---

[53] Tournament no limit is different. With short stacks and antes, blind stealing becomes the single most important reason to raise.

[54] Of course, the blind money isn't entirely insignificant. If it were, players could simply play extremely tightly and reraise only with top notch hands. Though the blind money is a small portion of the total money at stake, it's still required to keep the action going.

ensure that most of the money will go in on the flop and turn betting rounds. But this particular hand flops a lot of draws and plays very well on the turn and river betting rounds. You don't want big flop bets; you want big river bets instead.

Say the flop comes

and your opponent has a king. You don't want the flop bet to be $60 (the size of the raised pot); you want it to be $20 or less. If the flop bet is $60, most of the rest of the money will go in on the turn, and you won't be able to continue drawing. You want most of the betting to happen after you make a straight, not before.

Raising preflop in this scenario isn't an aggressive blind steal; it needlessly stunts your implied odds and limits your potential win when you catch a hand.[55]

If the stacks were much deeper, however, then you might again want to raise. Once there is enough money behind that a preflop raise doesn't force the turn betting to be prohibitively large compared to the money remaining for the river, then you might again want to raise to take advantage of your positional advantage.

Don't think that raising preflop in late or even last position when all have folded is an automatic play as it is in limit. It's not. Don't raise out of habit. Sometimes limping will get you the money.

Concept No. 56: Pot odds (as opposed to implied odds) matter a lot less in deep stack no limit than in limit. In limit, calculating your pot odds is often a useful tool. Compare the odds of making

---

[55] If, however, limps like this entice raises from the blinds that you don't want to call, an alternative might be to raise the minimum.

your hand to the odds that the pot is laying, and decide whether to call. If there's $360 in the pot, usually you should call a $30 turn bet with a gutshot draw. If there's only $210, you should fold. On a 10.5-to-1 draw, you call getting 12-to-1 and fold getting 7-to-1.

You'll also hear some more questionable invocations of pot odds. You might hear arguments such as this one: "You are getting 5-to-1 pot odds on your preflop call. With king-jack, you are a 5-to-1 dog only against two hands: pocket aces and kings. Since you'll almost always be better than 5-to-1 to win the hand, you should call."

In limit, arguments like this one are questionable because so much betting happens after the flop. You're not really risking $10 to win $50. You're risking $10 on this round, but possibly an additional $60 to $100 for the whole hand. Your preflop pot odds of 5-to-1 with king-jack can easily turn into effective odds of 3-to-2 or worse for the entire hand. You may not lose 83 percent of the time, but you can easily lose 60 percent, and that turns the hand into a loser.

In deep stack no limit, however, such an argument isn't just questionable. It's absurd. If you are playing $1-$2 with $200 stacks, what does it matter if there's $6 in the pot versus $10 when you think about making your $2 call? You aren't calling to win that $4 extra; you're calling for the $200 behind it. Obviously you'd prefer that the extra $4 be in the pot, but both $6 and $10 are small compared to the $200 you'll be risking.

An extra $4 teaser is no excuse to play a bad hand or put yourself into a tough situation. When the preflop betting is very small compared to the stack sizes, it doesn't really matter much whether you're getting 2-to-1 or 4-to-1 or even 8-to-1 pot odds. What matters is how well you (and your holding) will perform throughout the entire hand. Don't make preflop decisions based on pot odds when there is a lot of money behind, and don't allow others to persuade you using pot odds-based arguments. (Again, this advice is for deep stacks. With short stacks, pot odds matter a lot more.)

Concept No. 57: Don't be fooled by players who have giant amounts of cash in front of them. Many players who buy-in for extremely large amounts are trying to misrepresent their intentions in the following ways:

- They want you to think that you have higher implied odds than you actually do. They are trying to induce loose calls from their opponents with drawing hands by implying that they are prepared to lose a large amount when they are outdrawn.

- They want you to think that they are bored with small bets and pots. They want you to take their preflop and flop bets and calls less seriously than you would a normally-stacked player because the amount seems "insignificant" compared to their enormous stack.

In reality, many players who make outsized buy-ins (e.g., $4,000 in a $2-$5 game or $15,000 in a $10-$20 game) play exactly as they would if they had bought in for a "normal" amount. They are not really trying to win (or expecting to win) any more money than you are. They just try to mislead their opponents with the extra cash on the table. Don't be tricked.

Concept No. 58: Any strategy relatively close to a game theoretical strategy is at least almost as good as the optimal strategy, and sometimes it's better. Throughout this book, we've stressed the importance of balancing your play — making randomizing plays to avoid betraying the nature of your hand. Game theory, a branch of mathematics, can tell you the optimal way to vary your strategy so that it absolutely cannot be exploited, no matter how cagey your opponent may be.

Unfortunately, figuring out the game theoretical strategy for any given decision can be very complex. Many seemingly simple situations get too involved to figure out even away from the table when you have hours and hours to think about it. At the table, solving these problems is usually impossible.

But you don't have to solve the problems to use game theory to your advantage. A strategy that is relatively close to the game theoretically optimal one is, for all intents and purposes, good enough.

For instance, if game theory says you should bet all your good hands and bluff an additional 22 percent of the time, you'll do just fine if you bluff 15 percent or 30 percent instead. You'll even be fine at 10 percent. Just avoid 2 percent or 80 percent, and you'll be a tough nut for anyone to crack.

And remember that if you play better than your opponents, you rarely need to think along these lines at all. Rather, think about what your opponents put you on, and what they think you put them on. If you plan to make a play that will give away your hand, choose a different play occasionally and make the same play sometimes with a different holding. If you do this consistently as you play, you'll usually do even better than the game theoretical strategy.

Concept No. 59: Don't help your opponents play correctly. Your job is to try to avoid difficult decisions for yourself, but to impose them on your opponents. Whenever you confront an opponent with a tough situation, you've created an opportunity for him to make a mistake. (Either that, or you've put him in a lose-lose situation which is even better.) You make money when your opponents make mistakes, so always try to entice them to make a mistake (given your hand).

One obvious way that people make things easy on their opponents is they make bets on the river that no better hands will fold to and no worse hands will call.

Less obvious situations occur when there are more cards to come. In a nutshell, the idea is to avoid betting so much that a hand you want to call won't, or betting so little that a hand you don't want to call will.

Another error is to size a bet that would tend to entice a raise that is about the size you don't want to face. Hopefully the text has shown you many examples of where we are coming from here.

Concept No. 60: If someone bets into several players, and you have a hand that is somewhat likely to be best, but unlikely to improve, you often have to fold. For example, in a $5-$10 game with $2,000 stacks, three players limp, the small blind completes, and you check the big blind with Q♣8♠. ($50 in the pot.) The flop is 8♥7♥3♣. The small blind bets $50. You typically should fold.

Your problem is that there are still several players yet to act, and you have a modest hand, unlikely to improve. If you raise now, you're risking too many chips compared to the chance that you are already beaten. Even if you aren't already beaten, you may be called by a strong draw and drawn out on or pushed off your hand later.

If you just call, then you allow any of the three players behind you either to raise (forcing you to fold) or call cheaply, leaving you out of position with a weak holding for the later betting rounds.

Furthermore, the small blind's holding is likely to be fairly strong. Betting out on a coordinated board is a strong move, likely either to be a strong pair or better or a good draw. So even if you call the flop, and all three players behind you fold, you still aren't out of the woods. The small blind may make a big bet on the turn that will be difficult to respond correctly to.

So even though there's a fair chance you have the best hand, the small pot, deep stacks, and multiple opponents with position on you force a fold.

The same analysis would generally hold even if your hand were as strong as A♥T♠ on an A♣J♣9♥ flop. The coordinated board and the many available threats force you to fold.

For many of our readers, this practical concept may be the single most valuable one in the book. So we can't think of a better one to end on.

Conclusion

In the early chapter "Skills for Success" we enumerated five important no limit skills:

1. Manipulating the pot size
2. Adjusting correctly to stack sizes
3. Winning the battle of mistakes
4. Reading hands
5. Manipulating opponents into playing badly

Hopefully now you understand the role that each of these skills plays in a winning no limit strategy. Good play involves mastering these skills and applying them at the appropriate times. What's right with $50 left might be very wrong with $500 left. You might usually do one thing, but your knowledge that your opponent makes a certain kind of mistake will lead you to do another.

These skills are difficult to master. Your best bet is to go play for a while and try to consider everything we've discussed. Then come back to this book and look for ideas you missed the first time around. If you repeat that process multiple times — gaining experience then revisiting this book — you'll soon find yourself thinking automatically about the right things while you play. While that isn't guaranteed to make you a big winner, it will give you a significant advantage over many of your opponents.

Finally, you can use the concepts in this book to help you evaluate other advice you get. Did your friend just give you a new tip? If he didn't tell you about what stack sizes the advice applies to, he may not have thought it through fully. If he has you consistently building big pots with weak hands, you should likewise question the advice.

The beauty of no limit hold 'em is that it's a complex enough game that many of your opponents will never "get it." They'll always make mistakes, and you'll always be there to profit from them. The thorough theoretical knowledge you learned from this book will forever help you keep your losses small and your wins big.

The Sklansky-
Chubukov Rankings

These tables provide the Sklansky-Chubukov numbers for every possible hand. (Find an explanation for these values in the section "When to (and When Not to) Use the Sklansky-Chubukov Rankings," beginning on p.222.)

Table I lists them in order of descending S-C number, and Tables IIa and IIb list them sorted by hand (pocket pairs and unpaired hands respectively). Table III provides S-C numbers along with some auxiliary information: how many hands can call a move-in profitably, how many must fold, and what percentage of the time the hand will win when called. This information can be used to determine whether a hand is robust or vulnerable: the more hands that can call and the higher the win percentage when called, the more robust a hand is and vice versa.

Table I: The Sklansky -Chubukov Ratings (in Descending Order) of all 169 Hands	
Hand	**Sklansky-Chubukov Number**
AA	Inf
KK	953.9955
AKs	554.51
QQ	478.0082
AKo	331.8872
JJ	319.2136
AQs	274.2112
TT	239.821
AQo	192.6702

99	191.4139
AJs	183.2213
88	159.2969
ATs	138.9131
AJo	136.3105
77	134.8477
66	115.3485
ATo	106.2647
A9s	104.1248
55	98.62987
A8s	89.86565
KQs	86.6277
44	81.97959
A9o	81.7162
A7s	79.17591
KJs	72.62126

A5s	72.29213	Q8s	26.71855
A8o	70.95651	K6o	26.67571
A6s	70.74453	J9s	25.71252
A4s	66.65053	K5o	24.68097
33	65.44082	Q9o	23.41954
KTs	62.80556	JTo	23.08525
A7o	62.74775	K4o	22.84502
A3s	62.27532	Q7s	22.68524
KQo	58.77166	T9s	22.49148
A2s	58.14199	Q6s	21.78516
A5o	56.54209	K3o	21.39222
A6o	56.15123	J8s	20.63624
A4o	51.93949	Q5s	20.32186
KJo	50.83879	K2o	19.99942
QJs	49.51544	Q8o	19.81933
A3o	48.44544	Q4s	18.91635
22	48.05412	J9o	17.79938
K9s	47.81236	Q3s	17.73401
A2o	45.17234	T8s	17.46571
KTo	44.94654	J7s	17.19452
QTs	43.80946	Q7o	17.07734
K8s	39.91081	Q2s	16.64103
K7s	37.33065	Q6o	16.29514
JTs	36.10652	98s	15.29334
K9o	35.75415	Q5o	15.03498
K6s	34.89	J8o	14.86776
QJo	32.81682	T9o	14.83221
Q9s	32.51971	J6s	14.7186
K5s	32.30333	T7s	14.19943
K8o	30.47389	J5s	14.04842
K4s	30.16328	Q4o	13.66217
QTo	29.7164	J4s	12.95547
K7o	28.54118	J7o	12.66604
K3s	28.38181	Q3o	12.50323
K2s	26.73084	97s	12.25142

T8o	12.15698		T3o	5.480421
J3s	12.04034		76o	5.439126
T6s	11.92109		92s	5.359298
Q2o	11.30295		74s	5.109201
J2s	11.13873		54s	4.850294
87s	11.11055		T2o	4.832254
J6o	10.78068		85o	4.81223
98o	10.27126		64s	4.769221
T7o	10.20476		83s	4.463809
96s	10.09767		94o	4.345783
J5o	9.987293		75o	4.269797
T5s	9.9469		82s	4.129509
T4s	9.260066		73s	4.018033
86s	8.994746		93o	4.000304
J4o	8.906238		65o	3.972305
T6o	8.571955		53s	3.851054
97o	8.570963		63s	3.777173
T3s	8.415718		84o	3.737896
76s	8.318417		92o	3.585219
95s	8.261043		43s	3.402163
J3o	7.914721		74o	3.366747
T2s	7.538836		72s	3.221509
87o	7.505732		54o	3.221293
85s	7.239171		64o	3.170312
96o	7.074151		52s	3.114999
T5o	6.920957		62s	3.054809
J2o	6.885765		83o	2.994827
75s	6.59416		42s	2.796223
94s	6.583641		82o	2.795837
T4o	6.248512		73o	2.731972
65s	6.207388		53o	2.640274
86o	6.099835		63o	2.591343
93s	6.058991		32s	2.567461
84s	5.692773		43o	2.366073
95o	5.650827		72o	2.243309

52o	2.181602
62o	2.139745
42o	1.976146
32o	1.825374

Table IIa:
The Sklansky-Chubukov
Rankings for Pocket Pairs

Hand	Sklansky-Chubukov Number
AA	Inf
KK	953.9955
QQ	478.0082
JJ	319.2136
TT	239.821
99	191.4139
88	159.2969
77	134.8477
66	115.3485
55	98.62987
44	81.97959
33	65.44082
22	48.05412

Table IIb:
The Sklansky-
Chubukov Rankings
for Unpaired Hands

Hand	Sklansky-Chubukov Number
AKs	554.50999
AKo	331.88718
AQs	274.21119
AQo	192.67022
AJs	183.22134
AJo	136.31047
ATs	138.91308
ATo	106.26471
A9s	104.12479
A9o	81.716196
A8s	89.865649
A8o	70.956513
A7s	79.175905
A7o	62.747746
A6s	70.744533
A6o	56.15123
A5s	72.292128
A5o	56.542087
A4s	66.650529
A4o	51.93949
A3s	62.275315
A3o	48.445438
A2s	58.141993
A2o	45.172344
KQs	86.627695
KQo	58.771664
KJs	72.621257
KJo	50.838788
KTs	62.805558
KTo	44.946538
K9s	47.812358
K9o	35.754152
K8s	39.91081
K8o	30.473887
K7s	37.330652
K7o	28.541184
K6s	34.890001
K6o	26.675708
K5s	32.303331
K5o	24.680974
K4s	30.163283
K4o	22.845021
K3s	28.381805
K3o	21.392219
K2s	26.730843
K2o	19.999415
QJs	49.51544
QJo	32.816822
QTs	43.809464
QTo	29.716401
Q9s	32.519706
Q9o	23.419539
Q8s	26.718552
Q8o	19.819326
Q7s	22.685237
Q7o	17.077335
Q6s	21.785164
Q6o	16.295139
Q5s	20.32186
Q5o	15.034981
Q4s	18.916352
Q4o	13.662167
Q3s	17.734011

Q3o	12.503232	T2s	7.538836
Q2s	16.641032	T2o	4.832254
Q2o	11.30295	98s	15.293343
JTs	36.106522	98o	10.271257
JTo	23.085252	97s	12.251417
J9s	25.712524	97o	8.570963
J9o	17.79938	96s	10.097673
J8s	20.636243	96o	7.074151
J8o	14.867761	95s	8.261043
J7s	17.194521	95o	5.650827
J7o	12.666038	94s	6.583641
J6s	14.718597	94o	4.345783
J6o	10.780675	93s	6.058991
J5s	14.048416	93o	4.000304
J5o	9.987293	92s	5.359298
J4s	12.955471	92o	3.585219
J4o	8.906238	87s	11.110552
J3s	12.040344	87o	7.505732
J3o	7.914721	86s	8.994746
J2s	11.138727	86o	6.099835
J2o	6.885765	85s	7.239171
T9s	22.491482	85o	4.81223
T9o	14.832206	84s	5.692773
T8s	17.465705	84o	3.737896
T8o	12.156984	83s	4.463809
T7s	14.199426	83o	2.994827
T7o	10.204755	82s	4.129509
T6s	11.921088	82o	2.795837
T6o	8.571955	76s	8.318417
T5s	9.9469	76o	5.439126
T5o	6.920957	75s	6.59416
T4s	9.260066	75o	4.269797
T4o	6.248512	74s	5.109201
T3s	8.415718	74o	3.366747
T3o	5.480421	73s	4.018033

73o	2.731972
72s	3.221509
72o	2.243309
65s	6.207388
65o	3.972305
64s	4.769221
64o	3.170312
63s	3.777173
63o	2.591343
62s	3.054809
62o	2.139745
54s	4.850294
54o	3.221293
53s	3.851054
53o	2.640274
52s	3.114999
52o	2.181602
43s	3.402163
43o	2.366073
42s	2.796223
42o	1.976146
32s	2.567461
32o	1.825374

Table III: The Sklansky-Chubukov Numbers with Extra Information

Hand	Number of hands (out of 1225) that can call	Number of hands (out of 1225) that should fold	Win percentage when called	Sklansky-Chubukov Number
AA	1	1224	0.5	Inf
KK	7	1218	0.226177	953.9955
AKs	75	1150	0.457697	554.51
QQ	13	1212	0.207007	478.0082
AKo	79	1146	0.433132	331.8872
JJ	19	1206	0.201104	319.2136
AQs	84	1141	0.424149	274.2112
TT	25	1200	0.198947	239.821
AQo	93	1132	0.403144	192.6702
99	31	1194	0.197142	191.4139
AJs	96	1129	0.401528	183.2213
88	41	1184	0.226651	159.2969
ATs	108	1117	0.385544	138.9131
AJo	105	1120	0.379834	136.3105
77	61	1164	0.285621	134.8477
66	103	1122	0.355264	115.3485
ATo	117	1108	0.362908	106.2647
A9s	123	1102	0.367405	104.1248
55	153	1072	0.389493	98.62987
A8s	135	1090	0.361211	89.86565
KQs	256	969	0.4295	86.6277
44	275	950	0.431528	81.97959
A9o	129	1096	0.339884	81.7162
A7s	147	1078	0.356565	79.17591
KJs	265	960	0.419399	72.62126
A5s	171	1054	0.367031	72.29213
A8o	141	1084	0.332789	70.95651
A6s	159	1066	0.352858	70.74453
A4s	183	1042	0.366358	66.65053

33	455	770	0.454268	65.44082
KTs	277	948	0.411707	62.80556
A7o	155	1070	0.329722	62.74775
A3s	195	1030	0.366882	62.27532
KQo	265	960	0.400723	58.77166
A2s	207	1018	0.366815	58.14199
A5o	181	1044	0.340952	56.54209
A6o	171	1054	0.329477	56.15123
A4o	202	1023	0.347061	51.93949
KJo	277	948	0.391325	50.83879
QJs	418	807	0.432774	49.51544
A3o	220	1005	0.351305	48.44544
22	709	516	0.467553	48.05412
K9s	295	930	0.392879	47.81236
A2o	240	985	0.355839	45.17234
KTo	289	936	0.383383	44.94654
QTs	430	795	0.426952	43.80946
K8s	307	918	0.378141	39.91081
K7s	325	900	0.378587	37.33065
JTs	570	655	0.440073	36.10652
K9o	301	924	0.361114	35.75415
K6s	337	888	0.37594	34.89
QJo	433	792	0.404082	32.81682
Q9s	457	768	0.40988	32.51971
K5s	349	876	0.371933	32.30333
K8o	324	901	0.351582	30.47389
K4s	367	858	0.371425	30.16328
QTo	445	780	0.398126	29.7164
K7o	344	881	0.353033	28.54118
K3s	379	846	0.369025	28.38181
K2s	394	831	0.367883	26.73084
Q8s	469	756	0.394731	26.71855
K6o	368	857	0.355714	26.67571
J9s	597	628	0.422213	25.71252
K5o	408	817	0.363569	24.68097

Q9o	459	766	0.377014	23.41954
JTo	585	640	0.411106	23.08525
K4o	458	767	0.373684	22.84502
Q7s	484	741	0.381931	22.68524
T9s	721	504	0.434081	22.49148
Q6s	499	726	0.382276	21.78516
K3o	508	717	0.383123	21.39222
J8s	609	616	0.406766	20.63624
Q5s	514	711	0.379236	20.32186
K2o	555	670	0.389958	19.99942
Q8o	479	746	0.363775	19.81933
Q4s	547	678	0.381543	18.91635
J9o	597	628	0.38947	17.79938
Q3s	568	657	0.380696	17.73401
T8s	733	492	0.418399	17.46571
J7s	624	601	0.393116	17.19452
Q7o	520	705	0.359844	17.07734
Q2s	591	634	0.380441	16.64103
Q6o	566	659	0.37011	16.29514
98s	841	384	0.427277	15.29334
Q5o	652	573	0.386607	15.03498
J8o	613	612	0.374112	14.86776
T9o	721	504	0.40219	14.83221
J6s	648	577	0.383218	14.7186
T7s	748	477	0.404171	14.19943
J5s	686	539	0.388455	14.04842
Q4o	748	477	0.400659	13.66217
J4s	751	474	0.396332	12.95547
J7o	657	568	0.368521	12.66604
Q3o	857	368	0.415272	12.50323
97s	853	372	0.412903	12.25142
T8o	733	492	0.385474	12.15698
J3s	792	433	0.39877	12.04034
T6s	767	458	0.391983	11.92109
Q2o	975	250	0.428097	11.30295

J2s	891	334	0.412488	11.13873
87s	945	280	0.422015	11.11055
J6o	755	470	0.378294	10.78068
98o	841	384	0.394874	10.27126
T7o	765	460	0.374878	10.20476
96s	878	347	0.401527	10.09767
J5o	855	370	0.395413	9.987293
T5s	886	339	0.401897	9.9469
T4s	949	276	0.408748	9.260066
86s	969	256	0.410324	8.994746
J4o	947	278	0.405076	8.906238
T6o	877	348	0.385581	8.571955
97o	873	352	0.384566	8.570963
T3s	1,026	199	0.415998	8.415718
76s	1,045	180	0.418616	8.318417
95s	970	255	0.403431	8.261043
J3o	1,047	178	0.415307	7.914721
T2s	1,123	102	0.425488	7.538836
87o	976	249	0.396225	7.505732
85s	1,039	186	0.406723	7.239171
96o	987	238	0.393276	7.074151
T5o	1,003	222	0.394962	6.920957
J2o	1,129	96	0.42042	6.885765
75s	1,115	110	0.414674	6.59416
94s	1,063	162	0.403925	6.583641
T4o	1,097	128	0.406874	6.248512
65s	1,159	66	0.418775	6.207388
86o	1,087	138	0.402754	6.099835
93s	1,121	104	0.409454	6.058991
84s	1,145	80	0.409633	5.692773
95o	1,133	92	0.406508	5.650827
T3o	1,145	80	0.406672	5.480421
76o	1,164	61	0.410142	5.439126
92s	1,153	72	0.406646	5.359298
74s	1,198	27	0.412623	5.109201

54s	1,225	0	0.414534	4.850294
T2o	1,149	76	0.397258	4.832254
85o	1,197	28	0.407938	4.81223
64s	1,225	0	0.413333	4.769221
83s	1,201	24	0.403003	4.463809
94o	1,201	24	0.400861	4.345783
75o	1,225	0	0.40512	4.269797
82s	1,207	18	0.398164	4.129509
73s	1,225	0	0.400359	4.018033
93o	1,200	25	0.393756	4.000304
65o	1,225	0	0.399443	3.972305
53s	1,225	0	0.39693	3.851054
63s	1,225	0	0.395336	3.777173
84o	1,225	0	0.394468	3.737896
92o	1,215	10	0.388261	3.585219
43s	1,225	0	0.386419	3.402163
74o	1,225	0	0.385498	3.366747
72s	1,225	0	0.381559	3.221509
54o	1,225	0	0.381553	3.221293
64o	1,225	0	0.380105	3.170312
52s	1,225	0	0.378493	3.114999
62s	1,225	0	0.37669	3.054809
83o	1,225	0	0.374838	2.994827
42s	1,225	0	0.36829	2.796223
82o	1,225	0	0.368277	2.795837
73o	1,225	0	0.366023	2.731972
53o	1,225	0	0.362648	2.640274
63o	1,225	0	0.360776	2.591343
32s	1,225	0	0.359844	2.567461
43o	1,225	0	0.351459	2.366073
72o	1,225	0	0.345836	2.243309
52o	1,225	0	0.342846	2.181602
62o	1,225	0	0.340751	2.139745
42o	1,225	0	0.331998	1.976146
32o	1,225	0	0.323032	1.825374

Index

NOTES

NOTES

NOTES

NOTES

NOTES

NOTES

NOTES